OKBOMB!

Conspiracy and Cover-up

Also by Jim Keith

The Gemstone File
Secret and Suppressed
Casebook on Alternative 3
Black Helicopters Over America
The Octopus (with Kenn Thomas)

OKBOMB!

Conspiracy and Cover-up

Jim Keith

Library of Congress Cataloging in Publication Data

Keith, Jim, 1949—
    Okbomb! : conspiracy and cover-up / by Jim Keith.
        p.   cm.
    Includes bibliographical references and index.
    ISBN: 1-881532-08-9
    1.   Oklahoma City Federal Building Bombing, Oklahoma City, Okla.,
1995.
    2.   Conspiracies—United States.
    3.   Terrorism—Government policy—United States.   I. Title
HV6432.K45   1996
364.1'64—dc20   95-48365

IllumiNet Press
P.O. Box 2808
Lilburn, Georgia 30226

10 9 8 7 6 5 4 3 2 1

Printed in the United States of America

Dedicated to the victims of terrorism
at Oklahoma City, Oklahoma and at Waco, Texas

With thanks and appreciation for my family, Ron and Nancy Bonds, Karl Granse, J.D. Cash, Rep. Charles Key, Greg Krupey, Matt Love, David Alexander, Jan Brown, Juanita Cox, Joan D'Arc, Hawthorne Abendsen, Adam Parfrey, John Driessler, Kenn Thomas, Wayne Henderson, Ted Gunderson, Paul Larson, Mary Ann Dickens, Susan Alexander, Donna Brown, Richard Sherrow, and all the Saturday Night Spetsnaz, with particular thanks to Barbara, Eric, Art, and Gayla. I would like to offer a special note of gratitude to Bob Sonderfan, friend and researcher extraordinaire.

"A covert operation is, in its nature, a lie."
— Oliver North
testifying before the Iran-Contra congressional investigations

Contents

1

Explosion

It was a clear spring morning on Wednesday, April 19, 1995 in Oklahoma City, Oklahoma. Just before 9 a.m. a 24-foot Ryder rental truck was driven to the curb outside the nine-story Alfred P. Murrah Federal Building, on Fifth Street.

Eyewitnesses who first came forward described two men in blue jogging suits who exited the truck and got into another vehicle, which was possibly driven by a third person. [1]

An Oklahoma City meter maid informed federal officials that immediately prior to the bombing she saw a man driving a Ryder truck toward the front entrance of the Murrah Building, and that the man appeared to be lost. According to her account, she expected him to stop and ask her for directions. She watched as the vehicle entered the parking lot of the Murrah Building and parked in a no parking zone. [2]

Another woman, driving on Northwest Fifth Street near the federal building, had to brake her car to avoid hitting a person walking away from the building, a man later identified as a suspect in the bombing. [3]

Another witness observed two men speeding away from the crime scene in a yellow Mercury just before the blast. Other witnesses would later come forward with additional details of possible conspirators in the bombing, although much of this information would inexplicably not find its way into the national media. [4]

At two minutes past 9 a.m., many of the federal employees in the building were sipping their morning coffee, shuffling papers, and beginning their work day. The payload in the Ryder truck disintegrated in a blast that was heard 70 miles away and which consumed the entire north face of the Murrah Building, annihilating one third of the structure. One hundred sixty-nine persons, including 19 children, died in the explosion and in the collapse of the front of the building which followed. The explosion left a crater that was reported by authorities to be 30 feet wide and eight feet deep. Two hundred buildings and 300 homes in the area, some as far as three blocks away, had severe structural damage from the explosive force. [5]

Inside, approximately 550 people had been working or visiting the facility, which housed the offices of a dozen agencies of the federal government. Those agencies included the Drug Enforcement Agency (the DEA), the Defense Investigative Service, the General Accounting Office, General Services Administration, U.S. Army and Marines recruiting offices, Housing and Urban Development, the Social Security Administration, Veterans Administration, U.S. Customs Service, Secret Service, and the Bureau of Alcohol, Tobacco and Firearms (ATF). On the second floor of the building there had been a day care center for the children of employees, where approximately 25 youngsters had been enrolled. [6]

Federal investigators were quick to conclude, without any substantiating documentation offered to the public, that the explosion had been caused by an ammonium nitrate and fuel oil bomb, a chemical mixture known by the acronym ANFO. Jack McGeorge, an explosives expert interviewed by CBS News on the day of the bombing, admitted that designating the bomb as ANFO was only a "logical guess." [7]

ANFO is the explosive substance whose usage was pioneered by the Irish Republican Army, and which was later employed by Islamic militants in the 1993 World Trade Center bombing in New York City, and in bombings in Beirut, Buenos Aires, and other locations. [8]

Ammonium nitrate is a chemical commonly used in fertilizer, and is readily obtainable in farm supply stores. Industry and farmers often mix ammonium nitrate with fuel oil or other combustible substances for use as an explosive, setting it off with a blasting cap and dynamite, or even a large firecracker.

On the day of the bombing Oklahoma City television stations reported that pieces of a maroon mini-van that may have been used to carry the bomb, including portions of a license plate, had been discovered in the ruins of the Murrah Building. Reports said that the van had been rented from a National Car Rental agency in Dallas, Texas, although federal investigators later retracted these claims. [9]

Initial estimates of the weight of the bomb were from 1,000 to 2,000 pounds, but on April 27 federal authorities changed the estimated weight to 5,000 pounds, again without offering information on what their initial estimates had been based upon, and why these weights had been adjusted so dramatically upward. Officials were specific enough to later say that the bomb had been composed of 20 blue plastic barrels ("blue or white," and "blue and white" in other accounts, "blue tubs" in another), holding about 55 gallons each, and that they had probably been detonated with a safety fuse, lit by hand. [10]

NOTES

1. *Information Digest*, Vol. XXVIII #8, April 21, 1995
2. Rappoport, John. *Oklahoma City Bombing, The Suppressed Truth*, Blue Press, Los Angeles, 1995; "The Bomb... in Oklahoma," video by *Star Investigative Reports,* 1995
3. Rappoport
4. "Evidence Linking Suspect To Blast Is Offered in Court," *New York Times*, April 28, 1995
5. *Information Digest*
6. Ibid.
7. *CBS News,* April 19, 1995
8. *Information Digest*
9. "At Least 31 Dead and Scores Missing After Car Bomb Attack in Oklahoma City," *New York Times*, April 20, 1995; "An Intensive Hunt Gets Under Way, but for Whom?," *New York Times*, April 20, 1995
10. Johnson, Kevin. "Investigators follow bombing trail to Kansas," *USA Today*, June 14, 1995; Meddis and Howlett. "FBI: Nichols got supplies for bombing," *USA Today*, May 12, 1995; *Facts on File,* April 27, 1995

2

Bombshells

L ittle reported is that about 11:00 a.m. on the morning of the blast rescue efforts were halted when some workers reported seeing another bomb in the rubble of the building.[1] An emergency radio call was broadcast, which was later reported by *Associated Press:*

"Remove all your personnel from the building immediately, possible explosives planted in the building. I repeat, evacuate the building immediately." [2] The incident was reported live by the Cable News Network between 11:29 EST and 11:35 EST.

Here is the live, on-location account of a reporter from KWTW-TV in Oklahoma City:

"All right, we just saw, if you were watching, there, there was a white pickup truck backing a trailer into the scene here. They are trying to get people out of the way so that they can get it in. Appears to be the Oklahoma Bomb Squad. It's their bomb disposal unit, is what it is, and it is what they would use if, if, the report that we gave you just a few minutes ago is correct, that a second explosive device of some kind is inside the building. They'll back that trailer in there, and the bomb squad folks will go in and they'll use that trailer. You see the bucket on the back? This is how they would transport the explosive device away from this populated area. They would try to do something."

Approximately two minutes later, a reporter for KFOR-TV conveyed the following commentary:

"The FBI has confirmed there is another bomb in the federal building. It's in the east side of the building. They've moved everybody back several blocks, obviously to, uh, unplug it so it won't go off. They're moving everybody back. It's a, it's a weird scene because at first everybody was running when they gave the word to get everybody away from the scene, but now people are just standing around kind of staring. It's a very surreal, very strange scene. Now, we want to get some information out to people, to people who are in the downtown area. You don't want to stand on the sidewalk, and the reason for that is there are gas mains underneath and if there's a second explosion, that those gas mains could blow. But again, we do have confirmation. There is a second bomb in the federal building. We know it's on the east side. We're not sure what floor, what level, but there is definitely danger of a major second explosion. They're warning everybody to get as far back as they can. They're trying to get the bomb defused right now. They are in the process of doing it, but this could take some time. They're telling people that this is something to take very seriously, and not to slip forward to get a look at this, because this thing could definitely go off." [3]

According to one report, three radio operators monitoring communications traffic heard the same conversation on the morning of April 19:

First voice: "Boy, you're not gonna believe this!"

Second voice: "Believe what?"

First voice: "I can't believe it... this is a military bomb!" [4]

An hour and a half after the first bomb report, a bomb squad member stated that the reports of an unexploded bomb or bombs had been a false alarm, although two days later a newspaper in London, England was still reporting the additional bomb as fact.

Two people identifying themselves as firemen are reported to have described a second (or perhaps third) bomb, with an additional confirmation provided the following day by the father of one of the men. They are said to have identified the weapon as actually being several bombs, labelled, olive-drab barrels of fulminate of mercury with MilSpec (military specification) numbers. [5]

Corroborating the above report, investigator Phil O'Halloran quotes the head of the Oklahoma City Police Department, Bill Martin, as having stated that he believes that workers found containers of mercury fulminate in the federal building after the blast. [6]

Witnesses also inform us that on April 19, K-TOK radio in Oklahoma City reported that explosives (including plastique) were found in the ruins of the Murrah Building, and that they were alleged to have been kept in the offices of the ATF. A spokesperson for K-TOK now denies that the report was ever broadcast. [7]

In an interview, investigator Pat Shannon quoted the maintenance foreman of the Murrah Building as saying that there had definitely been two explosions at the Murrah Building, and the foreman also stated that three bombs had been removed from the site. [8]

David Hall, the general manager of KPOC-TV in Oklahoma, interviewed the assistant Oklahoma City firechief, John Hanson, who told him, "that they had found two undetonated bombs in the building as well as one rocket launcher in the building." According to Hall, "We have confirmed that they were there, but we have not been able to get any comments from the FBI or ATF." [9]

Researcher Devvy Kidd says that unedited KFOR-TV video footage includes "startling news that two or more bombs were found inside the building. That due to the diligence of bomb-sniffing dogs, another disaster was averted. Much is made about these two bombs, the second one having already been diffused at this point in the tape, the third underway. It is confirmed [by the television commentators] that both of these bombs were far larger in magnitude than the first that went off inside the building."

Ms. Kidd relates that, "Around the noon hour, Channel 4 has as their guest Dr. Randall Heather, a terrorist expert. Dr. Heather stated: 'We got lucky today, if you can consider anything about this tragedy lucky. We have both of the bombs that were defused at the site and they are being taken apart. We will be able to find out how they were made, and possibly who made them. These bombs are very sophisticated high explosives with maybe a little fertilizer damped around them.'"

Ms. Kidd additionally states of the unedited footage, "There is discussion about another bomb found in the west side of the building. This is where the major damage occurred. Also, another device found strapped to the column next to the day care center on the 2nd floor. There is the discussion that perhaps the ATF kept explosives for training exercises in the basement." [10]

One person who was on the scene immediately after the bombing was rescue worker Toni Garrett. She has stated in an interview that, "There was at least four other people that had told me that there was another bomb inside the building... and there was a couple of people that had actually seen them remove the bomb when the bomb squad had come down to the Murrah Building... There was a timing device on the bomb that they had secured earlier that morning, and that had been set to go off ten minutes after the bombs had gone off that morning... They assumed that the mechanism of the bomb malfunctioned because of the blast, so that's what caused that bomb not to explode." Questioned about whether these witnesses had said that it definitely had been an active bomb discovered, she responded: "Yes." [11]

Accounts of "dummy bombs," according to explosives expert Brigadier General Benton Partin, "impute either the highest stupidity to the bomb technicians — since training aids are always clearly labeled as such — or gross incompetence on the part of the ATF for not marking the devices as 'training aids' in the first place." [12]

With all the reports of unexploded bombs, why has almost nothing been mentioned of their existence in the national media, except for an occasional cynical debunking denying the possibility that additional bombs could exist? Why has information of other bombs found in the federal building been covered up? It was only later in the course of the investigation that credible answers were found.

After 10 hours the FBI suspended the search for victims in the rubble of the bombing. The search was called off for 12 hours, with the number of rescue workers reduced to 12. According to the New York *Daily News*:

"Hours after a truck bomb ripped apart the Oklahoma City federal building, some rescue workers were ordered to stop searching for survivors while federal officials removed boxes of documents, the *Daily News* has learned.

"'You'd think they would have let their evidence and files sit at least until the last survivor was pulled out,' one angry rescue worker told the *News*.

"'They had guys carrying out boxes while the rescue workers were forced to sit on their hands,' said the worker, a member of a canine rescue squad who requested anonymity.

"The rescue worker and an Oklahoma City firefighter, who also asked that his name be withheld, offered similar accounts in separate interviews with the *News*.

"The two said about 10 to 12 hours after the 9 a.m. April 19 blast, federal officials began limiting the number of rescue workers allowed in the building to about a dozen, confining them largely to the lower right side of the battered structure.

"Meanwhile, groups of 40 to 50 federal agents spent much of the night carrying dozens of boxes from the seventh and ninth floors, where the federal Drug Enforcement Administration and the Bureau of Alcohol, Tobacco and Firearms have offices." [13]

One might wonder what it was in those FBI and BATF files that was more important than the lives of the victims, the last live victim being rescued 36 hours after the explosion, as well as whether any victims died because of the delay while files were recovered.

NOTES:

1. *Information Digest*, Vol. XXVIII #8, April 21, 1995; "News in Brief," *The European*, 21-27 April, 1995
2. "Radio, phone calls began pouring in," *Associated Press,* April 29, 1995
3. Transcript of April 19, 1995 CNN broadcast, copy in author's possession
4. Cooper, William, "Oklahoma City Bombing, Truth among casualties, buried under mountain of lies," *Veritas*, May 9, 1995
5. Ibid.
6. Rappoport
7. Cooper
8. Zeps, Charles. "OKC Victims Deliver Petition," Internet computer posting, June 15, 1995
9. Hall, David. "FBI Stonewalls Evidence Discovered by TV Station," *The Spotlight*, July 17, 1995
10. Kidd, Devvy. "Live Unedited KFOR [Ch. 4.] Film — Oklahoma City Bombing," photocopy of essay in author's possession
11. "Oklahoma City: What Really Happened?", video, Charles Allen, 1995
12. Jasper, William F. "Explosive Evidence of a Cover-up," *The New American*, August 7, 1995
13. "Files Before Victims," New York *Daily News*, May 1, 1995

3

Preliminary Investigation

On the day of the bombing, orders were issued nationwide by the FBI to deploy more than 1,000 federal agents to work on the Oklahoma City case, which was dubbed OKBomb. Within days federal agents had received 14,000 tips and 35,000 phone calls to a 1-800 number bomb hotline that had been set up. [1]

Early in the investigation, the FBI announced that they possessed videotape of two suspects in the bombing getting into a "brown Ford pickup with tinted glass" and leaving the bombing scene. ABC Television News announced on April 19 that three Middle Eastern men were observed leaving the crime scene in a brown truck. Later it was claimed that the identification of the men and pickup truck had been mistaken. [2]

Within hours of the bombing, a piece of the axle of the truck that allegedly carried the bomb was said to have been discovered (it was the "undercarriage," in another account) by Oklahoma City Police officer Mike McPherson (or an FBI agent, or a BATF agent, or by a group of which Governor Frank Keating was a member, in other accounts) two blocks away from the Murrah Building (or, in another account, in the bomb crater). The axle was reported to have been imprinted with a VIN, a vehicle identification number, and this information was entered by investigators into the FBI's computerized Rapid Start System. Also found in the wreckage of the bombing was a Florida license plate, which investigators at the time believed had been attached to the vehicle that had carried the bomb. [3]

At approximately 2 a.m. on April 20, CNN television news announced that the VIN on the axle had been traced to a rental car out of Dallas, Texas. This story was never repeated so far as we can ascertain, but was quickly replaced by the story that the VIN had been traced to a Ryder truck rented from Elliott's Body Shop, in Junction City, Kansas, 270 miles north of Oklahoma City, a town located near the Fort Riley Army base. [4]

It is interesting that the method by which the alleged perpetrators were located, by the VIN on the axle of the Ryder truck, was identical to the lead which supposedly provided the break in tracking suspects in the World Trade Center bombing two years earlier, a bombing that conformed in many respects to the one in Oklahoma City. While this coincidence and its ramifications are rarely mentioned in the mainstream media, they will be discussed later in this text.

There are other problems with the VIN story, pointed out by Adam Parfrey in an essay about the Oklahoma City bombing:

"No rear axle is imprinted with the vehicle indentification number, even after recent legislation forcing manufacturers to place multiple VINs on the engine, firewall, and frame to discourage chop shops. When queried, a spokesman for Ryder told me that it does not imprint additional VINs on its trucks. The only conceivable number available on a rear axle is a part number, but a part number couldn't lead to the identification of a specific vehicle. Where did the VIN story come from? And why?" [5]

Oklahoma City investigator Pat Briley confirms this information. He has stated, "Two very credible sources have told me that if you look at the Ford Motor Company manual for the Ryder truck, there are no VIN (vehicle identification numbers) on the parts the government claims they found." [6]

An alternate version of the story describing the tracking of the bombing suspects, which was broadcast on April 20 on ABC television news, was that videotape from a surveillance camera near the Federal Building had captured images that, when enhanced, revealed a Ryder truck parked in front of the Murrah Building. "That's what took them to Kansas," ABC's commentator stated.

Also on April 20, ABC news released the information that the Oklahoma City police had found a suspected getaway car, that it was a Chevy Cavalier, and that the vehicle had been turned over to the FBI. So far as we can determine, the Chevy Cavalier has never been mentioned again. [7]

In whatever manner the vehicle was actually located, it was finally identified as a 1993 Ford van that had been rented two days earlier by "Robert Kling" (in another account, "Bob Kling," and in another, "William B. Kling"), Social Security number 962-42-9694, South Dakota driver's license number YF942A6, with an issue date of April 19, 1993.

The license was false. Employees of the rental company were, however, able to provide descriptions of "Kling" and another man who had been with him at the time of the rental, and these descriptions were used in the creation of composite drawings by the FBI. One man was tall and slim with a light brown crew cut (termed John Doe 1 by the authorities), while the other man was muscular and "swarthy," with longer dark brown hair, full lips, a wide nose, and a tattoo on his left arm (John Doe 2). [8]

While there was more interest in John Doe 2 the major U.S. news media seemed to avoid reporting it. After the release of the composite sketch of John Doe 2, the manager of the Great Western Motel in Junction City, Kansas immediately recognized the man. "He spoke broken English," the manager stated. "It was a foreign name. He said he was from Colorado. He drove a Ryder truck." The manager also said of John Doe 2 that, "He was scared. He didn't want to talk too much." According to the Motel manager the man had an eight-inch tattoo of a "snake or serpent" on his upper left arm. [9]

A delivery person for a Chinese restaurant in Junction City also identified another man at the Motel, not John Doe 1 or 2, said to have had "longer hair and a fuller face." [10]

Apparently the information of a possible foreign involvement in the Oklahoma bombing has been suppressed for fear that it might encourage reprisals against innocent immigrants and other persons of Middle Eastern descent, but these same sources and media outlets have not exhibited much reticence in linking the bombing to conspiracy researchers, to the militia movement, and to other segments of the populist right wing.

Composite sketches of the two John Does were released to the news media on April 20. As late as May 8 the media was reporting that the FBI believed at least three or four people were involved in the bombing. As of May 18, federal investigators were going door to door in Junction City, Kansas, circulating photos of six men who might have been involved in the bomb plot. [11]

NOTES:

1. Achenbach, Joel. "Dead Ends," *Washington Post*, June 11, 1995; *Facts on File*, May 4, 1995
2. Broward, Horne. Internet computer posting, May 28, 1995, in the possession of the author
3. Loftis, Randy Lee. "The kindness of strangers," *Dallas Morning*

News, April 30, 1995; Tharp, Mike. "The end of innocence," *U.S. News & World Report*, May 1, 1995; Howlett, Debbie. "Fragments tell history of bomb," *USA Today*, May 1, 1995

4. Hopkins, Ken. Interview conducted by Jim Keith on July 15, 1995
5. Parfrey, Adam. "Finding Our Way Out Of Oklahoma," *Cult Rapture*, Feral House, Portland, Oregon, 1995
6. Briley, Pat. "Federals Know Identity of Oklahoma's John Doe No. 2," *The Spotlight*, October 2, 1995
7. ABC television news broadcast, April 19, 1995
8. *Information Digest*, Vol. XXVIII #8, April 21, 1995; Johnston, David. "U.S. Trying to Hold 2 Witnesses in Jail," *New York Times*, April 24, 1995
9. "The manhunt: Twisting trail," *U.S. News and World Report*, May 8, 1995; "Motel manager says he saw bombing suspect," *Associated Press,* April 26, 1995; Johnston, David. "Nichols brothers are charged in bombing conspiracy," *New York Times News Service*, April 26, 1995
10. Thomas, Evan et al. "This Doesn't Happen Here," *Newsweek*, May 1, 1995
11. Thomas, Evan, et al. "The Plot," *Newsweek*, May 8, 1995; Johnson, Kevin. "Blast investigators' pace slows to a walk," *USA Today*, May 18, 1995

4

McVeigh

L ess than 90 minutes after the explosion in Oklahoma City, at about 10:20 a.m., a 1977 yellow Mercury Marquis was pulled over in the town of Perry, Oklahoma, 60 miles north of Oklahoma City. Charles Hanger, the police officer who stopped the car, reported that he had noticed that it lacked license plates, and that it was travelling at over 80 miles per hour. All the car seemingly lacked was a big sign saying "Arrest me!"

When Officer Hanger approached the window of the Mercury he reportedly spotted the bulge of a shoulder holster under the driver's jacket. The driver volunteered the information that he was carrying a gun to the officer, who had still not unholstered his own weapon. At this point, the policeman drew his gun and put it to the driver's head, taking from the man a .45 caliber Glock pistol loaded with hollow point bullets (called a "9mm assault pistol" with "cop killer bullets" by the media) and a five-inch knife. No media source I have come across has bothered to mention that the knife was legally sheathed. According to Officer Hanger, when he took McVeigh's gun, "there was no reaction, no shock, that didn't seem right, either." [1]

The driver was 26-year-old Timothy James McVeigh. His driver's license listed his residence as 3616 Van Dyke Street, Decker, Michigan. McVeigh had served with distinction in the Persian Gulf War and had been discharged from the U.S. Army in 1991. McVeigh had been stationed at Fort Riley, Kansas (taking his basic training at Fort Benning, Georgia), and his specialty, according to *Information Digest*, was demolitions. While in the Army, McVeigh had received the Bronze Star medal, Army Commendation medal, Army Achievement medal, National Defense Service medal, Southwest Asia Service medal with two bronze stars, Kuwait Liberation medal, Combat Infantryman badge, and the Army Service ribbon. McVeigh had been promoted to sergeant while in the Gulf War, ahead of everyone else in his unit. [2]

After his arrest, McVeigh's Army records were sealed by federal agents. According to the *Washington Post*, "During the end of his military career, according to former comrades, McVeigh apparently started spending much of his time off-base associating with paramilitary rightwing groups." [3]

When McVeigh was taken to jail, he reportedly dropped a business card inside the police car. The card advertised Paulsen's Military Supply in Wisconsin, and McVeigh had apparently noted on the card "Dave" (presumably Dave Paulsen, the owner of the store) and "more five pound sticks of TNT by May 1." [4] Paulsen was later given a lie detector test regarding his connections to the Oklahoma City bombing and is reported to have failed it, but as of this writing Paulsen remained free, although under federal surveillance.

According to Cable News Network, in the glove compartment of the Mercury Marquis was a letter written by McVeigh to a girlfriend indicating plans to bomb other locations. This is curious becauseother sources maintain that McVeigh did not have a girlfriend and was almost pathologically shy of women. A newspaper account alleges that, "Correspondence found in Mr. McVeigh's car vows revenge for the 1993 federal raid on the Branch Davidian complex, investigators say." If that is, indeed, what the letter says, why release the information in this piecemeal fashion, leaked by factions hostile to McVeigh's legal case, rather than offering the letter itself for public scrutiny? [5]

Former FBI agent Ted L. Gunderson informs us that the Anti-Defamation League of the B'nai B'rith (ADL) leaked information that McVeigh was carrying another card at the time of his arrest, this being a *Spotlight* newspaper prepaid calling card. *The Spotlight*, a popular conservative newspaper, had previously come under fire from precisely this source, the ADL. So far it has not been revealed how the ADL obtained this information. It is also important to note that *The Spotlight* debit card (or any other item mentioning *The Spotlight*) was not listed in the inventory of his possessions made at the time of his arrest. This opens wide the possibility that McVeigh was located through an informant who was in touch with him prior to the bombing.

McVeigh did, apparently, use a *Spotlight* phone debit account that had been obtained in November 1993 under the name "Darryl Bridges" (named by another source "Brigadier"). The debit account has been referred to as "the backbone of the government's case" against McVeigh and was used to track leads including reported calls to fertilizer companies, to companies that manufacture plastic barrels, and to Michael Fortier and Jennifer McVeigh. The records of the calls were also used by the FBI to create a timeline of the pre-bombing activities of the accused. [6]

After his arrest, McVeigh was charged with the transportation of a loaded weapon, carrying a concealed weapon and the lack of license plates on his vehicle; curiously enough, however, not charged for speeding, even though he had been travelling over 80 miles per hour. His name and social security number are said to have been routinely entered into the National Crime Information Computer (or so most reports have it). [7]

Almost all published reports indicate that McVeigh had $225 on him at the time of the arrest, but the *New York Times* on April 22, 1995 asserted that he was carrying $2,000 in cash. [8] Later information revealed that the "partially employed" McVeigh had over $10,000 hidden away in a number of bank accounts, and several thousand dollars stashed in storage units. [9]

Noble County Sheriff Jerry R. Cook states that McVeigh listed James Nichols as his next of kin at the jail, although he provided the wrong phone number for Nichols' Decker, Michigan farm. According to the sheriff, McVeigh's only question prior to being taken to the jail holding area was, "When's chow?" [10]

There are remarkable discrepancies in the record of the arrest of Timothy McVeigh. David Hall, the general manager of KPOC-TV in Oklahoma, has stated that authorities "indicated that McVeigh was arrested at 10:45 on the morning of Wednesday, April 19 and that the vehicle he was driving was the 1978 Mercury. I happened to be sitting by my radio scanner on Friday, April 21, about one o'clock in the afternoon, and I heard a broadcast coming over from the Oklahoma Highway Patrol that they had a car on I-35 and that the car, most likely, had been involved in the bombing. I dispatched a [television] crew over from the station and they got there and a lady there told us that she witnessed the arrest of a man about 1:30 p.m. She said he was taken out of the vehicle, put in a military helicopter and [it] went south with him. We broadcast that story as did Channel 4 in Oklahoma City as well as the *Oklahoma News Network* for radio.

"If that wasn't enough, then, the following Monday we had our insurance agent for the station who came in that day to visit. He lives in

Perry, Oklahoma. I mentioned this report to him and he said, 'I was coming down I-35 on Friday and a highway patrolman passed me with his red lights and siren on at a high rate of speed.' He said that when he got up to where the patrolman had gone there were all sorts of vehicles and all sorts of police (including plainclothesmen). There was a helicopter flying away. So that substantiates the story that the lady had told. Our insurance man is a former Oklahoma City police officer.

"So, we are trying to determine who was arrested on Friday. Was McVeigh arrested on Wednesday (as they say) or on Friday? It may be that there is a reasonable explanation for this. It may be that the car McVeigh was driving was left on the spot for two days [to explain its presence there on the 21st] but that's not likely. The Oklahoma Highway Patrol has a policy in the types of arrest that McVeigh was involved in. The car would be impounded and searched and taken off the highway. At any rate they don't let a car sit for a 48-hour period on I-35."

Hall omits saying that if they do allow a car to sit unsecured for 48 hours, this irrevocably breaks the chain of evidence, allowing any manner of tampering to take place with the car.

Substantiating the above account by Hall, according to investigator Devvy Kidd, "There are three eyewitnesses who have absolutely no connection to McVeigh at all. All tried to give statements to the FBI and law enforcement in Perry that they recognized McVeigh from the TV and that he was not in jail the day of the bombing or the following day as the media tells it." [11]

Apparently something very strange took place in Perry, Oklahoma.

Supposedly due to a delay in the court, Timothy McVeigh was held until Friday morning, April 21, in a cell at the Noble County Courthouse in Perry, at which time the judge was scheduled to set bail for him. By that time, it is reported, a former co-worker of McVeigh's had phoned the FBI with additional information about the man, linking him to the bombing. More probably, McVeigh had been linked to the crime by having given his real name to the manager at the Dreamland Motel in Junction City, where he had stayed. [12]

Still another version of the way in which McVeigh was identified as a suspect in the bombing was circulated by *Associated Press*, stating that, "He had nearly gotten out on bail before the trooper who stopped him spotted a resemblance to an FBI sketch of one of the men wanted in the bombing." This is the height of absurdity. Wouldn't the police in a small town in Oklahoma near Oklahoma City have been at a high state of alert after the bombing — certainly the biggest thing to have happened in those parts since the Land Rush — and have immediately noticed that the arrested McVeigh was a dead ringer for one of the composite drawings? Everyone arrested in Perry, Oklahoma, and probably everyone who even motored through the town for several days after the bombing, would have been carefully scrutinized as a possible suspect, and it would have been obvious from the first that McVeigh was a dead ringer for John Doe 1. [13]

FBI investigators, who arrived by helicopter on Friday, took custody of McVeigh just prior to his scheduled 10:30 a.m. court hearing. McVeigh was escorted by the FBI past a crowd shouting "Baby killer!" and was escorted to a helicopter that flew him to a federal magistrate at Tinker Air Force Base in Oklahoma. One questions what part of the judicial process dictated that McVeigh be taken to an Air Force base, rather than to a prison.

At the base, McVeigh allegedly responded to the questions of investigators with his name, army rank and date of birth (or serial number, depending on the account). "I am a prisoner of war," he is reported to have stated, although he later denied this allegation. Later, McVeigh entered "no plea" to charges of malicious damage of federal property, which I assume is the same thing as saying that he offered no response to the charges. [14]

From Tinker Air Force Base, McVeigh was transferred to solitary confinement at the Federal Correctional Institute at El Reno, Oklahoma. He was placed in a 12-by-12-foot glass cell, the only inmate in a 40-cell block in the prison. The cell was illuminated 24 hours a day, and was likened colorfully in the media to the glass cell that confined the fictional monster Hannibal Lecter in the motion picture *Silence of the Lambs*. [15] McVeigh's guards were under instructions not to talk to McVeigh, and he is reported to have said nothing to them.

In an affidavit filed by the FBI in connection with the arrest of McVeigh it was stated that he had visited the Branch Davidian compound during the 51-day siege, and was "extremely angry" about what had taken place.

It is apparently true that McVeigh was very concerned about the government's stormtrooper tactics at the Branch Davidian complex in Waco, although this hardly implicates him in the Oklahoma City bombing. A wide cross-section of the populace was justifiably appalled at what took place there.

As evidence of McVeigh's concern about the Waco incident, gun dealer Chuck Halley indicated in an interview with the author that

McVeigh, under the alias Tim Tuttle, had set up a table at a California gun show for the purpose of distributing literature about the Branch Davidian massacre. Halley stated that "McVeigh knew everything about the Branch Davidian stand-off, but he didn't know that much about the New World Order." According to Halley, McVeigh informed him that he had left the military because he didn't like the direction it had taken, post-Clinton. The two men had a friendly talk and exchanged addresses — at the time, McVeigh's was 1711 Stockton Hill #206, Kingman, Arizona — and McVeigh later mailed Halley free of charge a copy of the Linda Thompson videotape expose of Waco, with a handwritten recommendation of the video attached. [16]

Among other information linking McVeigh to the right wing are the statements of a "paramilitary group" in Florida. According to them, McVeigh had attended meetings of the group with Mark Koernke, of Dexter, Michigan ("Mark from Michigan" as he is sometimes called), and some witnesses have stated that he was Koernke's bodyguard. [17]

In a similarity to the case of Lee Harvey Oswald, who allegedly left behind a diary widely claimed to be a CIA forgery, McVeigh is also alleged to have well documented his extremist position. According to the *New York Times*, "Law enforcement officials said Mr. McVeigh left behind a large body of writings about his ideological leanings, including extensive tracts in letters to friends and relatives, that describe his belief in the Constitutional principles that he adamantly maintained allowed him to carry firearms and live without any restraints from the Government. Prosecutors are likely to use such documents to establish his motive at a trial." [18]

Everything is not quite so cut and dried, however. Examples of evidence that are being carefully avoided by the media and by prosecutors are striking incongruities in the behavior of Timothy McVeigh prior to and during his arrest. These examples include:

A. McVeigh is alleged to have been only sporadically employed during the year prior to the bombing, strange because the OKBomb had probably cost several thousand dollars to construct, and he is alleged to "have travelled with a large amount of cash." [19]

B. Of high curiosity is the fact that McVeigh, even though reported to possess fake I.D. under the name Robert or Bob or William B. Kling (depending on who is asked), chose to give his correct name and address to the owner of the Dreamland Motel he was staying at in Junction City. This is hardly the behavior of a man planning on committing a crime of the magnitude of the Oklahoma City bombing. It should also be noted that McVeigh was not carrying the false I.D. when he was arrested in Perry, Oklahoma.

C. When filling out the agreement for the Ryder rental truck in Junction City, Kansas, McVeigh allegedly listed his (i.e. Kling's) home address as 428 Malt Drive, in Redfield, South Dakota. He listed his destination as 428 Maple Drive, in Omaha, Nebraska. Wouldn't the identical address numbers and similar street names have been calculated to create suspicion at the rental agency, perhaps causing them to demand further substantiation and identification?

D. Based upon inquiries to several Ryder agencies, McVeigh could not have rented a Ryder truck with his only identification being a single piece of out-of-state documentation.

E. McVeigh is said to have visited the Murrah Building, where the bombing took place, 3 1/2 weeks prior to the crime. During this time he wore Army dog tags, and mentioned to employees at the Murrah Building that he had been posted to Oklahoma City, from Fort Riley, Kansas. Strange behavior indeed for someone who presumably would have wanted to keep his identity secret. [20]

Additionally, if McVeigh had cased the federal building and specifically inquired about the location of the BATF offices in the building — the supposed target of the bombing because of the agency's participation in the Waco debacle — why was the truck bomb positioned on the opposite side of the structure from the BATF offices?

F. According to the *New York Times*, "The day before he became one of the most hunted men in the world, Timothy McVeigh, or a look-alike, showed up at a hair salon here [in Junction City] with a friend who wanted a haircut, said the salon owner, Kathy Henderson... They were together when they walked into Gracie & Company looking for a haircut, Ms. Henderson said. She did not see them get out of a car or a truck as they walked across the parking lot and into the shop. The dark-haired man did the talking.

"'He said they needed haircuts and I told them we were booked up,' Ms. Henderson said. 'It was strange. He did not need a haircut. He was very well groomed.' She said they seemed disappointed as they walked away."

With the construction of the bomb apparently still to be accomplished, and the drive to Oklahoma City still ahead of him, time would have been at a premium for Timothy McVeigh. Would he have taken the time out for a haircut he didn't need? Would he have even thought about getting a haircut, considering the crime that he was allegedly planning to commit?

G. The suspect drove without license plates on his car. This is an act calculated to draw attention to oneself — and drawing attention would seemingly be the last thing that an escaping murderer would want to do. According to the *New York Times*, McVeigh told anonymous sources that he had parked his yellow Mercury in Oklahoma City a few days before the bombing, "but forgot to put the license plate on the car. That oversight led to his arrest." [21] This "oversight," and other acts of seeming stupidity and forgetfulness on McVeigh's part, are especially odd in light of the fact that he was supposedly intelligent enough to construct and detonate a complex bomb.

Where was the license plate that was taken off of the Mercury? An *Associated Press* release from early in the investigation, April 29, states that, "Timothy McVeigh's missing Arizona license plate appears on a mystery vehicle in a videotape taken just before the Oklahoma bombing." This does not resolve the mystery of the missing plate, however. It suggests that McVeigh purposely removed the plate and did not replace it, which would not have been that difficult to do, given the large number of license plates available for the picking. It also does not resolve the large number of mystery vehicles in this case, which the FBI remains mum about while releasing all of the incriminating evidence about the alleged perpetrators that they can. [22]

H. If McVeigh had just taken part in the bombing of the Murrah Building in Oklahoma City, is it likely that he, armed with a pistol, would have let a police officer approach his car without resisting him? As a man trained in the use of small arms, McVeigh would not have had much trouble in gunning the police officer down from within the protection of his car. Also, according to the affidavit of State Trooper Hanger, McVeigh volunteered the information that he was carrying a gun under his jacket before the officer unholstered his own gun.

I. McVeigh's possessing, and leaving in the police cruiser, a business card that seems to note his ordering of a quantity of TNT is also strange. This is just the sort of evidence that could be easily manufactured and planted after the suspect's arrest in order to incriminate him. Remember the allegedly doctored photos of Lee Harvey Oswald holding a rifle and a Communist newspaper published in *Life* magazine? Remember the photo of one of the alleged perpetrators in the World Trade Center bombing posed with grenade and Palestinian flag?

It is also extremely convenient for the prosecution that a letter is reported to have been found in the glove compartment of the Mercury, outlining plans for bombing additional sites, addressed to a "girlfriend" of Timothy McVeigh, which he supposedly did not have. [23]

J. When McVeigh was arrested he gave 3616 North Van Dyke Road, Decker, Michigan as his address. This is the property of James Nichols, and McVeigh's admission led authorities directly to both of the Nichols brothers. Does it make any sense that McVeigh would have pointed the FBI to his alleged partner or partners in crime and to Terry Nichols' property, which was reportedly used to store bomb-making ingredients?

K. According to an anonymous writer for the Militia of Montana newsletter *Taking Aim*, "Also another strange part of his story is McVeigh is not talking the party line of a Constitutionalist. This writer was involved in arguing Constitutional issues in the past. Some of the key arguments that McVeigh would be using is: A. 'You are violating my rights'; B. 'I will not speak without counsel of my choice.' (meaning anybody he chooses, not just an attorney); C. 'You have no jurisdiction over me.'

"McVeigh is only giving his name, rank and serial number. Something definitely smells bad here. If McVeigh were a Constitutionalist he would emphatically deny that he would have a serial number. You see, a Constitutionalist rescinds his social security number and would never admit to having one. It smells purely of military." [24]

There is other evidence that Timothy McVeigh is not quite the dyed-in-the-wool camouflage-bedecked militia man that the government and the press would have him be. Here is a quote from one of two letters that McVeigh allegedly wrote to the Lockport, New York *Union-Sun and Journal* after leaving the Army:

"At a point when the world has seen communism falter as an imperfect system to manage people; democracy seems to be headed down the same road. No one is seeing the "big" picture.

"Maybe we have to combine ideologies to achieve the perfect utopian government. Remember, government-sponsored health care was a communist idea. Should only the rich be allowed to live long? Does that say that because a person is poor, he is a lesser human being; and doesn't deserve to live as long, because he doesn't wear a tie to work?"

The idea of combining democracy and communism "to achieve the perfect utopian government" is absolute anathema to the populist right in almost all of its manifestations; it is pure New World Orderism. So just what are McVeigh's real political convictions?

Although these oddities in McVeigh's behavior do not prove that he was innocent of the Oklahoma bombing, they are almost as strange as the behavior of the self-professed "patsy" Lee Harvey Oswald prior to his arrest, and do point out the need to not accept easy answers and for further investigation. The quick apprehension of McVeigh after the bombing also strains belief, and opens up the possibility of a set-up. Is McVeigh a patsy in the classic mold? Will he make it to trial, or will he be dealt with before he is able to defend himself before a jury?

Documentably, there are those who would like him out of the way. On the May 8, 1995 issue of the *Oregon Commentator* from the University of Oregon, the back cover features a picture of Timothy McVeigh targeted in the crosshairs of a telescopic rifle sight. The picture is captioned "Jack Ruby Memorial Marksmanship Contest," and the caption says, "The object: Ventilate Timothy McVeigh. The Purpose: Show him how a true patriot enacts justice. The Rules: Do it before his eight year trial and subsequent stay of execution make a complete mockery of the justice system."

Still, not everyone was duped by the official explanations. Within minutes of the Oklahoma City explosion, the debate began as to who was responsible for the crime. Governmental sources initially said the answer was easy: Islamic militants. Then they turned around and said that it had been rightist militia types who had done the bombing. But by this time, by 1995, people had begun to doubt just about everything that the government had to say. They had lied to the public too much in the past, they had covered up too much, and they had committed too many crimes without being held accountable. Evidence quickly surfaced suggesting that we were not being told the whole story, and, indeed, that a cover-up of the facts and a gross miscarriage of justice might be taking place.

NOTES:

1. *Information Digest*, Vol. XXVIII #8, April 21, 1995; Thomas,

Evan, et al. "This Doesn't Happen Here," *Newsweek*, May 1, 1995; Henneberger, Melinda. "A By-the-Book Officer, 'Suspicious by Nature,' Spots Trouble and Acts Fast," *New York Times*, April 23, 1995

2. "McVeigh a dedicated soldier and a loner," *Associated Press*, August 11, 1995; *Information Digest*, Vol. XXVIII #8, April 21, 1995; Johnston, David. "Nichols brothers are charged in bombing conspiracy," *New York Times News Service*, April 26, 1995

3. Maraniss, David, and Thomas, Pierre. "More bomb suspects," *The Washington Post*, April 23, 1995

4. Thomas, Evan, et al. "The Plot," *Newsweek*, May 8, 1995

5. Sennott, Charles M., and Howe, Peter J. "'Something big is going to happen,' " *Boston Globe*, April 27, 1995; Loftis, Randy Lee. "The kindness of strangers," *Dallas Morning News*, April 30, 1995

6. Fields, Joe. "Patriots Meet at Palm Springs Despite Establishment Spasms," *The Spotlight*, May 29, 1995; Hansen, Chris. "Deadly Connections," *Dateline* television

7. *Information Digest*

8. Johnston, David. "Just Before He Was to Be Freed, Prime Bombing Suspect Is Identified in Jail," *New York Times*, April 22, 1995

9. "20 Questions About the Oklahoma City Bombing," *Media Bypass*, July 1995

10. Myers, Lawrence. "OKC Update," *Media Bypass*, October 1995

11. Kidd, Devvy. "A Quest for the Truth: My Visit to Oklahoma City, May 18th & 19th, 1995," May 21, 1995, copy obtained from *American Patriot Fax Network*, copy in author's possession

12. Thomas, Evan et al. "This Doesn't Happen Here," *Newsweek*, May 1, 1995

13. "Man arrested in bombing," *Associated Press*, April 22, 1995

14. *Facts on File*, April 27, 1995; Thomas, Evan, et al. "The Plot," *Newsweek*, May 8, 1995; Thomas, Evan et. al. "This Doesn't Happen Here," *Newsweek*, May 1, 1995

15. Thomas, Evan, et al. "The Plot," *Newsweek*, May 8, 1995

16. Halley, Chuck. Interview conducted by Jim Keith, July 29, 1995

17. Schneider, Keith. "Talk on Bombs Surges on Computer Network," *New York Times*, April 27, 1995

18. "Oklahoma Bombing Plotted for Months, Officials Say, but Suspect Is Not Talking," *New York Times*, April 25, 1995

19. *Information Digest*; *Facts on File*, May 4, 1995; "FBI: 4 or 5 were likely involved in blast," *Associated Press*, April 28, 1995; "The

Bomb... in Oklahoma," video by *Star Investigative Reports*, 1995

20. Duffy, David, et al. "Bomber Visited Day-Care Center Before Blast," *National Enquirer*, May 16, 1995
21. "McVeigh reportedly confesses," *Associated Press*, May 17, 1995
22. Sniffen, Michael J. "Videotape captures likely 2nd getaway car, source says," *Associated Press*, April 29, 1995
23. Sennott, Charles M., and Howe, Peter J. "'Something big is going to happen,'" *Boston Globe*, April 27, 1995
24. "Patriots' Worst Nightmare, Terrorism," *Taking Aim* newsletter, Volume 2, Issue No. 2, April 1995

5

The Nichols Brothers

W hen Timothy McVeigh purchased the Glock pistol he was carrying at the time of his arrest he listed his address as Fort Riley, Kansas. A search through his Army file reportedly revealed his demolitions specialty in the Army, and this provided the Bureau of Alcohol, Tobacco and Firearms enough justification to obtain a search warrant for the address listed on his driver's license, in Decker, Michigan, the property owned by James Douglas Nichols. A so-far-unsubstantiated allegation has circulated widely in the patriot underground press that a search warrant for the Nichols farm had been obtained seven days prior to Nichols' arrest, that is, four days before the Oklahoma City bombing took place.

During the search of the farm in Michigan, James Nichols was taken into custody as a material witness. James Nichols said in an interview, "I heard on the radio they were raiding a house in Decker, Michigan. I said, 'Wow, that's awful close to home.' Well, within an hour I found out. Mine."

Nichols feels that the rationale behind the raid on his house was simplistic. "His [McVeigh's] driver's license shows my address, same address as mine. Convenient. Here it is. Let's go get him." Nichols also stated, "I wasn't hiding anything. They come to put on a show, to show that they were doing something about the bombing. They were going to get someone."

According to Nichols, the FBI was not planning a simple arrest, but he believes that they were trying to set him up to be murdered to prevent him from testifying. Nichols says that an FBI agent asked him to retrieve a gun that was stored in the house. Nichols reports, "I said 'No, I won't go get it. I told you, send an agent or two in there to go do it.' [The agent said] 'Aw, go ahead. Go and do it,' and they all turned their backs, real nonchalantly. I said, 'Whoa, wait a minute...' They'd a shot me, because they would have just said 'He pulled a gun on us.' The fate of Terry and Tim would have been signed, sealed and delivered... Dead people don't testify." [1]

The FBI was soon to find that the description of the second suspect, John Doe 2, matched (according to them) Nichols' younger brother, Terry Lynn Nichols. Neighbors in Decker provided the information that Terry Nichols and McVeigh were close friends, and had served together at Fort Riley, Kansas, joining the Army on the same day although in different cities. McVeigh was said to have lived on the Nichols' farm for six to eight months. Locals also said that Nichols and McVeigh were members of the Michigan Militia. [2]

Independent investigator James McQuaid reports: "This afternoon I spoke with a militia leader from Sanilac County; this is the county which contains the Nichols residence located near Decker, Michigan. He indicated that the Nichols brothers were not members of the Michigan Militia, nor are they members of any of the independent units (located in the thumb [of Michigan], area.

"Approximately one month ago, one of the Nichols brothers came to a militia meeting (which are open to the public). During the open forum portion of the meeting, Mr. Nichols specifically indicated that he was not a member of any militia unit. Mr. Nichols encouraged those present at the meeting to 'cut up their driver's licenses.' In addition, Mr. Nichols sought to promote a discussion of tax protestor issues and attempted to distribute tax resistor material printed by someone from Minnesota, and was asked to leave the meeting.

"The militia leader I spoke with indicated that this was their only contact with either of the Nichols brothers (who live about ten minutes away). My source has not been interviewed by any law enforcement or media organization. The information provided by my source is consistent with that I've received from other sources in various militias." [3]

James Nichols later explained his contact with the militia: "I told everybody. I've been to two meetings in my whole life. I didn't like them, I told them what I thought, they told me. [I] said, 'You go your way, I'll go mine'... They have good ideas but they just seemed a little too radical."

One neighbor in Michigan, Dan Stomber, reported seeing the Nichols brother and Timothy McVeigh setting off homemade bombs in the farmyard. Les Phillips, another Decker, Michigan resident, said of the Nichols brothers, "They had a different outlook on things. They didn't want to pay taxes. They didn't want to get license plates." [4]

In 1992 Terry Nichols had sent a letter to the township clerk where he lived, renouncing his right to vote. "There is total corruption in the entire political system," Nichols told the clerk, "from the local government on up through and including the President of the United States of America, George Bush." [5]

A warrant for the arrest of Terry Nichols was issued, and an hour after the announcement of the federal raid on the Decker property, the younger Nichols turned himself into the local police in Herington, Kansas, where he lived. Herington is a farming community located 25 miles from the Ryder agency where the bomb truck had been rented. A search warrant was obtained for Terry Nichols' property, at 109 South Second Street in Herington, and a search was conducted. It is alleged that 33 firearms were found at the residence by BATF agents, including an anti-tank launcher. Also said to have been found were five 60-foot Primadet detonator cords, non-electric blasting caps, ground ammonium nitrate, nitrogen fertilizer, and 55-gallon blue plastic drums (although in another account they are described as white plastic drums with blue lids). Some accounts state that the plastic drums are "of the type used in the bombing," but the *New York Times* stated on April 30 that "it is not clear that they match blue plastic fragments found at the blast site." [6]

The presence of the detonator cords at the Nichols' property bears mention. In an interview with an ex-G.I. with extensive experience in the use of Primadet, I was told that one foot of the detonating cord is roughly equivalent in explosive power to one foot of dynamite, and that the material is so unstable that static electricity will set it off. According to the man, "Primadet is not something you leave laying around in a barn."

It was also reported that a September 1994 receipt for the purchase of 2,000 pounds of ammonium nitrate fertilizer by Terry Nichols under an alias was found, and another for a purchase of 55 gallons of diesel fuel. The receipt for the fertilizer is reported to have had McVeigh's fingerprint on it. I am reminded of the fact that a receipt for the Ryder truck supposedly involved in the World Trade Center bombing was reportedly covered with ANFO particles. [7] It is noteworthy that employees of the Mid-Kansas Cooperative Association in McPherson, Kansas, the place from which the fertilizer was reportedly purchased, are unable to identify Nichols or McVeigh. [8]

Unexplained were the large amounts of cash that Nichols had in his possession while being "partially employed" — over $45,000 — and the expenses required by McVeigh in the days preceding the bombing — in excess of $1,500, with an additional $225 in his wallet (or $2,000 according to the *New York Times*). [9]

According to U.S. Attorney Randy Rathbun, neighbors of Terry Nichols stated that a number of white males who they did not recognize stayed at the Nichols' home from April 12 to 14, 1995. Rathbun also said that the description of two of the visitors roughly corresponded to those of McVeigh and John Doe 2. [10]

When questioned by federal investigators, Terry Nichols said that McVeigh had called him from Oklahoma City on Sunday, April 16, asking him to pick him up. Nichols stated that he had driven to Oklahoma City, and that he had then driven McVeigh to Junction City, Kansas. [11] According to Oklahoma researcher J.D. Cash, accompanying Nichols on the trip was his 12-year-old son Josh. [12]

During the drive the following conversation reportedly took place:

McVeigh: "Something big is going to happen."

Nichols: "Are you going to rob a bank?"

McVeigh: "Something big is going to happen." [13]

On April 22, James Nichols appeared before Magistrate Thomas Carlson in U.S. District Court in Michigan. A request was issued by a U.S. prosecuting attorney that the audio tape of the hearing be sealed from public hearing, an act guaranteed to generate suspicion that facts were being withheld. The judge granted this request. Later, an order was obtained by an attorney for the *Detroit Free Press* for the unsealing of the tape. The tape was found to be blank, in an incident reminiscent of the famous "accidentally erased" 18 1/2 minute gap in the Nixon Watergate tapes or the "accidentally erased" tape in the Inslaw software piracy case. [14]

On April 25 the Nichols brothers were charged with conspiring with McVeigh and others to build explosives: "bottle bombs," actually, a charge unconnected to the Oklahoma City bombing. According to the affidavit contained in the complaint, the Nichols brothers had also criticized the government for the attack on the Branch Davidians. [15]

Lacking any solid evidence that would implicate James Nichols in the bombing, on May 22 a U.S. District Judge ordered his release from prison without bail after 32 days of incarceration.

"I am just glad to be free, so I can get on with my life," Nichols said, after his release on May 23. "It's a bad tragedy. Everyone should cooperate fully, and I have cooperated fully to get to the bottom of it." According to *USA Today*, Nichols had been "all but eliminated as a suspect in the Oklahoma bombing...," although at least one other media source maintained that James Nichols was still under federal scrutiny. [16]

James Nichols said that he believed the whole case against him had been trumped up to prevent him from talking in his brother's defense. "I know certain things," Nichols said. "I can tell the truth and dispel certain rumors and gossip." Nichols also stated that he believed his brother was innocent of the charges. "I don't think he's involved," he said. "I want to see some facts." Nichols staunchly defended his brother by saying, "He's not that character. He has a wife, and she's pregnant, he's planning for the future, he just bought a house, he's expanding his business. A person that's involved in a bombing like that isn't going to plan for the future."

James Nichols also stated that he had not seen anything which proved that Timothy McVeigh was guilty. He vouched for McVeigh's character by saying, "You'd probably like him. He's a likable guy. He likes to go out and shoot guns. So do I." When asked what Timothy McVeigh liked to talk about, Nichols responded, "Government issues, law and this and that, Constitution, the Randy Weaver case." [17]

As far as the "bottle bombs" that were supposedly constructed on James Nichols' Michigan farm, Nichols calls them, "Kids' play. Kids play with firecrackers, adults play with pop bottle bombs."

Who does James Nichols believe was responsible for the Oklahoma City bombing? Nichols suggests, "When you want laws passed that you can't get passed, you have to create a situation so they will get passed... It could be rogue agents, who knows?" When asked specifically whether he believes that the government was responsible for the bombing, he said, "Exactly. If you don't know history, you're doomed to repeat it... Government wouldn't shoot an innocent, unarmed woman, Randy Weaver's wife, would they? But they did. They wouldn't burn innocent people in Waco. But they did."

Nichols reiterated that he had not been involved in the bombing: "I'm not going to change their mind, you're not going to change their mind, they're the only ones that can change their mind. They're going to have to look at the facts. They have to live with that. I don't. I know in my heart and my mind I didn't do anything. I didn't help in any way, shape, or form." [18]

During a hearing in federal court in Milan, Michigan on May 2, a federal magistrate refused to release Terry Nichols from custody. During the hearing FBI agent Randall Farmerarmer, Randall testified that a witness had heard Nichols say that "the technology existed for a super bomb that could blow up a federal building." [19]

According to the judge, "There is not only probable cause to believe that the defendant committed or aided and abetted the commission of the most devastating bombing — in terms of loss of lives — in the peacetime history of this country, but the weight of the evidence that he committed that offense is great." [20]

As of May 3, 1995, federal officials were speculating in an affidavit that McVeigh and Terry Nichols might have been involved in a $60,000 robbery in Hot Springs, Arkansas in November, 1994, thus neatly accounting for the money which Nichols and McVeigh had at the time of arrest, and the funds needed to build the bomb and for other expenses. Evidence linking the duo to the robbery was a stolen safe deposit key, supposedly found at Terry Nichols' house, and the word of the victim, who reportedly "felt" that McVeigh may have been responsible. Unexplained are reports that McVeigh was in Dayton, Ohio at the time of the robbery, and that the robber had a "distinctive" hair color which has not been described further. [21]

On May 10, 1995 Terry Nichols was transported from Wichita, Kansas to the Federal Correctional Institute at El Reno, Oklahoma. On June 2, 1995 Terry Nichols' chief defense lawyer, Michael E. Tigar,gar, Michael E. protested to Judge David L. Russell that the lights were being kept on all night in Nichols' cell. Tigar also protested that Nichols had been sent twice to a psychologist without notification of defense. [22]

Terry Nichols telephoned Karl Granse, a legal researcher and Constitutional expert, on June 8. During a 20-minute conversation conducted from prison in which he sought legal advice, Nichols told Granse that he had not been involved in the bombing, and did not know McVeigh as well as news reports had suggested. According to the *New York Times*, Nichols said that he had only spent five weeks with him prior to the bombing, time that had been spent touring gun shows.

Lana Padilla, Terry Nichols' ex-wife, disagrees about the casual nature of the relationship between Nichols and McVeigh. "In the four years since their discharges [from the Army]," Padilla states, "they had become almost inseparable, traveling and partnering up to buy and sell guns and other items at various gun shows." She calls McVeigh "his closest friend." [23]

When I interviewed Karl Granse, he told me that Nichols had offered

several other revelations that have not been mentioned in the press. [24]
Press reports stated that a 60-mm antitank rocket launcher was also
found at Nichols' residence, although he denied this when he talked to
Karl Granse. Nichols informed him the antitank rocket launcher was
"just a casing... a veneer."

Terry Nichols had some interesting things to say to Granse about
Timothy McVeigh, characterizing him as not at all a calculated murderer,
but as a thoughtful person who would act as the designated driver when
soldiers from Fort Riley would go out drinking. Nichols also said that it
had been McVeigh who had worked for half an hour to try to revive
Nichols' infant son when he had died from suffocation from a plastic
bag, not an act in character with that of a man lacking any compunction
about blowing up a day care center.

In her book, ex-wife Lana Padilla (or perhaps co-author Ron Delpit)
put a curious spin on the "mysterious" suffocation of Nichols' son, coming close to suggesting that Timothy McVeigh was guilty of it. [25]

When asked directly about whether Timothy McVeigh was capable
of bombing the Oklahoma City federal building, however, Terry Nichols
responded: "I don't know." [26]

One matter that has remained untouched, unspeculated upon by national media, is that McVeigh and Nichols may have been the target of at
least one murder attempt, or that there may have been a plot to encourage one or both to commit suicide by providing them the means. Although the information is sketchy, Charles M. Mildner, the chief correctional supervisor at the El Reno Federal Correctional Institution, where
McVeigh and Nichols are incarcerated, was relieved of duty in August
1995. The reason was that Mildner wanted to "tighten safety restrictions," ordering only one officer to handle food trays for McVeigh and
Nichols. The reason for Mildner's concern, and his removal from duty,
was that syringes were found on food trays going into McVeigh and
Nichols' cell bloc. [27]

NOTES:

1. Hansen, Chris. "His Brother's Keeper," *Dateline* television production, 1995
2. *Facts on File*, April 27, 1995
3. McQuaid, James. Fax of April 21, 1995, released by *American Patriot Fax Network*. Copy in the author's possession
4. Nemeth, Mary. "Why Oklahoma City?", *Maclean's*, May 1, 1995;

Hansen
5. "2 radicals arrested in bomb attack," *The Weekend Sun,* British Columbia, April 22, 1995
6. *Information Digest,* Vol. XXVIII #8, April 21, 1995; Thomas, Evan, et al. "The Plot," *Newsweek,* May 8, 1995; "FBI affidavit details alleged plot," *Associated Press,* May 12, 1995; Johnston, David. "Agents in Kansas Hunt for Bomb Factory As Sense of Frustration Begins to Build," *New York Times,* April 30, 1995; "Terry Nichols Shows Up in Prison Court," *Reuters News Service,* May 12, 1995
7. *Facts on File,* May 4, 1995; Thomas, Evan. "Cracking Down on Hate," *Newsweek,* May 15, 1995; Cole, Patrick E., et al. "This Guy Is A National Tragedy," *Time,* May 15, 1995
8. Pincus and Lardner, Jr., "Nichols Lawyer Says McVeigh Rented Suspect Storage Shed," *Washington Post,* June 20, 1995
9. Sharn, Lori. "Probe follows money trail," June 16, 1995
10. Sennott, Charles M., and Howe, Peter J. "'Something big is going to happen,'" *Boston Globe,* April 27, 1995
11. "FBI affidavit details alleged plot," *Associated Press,* May 12, 1995
12. Cash, J.D. Interview conducted by Jim Keith, September 26, 1995
13. Belluck, Pam. "Affidavit Offers Clues About Suspect's Activities in the Days Before the Bombing," *New York Times,* April 27, 1995
14. Blair, Mike. "Mysterious 'Accident' Blanks Tape of Nichols Hearing," *The Spotlight,* May 15, 1995
15. *Facts on File,* April 27, 1995; Sennott, Charles M., and Howe, Peter J. "'Something big is going to happen,'" *Boston Globe,* April 27, 1995
16. Johnson, Kevin, and Sharn, Lori. *USA Today,* May 24, 1995
17. Bennet, James. "Charges Dropped, a Farmer Worries About His Reputation," *New York Times,* August 11, 1995; Gunderson, Ted. "The Gunderson Bomb Report," 1995.
18. Hansen, Chris. "His Brother's Keeper," *Dateline* television show, 1995
19. *Facts on File,* May 4, 1995
20. Serrano, Richard A. "Evidence Against Nichols Called 'Great'," *Los Angeles Times,* June 7, 1995
21. Padilla, Lana and Delpit, Ron. *By Blood Betrayed,* Harper Paperbacks, New York, 1995; "Missing duffel may hold clues to Oklahoma blast," *New York Times,* July 16, 1995
22. "Feds charge Terry Nichols in bombing," *Los Angeles Times,* May

10, 1995; "Judge orders suspect held in Oklahoma bombing," *Associated Press,* June 3, 1995
23. Padilla, Lana and Delpit, Ron.
24. Johnston, David. "A Man Charged in the Oklahoma Bombing Talks About His Co-Defendant," *New York Times*, June 24, 1995
25. Padilla, Lana and Delpit, Ron.
26. Granse, Karl. Interview conducted by Jim Keith in October, 1995
27. "Bombing suspects' security chief removed," *The Idaho Statesman, August 28, 1995*

6

The
Investigation Widens

USA *Today* summarized information in an FBI affidavit, released at a hearing for Terry Nichols, in a chronology printed on May 12:

"Sept. 22, 1994 — McVeigh rents a storage unit in Herington, Kan., using the name 'Shawn Rivers.' Nichols says he later retrieved items there, including a rifle.

"Sept. 30 — Forty 50-pound bags of ammonium nitrate are purchased from Mid-Kansas Cooperative Association in McPherson, Kan., by a 'Mike Havens.' A receipt for the fertilizer is eventually found at Terry Nichols' home in Herington. The receipt reportedly had McVeigh's fingerprint on it.

"Oct. 17 — A storage unit is rented in Council Grove, Kan., in the name of 'Joe Kyle.' An FBI search of Nichols' home finds a document citing that location and name.

"Oct. 18 — Forty more 50-pound bags of ammonium nitrate are purchased at the same store, also by 'Mike Havens.'

"Nov. 7 — Another storage unit is rented in Council Grove, under the name 'Ted Parker.' An FBI search of Nichols' home uncovers a document citing that location and name.

"Nov. 22 — Nichols writes a letter to McVeigh stating it should only be opened if he dies. The letter cites the locations of two units and tells McVeigh to 'Go for it.'

"April 15, 1995 — Nichols purchases diesel fuel from a Conoco service station in Manhattan, Kan.

"April 16 — Nichols purchases an additional 21.59 gallons of diesel fuel from a Conoco service station in Junction City.

"April 17 — Two men rent a yellow Ryder truck at Elliott's Body Shop in Junction City. The man who signs the rental agreement identifies himself as 'Bob Kling,' but a clerk subsequently identifies him as Timothy McVeigh.

"That same day a Ryder truck is seen parked behind Nichols' home.

"April 17 or 18 — An older model pickup with a camper shell is seen at the Herington storage shed.

"April 18 — A witness at Geary State Fishing Lake in rural Kansas sees a yellow Ryder truck parked next to a blue or brown pickup truck, possibly with a camper shell. Authorities believe the bomb may have been assembled there."

Early investigations centered around a search for a bomb factory in Kansas, where the bombers would have mixed and loaded the Ryder truck with approximately 5,000 pounds of ANFO in barrels, and rigged the payload with a detonator. When no suitable location was found that might have been the site for the bomb construction, the FBI reported that Geary State Fishing Lake in Kansas was the probable location because of the discovery of traces of fuel oil at that site, although one suspects that small quantities of fuel oil could be found at virtually any camping site. If the bomb had been built at that location, it seems likely that traces of ANFO would have been found, not just fuel oil.

Additionally, inspection of the Geary Lake area shows that bomb-building is somewhat unlikely in this locale, given the fact that the lake is completely exposed to view, and that in mid-April the trees in the area would have lacked concealing foliage.

Would the bomb making have been done out in the open? As demonstrated by information on preparations that were necessary for the World Trade Center bombing, constructing a bomb of this alleged composition and size is an arduous, messy, and time-consuming process, and would have been certain to attract the interest of passers-by in the area. If the bomb was constructed inside the Ryder truck, oxygen equipment would have been necessary for those who mixed it. Where are the stained mixing clothes, the oxygen equipment, the mixing paddles, the discarded cans and bags? Speculations were offered by the FBI that the bomb ingredients might have been combined in a cement mixer, but this is wishful thinking: no cement mixer has been found. For individuals who were so lax in leaving bomb-making materials and firearms around the Nichols residence, and who incriminated themselves so lavishly, it is amazing how well they concealed the actual creation of the bomb. [1]

Other information suggests that it is unlikely that Geary Lake was the site of the creation of the bomb. Bomb experts state that an ANFO mixture hauled 175 miles from Geary Lake to Oklahoma City would probably not detonate, because of settling out of the chemicals, and that this settling out would occur after only a few miles of driving. The idea that the bomb was driven from Kansas to Oklahoma City is, according to these experts, "beyond reason." [2]

Possibly the most damning evidence against the bomb being constructed at the Geary Lake location is that ammonium nitrate must be kept extremely dry in order for it to detonate, and that much of the ammonium nitrate available commercially is too damp to detonate. If one wanted to keep ammonium nitrate dry, would the bomb have been built next to a lake?

According to the FBI, after the bomb was constructed at Geary Lake, Nichols and McVeigh drove to Nichols' home in Herington, Kansas and spent the night there. Neighbors who were interviewed, however, cannot remember seeing the Ryder truck parked at Nichols home. Nichols' son Josh says that he never saw a Ryder truck at the residence, nor, for that matter, did he ever see any blue plastic barrels. [3]

Witnesses establish that the Ryder truck was driven down Highway 77 on the 18th of April. The Ryder truck was seen crossing the Kansas state line north of Newkirk, and it was accompanied by an older model blue half-ton pickup truck. At the E-Z Mart in Newkirk at approximately 3:15 p.m. on the 18th, Terry Nichols is said to have pulled the blue pickup up to the gas pump and filled the tank of the truck with gasoline. The yellow Ryder truck was backed up to the building, with McVeigh driving, according to a witness. Nichols is reported to have entered the store and paid for the gas. He also bought eight burritos and four soft drinks: possibly food for four people. The manager believes that there were at least two other persons waiting outside in the blue truck, which confirms this suspicion.

A report on CBS television stated that McVeigh had stopped to ask for directions to the federal building on the day of the bombing. David Hall has stated that, "We actually know where McVeigh stopped along the way and talked with people and we've talked with some of those people. The FBI knows that same thing that we know. They know that McVeigh was supposed to be in Oklahoma City at 3 a.m. in the morning and was delayed because he got lost and we've talked to the people who talked to him while he was lost and got him back on the road." [4]

The next reported observation of the Ryder truck and the blue pickup is at the McDonalds restaurant at Sheridan and Western streets in Oklahoma City, between 9 and 10 p.m. on April 18. Jerry Bohnen, the news director at K-TOK radio in Oklahoma City, was contacted by a homeless man who states that the night before the bombing McVeigh drove by the McDonalds at Sheridan and Western in Oklahoma City, and yelled to him, "Hey, want to have a few beers?" The homeless man agreed and after receiving money from McVeigh, bought two quarts of beer at the Total Store, the purchase verified by Ron Williams, one of the employees. Williams confirms that there was a Ryder truck parked at the McDonalds at the time the man bought beer. After the bombing the FBI questioned the homeless man about his encounter, and also confiscated surveillance videotape from the Total Store.

Terry Nichols has reportedly told investigator David Hall that McVeigh was, in fact, at the McDonalds on April 18th, and that the purpose was for a meeting with men who would provide a $2,000 payoff to McVeigh. Another Oklahoma City reporter who insists upon anonymity verifies the meeting through the account of a source in Oklahoma City. At 9:45 p.m. Nichols drove away from the McDonalds restaurant and reportedly drove back to Kansas. On the morning of the 19th of April, Nichols was observed at his home by several witnesses. [5]

On May 10, information was released that federal investigators were considering whether John Doe 2 was misidentified, and was actually Terry Nichols' 12-year-old son, Josh. According to a "Washington official" quoted by *Associated Press,* the FBI was questioning the accuracy of the composite sketches, "as evidenced by the fact that there are three versions of it now." The same official protested mightily when he discounted the description of Doe 2's tattoo by saying, "We've heard this was a kid who was into those temporary, stick-on tattoos." [6]

It is interesting that the FBI was trying to discount and distance themselves from the idea that there was a John Doe 2 just as independent researchers were beginning to sense that they were hot on the suspect's trail.

NOTES:

1. Achenbach, Joel. "Dead Ends," *Washington Post*, June 11, 1995
2. "The Bomb... in Oklahoma," video by *Star Investigative Reports,* 1995

3. Ibid; Padilla, Lana and Delpit, Ron. *By Blood Betrayed,* Harper Paperbacks, 1995

4. Hall, David. "FBI Stonewalls Evidence Discovered by TV Station," *The Spotlight*, July 17, 1995

5. Rappoport, John. *Oklahoma City Bombing, The Suppressed Truth*, Blue Press, Los Angeles, 1995; "The Bomb... in Oklahoma"

6. Howlett, Debbi, and Meddis, Sam Vincent. "John Doe 2 sketch may be witness' son," *USA Today*, May 10, 1995

7

Fortier

On May 8, 1995, Michael Fortier, who had served with McVeigh and Terry Nichols in the Army, characterized as "a close friend" of McVeigh, was interviewed on Cable News Network television, and he stated, "I do not believe Tim McVeigh blew up any building in Oklahoma. There's nothing for me to look back on and say, 'Yeah, that might have been. I should have seen it'... There's nothing like that."

Researcher John Judge interviewed Michael Fortier prior to his being contacted by the government, and Fortier denied that Timothy McVeigh could have possibly had anything to do with the Oklahoma bombing. Fortier, however, would soon do a turnabout in his beliefs about McVeigh's guilt. [1]

In the latter portion of May, Fortier was arrested, and then became more forthcoming with information on the bombing. According to federal investigators, Fortier stated that when he and McVeigh lived in Kingman, Arizona they had discussed blowing up the Oklahoma City federal building, as well as other sites, and that McVeigh had invited him to join in the bombing, but that he had declined. Fortier said that on December 22, 1994 he and McVeigh had travelled to Oklahoma City, and had posed as job applicants, going "floor to floor" in order to inspect the federal building as a possible target for bombing. Fortier implicated Terry Nichols in plans for the bombing, but denied any actual involvement by himself. [2]

In a chronology released by *Newsweek*, McVeigh and Fortier are described as transporting a load of guns from Kansas to Kingman, Arizona in January 1995, and selling them in Kingman in February. According to *Newsweek*, "McVeigh and Fortier allegedly sold the stockpiled guns to pay for expenses and bomb materials."

Federal officials, however, were "wary" about what Fortier had to say, on the basis that he might be trying to strike a deal with prosecutors for his own immunity from prosecution. By July 3, 1995, *Newsweek* would be quoting a federal official as saying that Fortier was "chest deep" in the alleged plot, and noting that prosecutors were discussing a 15-year prison term for Fortier in exchange for testimony which would presumably implicate McVeigh and Terry Nichols. [3]

By August, information on plea bargain negotiations with Fortier and his wife Lori was being released. According to *USA Today*, the process of plea bargaining had been "slow." A week had been spent agreeing on ground rules, with key decisions being deferred to FBI and Justice officials in Washington. According to published reports, Fortier "acknowledged helping transport stolen weapons to aid in financing the bombing and spoke of his knowledge of the bombing plans." Lori Fortier had been granted complete immunity from prosecution, and was soon to testify against McVeigh and Terry Nichols before a grand jury. Michael Fortier's sentencing was postponed until after his testimony against Terry Nichols and Timothy McVeigh. [4]

On August 10, 1995, Michael Fortier released the following statement as part of his plea bargain agreement with federal officials:

Factual Statement in Support of Plea Petition

"On December 15th and 16th I rode with Tim McVeigh from my home in Kingman, Arizona to Kansas. There I was to receive weapons that Tim McVeigh told me had been stolen by Terry Nichols and himself. While in Kansas, McVeigh and I loaded about twenty-five weapons into a car that I had rented. On December 17th, 1994, I drove the rental car back to Arizona through Oklahoma and Oklahoma City. Later, after returning to Arizona and at the request of Tim McVeigh, I sold some of the weapons and again at the request of Tim McVeigh I gave him some money to give to Terry Nichols.

Prior to April 1995, McVeigh told me about the plans that he and Terry Nichols had to blow up the Federal Building in Oklahoma City, Oklahoma. I did not as soon as possible make known my knowledge of the McVeigh and Nichols plot to any judge or any other persons in civil authority.

When F.B.I. agents questioned me later, about two days

after the bombing, and during the next three days, I lied about my knowledge and concealed information. For example, I falsely stated that I had no knowledge of plans to bomb the federal building.

I also gave certain items that I had received from McVeigh, including a bag of ammonium nitrate fertilizer, to a neighbor of mine so the items would not be found by law enforcement officers in a search of my residence.

The neighbor that Fortier refers to in his statement is Jim Rosencrans, who admitted in an interview with a magazine that he had been given a bag of ammonium nitrate fertilizer by Fortier, and that he had disposed of it in the desert. "Had I known [what] the fertilizer was for, I would have thrown the bag back in Fortier's yard," Rosencrans said. [5]

On September 3, Lori Fortier told a federal grand jury that Timothy McVeigh had once arranged soup cans in a triangle on her kitchen floor in demonstration of how to construct a "shaped" explosive charge. Mrs. Fortier also said that McVeigh had once drawn a diagram of how to blow up a building. [6]

NOTES:

1. Judge, John. Unpublished interview by Kenn Thomas, June 8, 1995
2. "Bombing suspect says he, McVeigh posed as job hunters to case building," *Los Angeles Times*, May 21, 1995
3. "Feds wary of bombing witness," *Los Angeles Times*, May 21, 1995; "McVeigh friend reportedly implicates Terry Nichols," *Washington Post*, May 24, 1995; Liu, Melinda. "A Case Built on a Web of Damning Detail," *Newsweek*, July 3, 1995; Thomas, Evan, with Murr, Collier, Hosenball, Liu, and Isikoff, "Inside the Plot," *Newsweek*, June 5, 1995
4. Johnson, Kevin. "Bomb negotiations touch and go," *USA Today*, August 14, 1995; Hansen, Chris. "Deadly Connections," *Dateline* television, 1995
5. Myers, Lawrence. "OKC Update," *Media Bypass*, October 1995
6. "Grand Jury Hears of Bomb Demonstration," *New York Times*, September 4, 1995

8

Colbern

On May 12, Steven Colbern, a UCLA graduate biochemist and former research associate in DNA studies at Cedars-Sinai Research Institute, who had spent time around Kingman, Arizona, was arrested in Oatman, Arizona after a nationwide manhunt. Colbern struggled with arresting officers, and pulled out a handgun in a show of resistance notably more vigorous than that of Timothy McVeigh, but was subdued. Federal officials were careful not to make statements suggesting that Colbern, who resembles the "John Doe 2" composite drawing, was actually the man. Colbern and McVeigh had shared a mailbox in Kingman, Arizona. [1] Colbern admitted to knowing McVeigh under the alias "Tim Tuttle," a pseudonym that some have speculated is based on the Robert DeNiro bomber character in the "1984"-esque movie "Brazil," but which may also refer to Tuttle Lake, near Junction City. The owner of the restaurant where Colbern worked said that the man hadn't been to work for a week before and a week after the bombing. She called him "a meticulous dishwasher who had a strong interest in UFOs." [2]

One official noted that Colbern was said to drive a brown pickup "that was recently spotted with a bag of ammonium nitrate fertilizer in the bed."

The *Chicago Tribune* noted, "officials said a witness told investigators that a brown pickup appeared to be traveling with McVeigh's car when it was pulled over in Oklahoma on the day of the bombing. As a state trooper arrested McVeigh, the pickup pulled to the side of the road, waited for a short time and then moved on, according to the witness." [3]

An Arizona newspaper revealed significantly more: "Authorities said Colbern owns the brown pickup that was caught on an Oklahoma trooper's video camera when McVeigh, the prime suspect in the April 19 bombing, was stopped on a traffic violation 90 minutes after the blast." [4] So the McVeigh arrest was videotaped? Why wasn't this information released until almost one month after the bombing, and why was it only leaked through the relatively unheard-of *Arizona Republic* newspaper? Another question. If someone was following McVeigh in the brown truck, wouldn't they have noticed that the Mercury was missing its license plate? Finally, wouldn't these alleged bombers have easily caught Officer Hanger in a crossfire of bullets after he had gotten out of the police car and as he was walking toward the Mercury Marquis? What did the alleged perpetrators have to lose?

Colbern was held without bail on charges of failure to appear on a 1994 firearms case in California, resisting arrest, and being a fugitive possessing a firearm.

According to an *Associated Press* news story, "Another possible connection emerged Saturday, when Mohave County [Arizona] authorities revealed that a roommate of Colbern's was being held in connection with a mysterious explosion that damaged a house outside Kingman, Ariz., on Feb. 21. The bomb was made of ammonium nitrate and fuel oil." [5] The roommate was Dennis Malzac, who was held in lieu of a $50,000 bond on a felony charge of arson. What the *Associated Press* release didn't mention was that the house that was damaged in the explosion was owned by Francis McPeak, a one-time business partner of Timothy McVeigh.

By May 16, authorities were saying that Colbern was not under suspicion as being involved in the bombing. [6]

NOTES:

1. Dellios, Hugh. "Federal marshals arrest chemist," *Chicago Tribune*, May 13, 1995
2. Shaffer, Mark. "Probe nets 2nd man in Oatman," *Arizona Republic*, May 14th, 1995
3. Delios
4. Shaffer
5. "Ties to bombing suspect explored," *Associated Press*, May 14, 1995
6. Shaffer; "Another arrest in bombing," *Associated Press*, May 13, 1995; *Facts on File*, May 18, 1995; "Feds order Colbern held without bond," *Associated Press*, May 14, 1995; Delios

9

Other Suspects

At least two Branch Davidians were arrested as suspects in the Oklahoma City bombing case. According to a report by Michael Mugrage, who was also arrested as a suspect at the time:

"Both Davidians Renos Avraam #60590-1080 and Livingston Fagan #60550-080, as well as myself, are under 'investigation' for the incident that occurred in Oklahoma City. We are all being held in isolation [as of June 19, 1995]. As for me, I was told that I was considered a 'suspect' (possibly the first one 'detained' — at approximately 11 am on April 19). The reason given was that I had made a 'statement or statements' that led the institution's administration to believe that I had 'knowledge' of this crime.

"I had only pointed out that the nineteenth was the second anniversary of the Mt. Carmel (Waco, Texas) massacre. I, along with millions of other Americans, knew that — so why single me out? Plenty of other individuals were talking about that possible 'connection,' even on the radio, prior to my 'arrest'...

"From what I've been able to find out about the other two men, Fagan (who's been in the 'hole' since early December of last year, for refusing to accept a work assignment) was 'interviewed' by staff here, on the same morning that I was arrested (April 19). He was returned to his cell, in segregation.

"Avraam, likewise, was 'interviewed,' then presumably let back out on the yard, only to learn, later that afternoon, that I had been 'locked up.' I'm not exactly sure what transpired after this, but within 24 hours, Avraam had also been placed in detention." [1]

On April 19, Asas Siddiqy, an Arab-American, was detained in

Oklahoma City, while two others, Anis Siddiqy and Mohammed Chafi, were detained in Dallas. All three men were later released. [2]

On April 20, Abrahim Ahmad, a U.S. citizen and resident of Oklahoma, was stopped and released at the airport by officials in Oklahoma City, then was detained in London, England. In London the man was strip-searched, denied food and water, and was returned that night in shackles to the United States. Ahmad was singled out based upon a profile of possible suspects issued by the FBI, whose investigations initially focused on Middle Easterners. He had been en route to Amman, Jordan, and was wearing a blue jogging suit like those described as worn by the bombing suspects immediately prior to the blast. His luggage continued on to Rome. When opened, the luggage contained three jogging suits, pliers, kitchen knives, aluminum foil, electric wire, silicon, photography materials, a VCR, and a photograph album with pictures of military weapons.

Researcher John Judge interviewed Mr. Ahmad, and the man explained that his suitcase had been full of presents for family and friends in the Middle East. American tools, he said, were of better quality than those he could obtain in Jordan, the electric wire had been for the VCR he was carrying, and the "silicon" was caulking for his uncle's sink. Judge suggests that if the FBI had really suspected Ahmad of being a terrorist, then they would have stopped his bag in Oklahoma City, rather than letting it proceed to Rome. Judge suspects that the authorities were "buying time" in the investigation, and possibly planning to set up Ahmad as a patsy. After his return to the U.S. and his interrogation, Ahmad was released. [3]

On April 21, Ray Jimboy, was arrested by FBI agents in Okemah, Oklahoma. Jimboy knew McVeigh in the Army and also physically resembles John Doe 2, but he was released after questioning. [4]

David Iniguez, a deserter from Fort Riley, Kansas, was arrested in California on April 23. He was later written off as a suspect. [5]

Also on April 23, Jennifer McVeigh, suspect Timothy McVeigh's sister, was detained by the FBI. She was interrogated and the house where she was staying was searched. According to one official, she was "burning papers on the grill" when federal agents arrived. [6] Jennifer McVeigh was released, although she was placed under surveillance. According to ABC News, the FBI had said that she might be charged, depending upon the degree to which she cooperated with the investigation. [7] Friends of McVeigh's sister reportedly remembered her making comments earlier in the year that "something big is going to happen in

March or April, and Tim's involved." [8]

A letter was later released, alleged to be the last sent by Timothy McVeigh to his sister prior to the bombing. The partial text follows:

> Still waiting on your letter as to whether you recv'd my last letter. (About being a 'rock.') That had a lot of sensitive material in it. So it's important to know if you received it, or if it was intercepted (either by G-men or Dad)... Please respond ASAP, only one letter. If one is already en route, Don't send another. Send no more after 01 APR, and then, even if it's an emergency — watch what you say, because I may not get it in time, and the G-men might get it out of my box, incriminating you.

By July 20, Stephen Jones, McVeigh's lawyer, was protesting "squadroom trickery" in the interrogation of Jennifer McVeigh. Reports had been leaked that Jennifer McVeigh had said that her brother had mentioned his involvement in a bank robbery, but Jones stated that he was certain that McVeigh had not committed any robberies. He also stated that Jennifer McVeigh had been subjected to "intimidating" interviews with federal investigators, which had been held in rooms filled with surveillance photos of her. Another report added that Jennifer McVeigh had been shown pictures of dead and burned babies, and quoted her as saying, "They put me and my mother in this room with all these huge posters with my name and a picture all blown up with all these possible charges against me... like life imprisonment, death penalty." These reports, if true, should render all interrogations conducted in the case by the FBI as suspect.

"It's standard trickery," Jones said. "They make it look like they've had an FBI agent behind every door since the doctor first slapped your bottom at birth." McVeigh's lawyer added that, "Before this investigation is all over with, the government will have Tim McVeigh standing next to Lee Harvey Oswald." Others have suggested the same possibility with a sinister difference: McVeigh might end up lying next to Oswald, in a figurative sense. [9]

In Valdosta, Georgia on April 24, Scott Sweely of Del City, Oklahoma, was arrested and forced to lay face down on the roadside while he was being handcuffed. Sweely was released four hours later. [10]

On April 26, federal authorities announced that there had been at least four and possibly more accomplices in the bombing.

Australian tourist Nick Morgan, a John Doe 2 look-alike, it is reported, was questioned by police in Ontario, Canada on April 30. [11]

By the end of April, federal investigators as well as media flagships like the *Washington Post* were saying that, judging from his behavior prior to the bomb's explosion, it was unlikely that McVeigh had been the mastermind of the bombing plot. [12]

On May 2 "drifters" Gary Land and Robert Jacks were arrested in Carthage, Missouri. The two were located using the Rapid Start Team FBI computer network, which had placed them in Kingman, Arizona and Perry, Oklahoma at the same times that McVeigh had been there. They were released after a day of questioning and a search of their belongings, but were subpoenaed to testify at a grand jury hearing to take place later. [13]

At the end of August 1995 a new suspect entered the picture; or at least a portion of a suspect. This was a severed leg found in the rubble of the federal building. On the leg were olive drab pants (camouflage pants in other reports), a black military-style boot, an elastic "blouse" for keeping tucked-in boots neat, and two pairs of socks (as worn in the military, and by members of BATF, FBI and other federal SWAT teams). The leg could not be matched to any of the other victims in the bombing, and thus was thought to be the leg of, perhaps, the elusive John Doe No. 2. "The limb probably belonged to a light-skinned man under the age of 30 with dark hair, Chief Medical Examiner Fred B. Jordan said in a statement." Later, investigators released the information that the leg had been misidentified, and that it belonged to a young Afro-American woman. A young Afro-American woman with curious taste in attire, I will add. [14]

Other officials doubted that the leg would offer any insight as to those guilty in the bombing. Ray Blakeney, director of operations at the Oklahoma Medical Examiner's Office, stated, "We have known about this [leg] for some time. I have never thought that it involved any other bomber. Nobody else has, either."

But according to *USA Today*, McVeigh's lawyer, Stephen Jones, suggested that the leg might provide a clue to the "real" conspirators involved in the Oklahoma City bombing. [15]

NOTES:

1. Mugrage, Michael. "You Decide Who Looks Paranoid," *The Spotlight, June 19, 1995*
2. "F.B.I. Seeking 2 in Blast; Search for Bodies Is Slow," *New York*

Times, April 21, 1995; Verhovek, Sam Howe. "Dallas Trip Turned Into 16-Hour Legal Ordeal, Student Says," *New York Times*, April 21, 1995; "Last of 3 Muslim men released," *Reno Gazette-Journal*, April 22, 1995
3. Ribadeneira, Diego, and Farrell, John Aloysius. "FBI sets sights on two suspects in blast," *Boston Globe*, April 21, 1995; Judge, John. Unpublished interview by Kenn Thomas, June 8, 1995
4. Eddings, Jerelyn. "Dry holes, dead ends," *U.S. News & World Report*, May 15, 1995
5. Ibid.
6. Jackson, David. "Prosecutors piece together case against McVeigh," *Dallas Morning News*, April 30, 1995
7. Eddings
8. Sniffen, Michael J. "Videotape captures likely 2nd getaway car, source says," *Associated Press,* April 29, 1995
9. Johnson, Kevin. "McVeigh lawyer says FBI agents using 'trickery'," *USA Today*, July 20, 1995; "Arraignments set for Tuesday," *USA Today,* August 14, 1995
10. Eddings
11. Ibid.
12. Pincus, Walter and Maraniss, David. "Clues to Bombing Suggest More Suspects," *Washington Post*, April 30, 1995
13. Eddings
14. "New disclosure in Okla. blast," *Associated Press,* August 8, 1995
15. Johnson, Kevin. "Officials doubt severed leg will provide clues," *USA Today*, August 9, 1995

10

The Changing Face of McVeigh

A bail hearing was held for McVeigh on April 27 at the Federal Correctional Institute at El Reno. There, FBI special agent John Hersley testified that three witnesses had seen a man who looked like McVeigh near the Oklahoma City Federal Building before the blast, and that bomb chemical residues had been found on the clothing that McVeigh had worn at the time of his arrest. [1]

On May 17, the *New York Times* released the dramatic news that Timothy McVeigh had confessed to the Oklahoma City bombing. According to the *Times*, "he chose his target because it housed so many government offices and was more vulnerable than other federal buildings." The confession was allegedly heard by anonymous sources who had talked to McVeigh while in jail. The *Times* further stated, "McVeigh told the sources, who spoke on condition of anonymity, that planning for the bombing began at least nine months ago and Oklahoma City was one of several cities that had been considered in the Midwest." [2] The following day, McVeigh's lawyer, Stephen Jones, disputed the report. "I'm not aware that he's confessed," Jones said. [3]

It seems curious to me that if McVeigh did in fact confess, that there have been no follow-up statements by the FBI. There was, however, a later statement by the sheriff of Noble County, Oklahoma, Jerry R. Cook. Cook doubted the correctness of the *Times* story, saying, "The individual who claims to have heard McVeigh admit to the bombing was not even in the Noble County Jail at the time McVeigh was in custody here." [4]

On June 25, 1995 the media released a statement by Eric Maloney, who had attended meetings of the Michigan Militia Corps, a citizens' militia group. Maloney said that he was present at meetings in late January in which Timothy McVeigh was present, and in which leaders of the group called for an attack on a National Guard base in northern Michigan. According to Maloney, McVeigh volunteered for the attack. Maloney stated that he had tried to dissuade the militia leaders from the plan, which they admitted was "suicidal," but failing that, he contacted the Bureau of Alcohol, Tobacco and Firearms. Accounts of others who had attended the meetings were at variance with Maloney's statements. More than one said that it was Maloney who was responsible for the plan to attack the National Guard base, and that it was he who had to be dissuaded from going any further with it. [5]

By June 26 the face of Tim McVeigh had changed. Now he was longer the silent, glowering monster that the media had compared with the fictional cannibal genius Hannibal Lecter. Now, in a series of photos and a videotape released by McVeigh's legal defense, the accused bomber looked positively amiable; boyish, even.

"The FBI wants to present him as they see him. I want to present him as he really is," attorney Stephen Jones said during a news conference. "The public is entitled to know more about Mr. McVeigh than the government has released anonymously." [6]

McVeigh broke his silence with an interview for *Newsweek* magazine that appeared on July 3, 1995. In the interview, McVeigh denied that he had confessed to the Oklahoma City bombing while in jail, and also denied early media reports that he had referred to himself as a "prisoner of war" while in jail. He indicated that reports that he belonged to, or had attended meetings of, the Michigan Militia were false.

McVeigh was asked, "What about the recent claims from [Michael] Fortier that you allegedly cased the federal building together last December?" Attorney Steven Jones responded, "Now, wait a second. I don't know that Fortier's made any such claims. That's a report." McVeigh responded, "I've been through Oklahoma City," but chose not to say whether he was with Fortier at the time.

Asked about "postwar hangover" (with the unstated implication that this might have put him in the mood for a bombing), McVeigh stated, "I think it was delayed in my case. I understand the feeling you're relating, that there's a natural adrenaline, you're way up and then it's way down when it's over... I think it did hit when everyone did get out." Note that

McVeigh has replied with what appears to be subconscious innocence, casually incriminating himself while assuming that the question merely refers to his Army career and its aftermath.

In response to a question about playing "with demolitions on the farm in Michigan," McVeigh stated, "It would amount to firecrackers... It was like popping a paper bag... They were plastic Pepsi [bottles] that burst because of air pressure." Specifically asked whether they were using ammonium nitrate in the Pepsi bombs, McVeigh did not respond.

In response to a question about the children killed in the bombing, McVeigh answered, "It's a very tragic thing."

In the interview, McVeigh also noted that he had "specifically requested" that he be given an armored vest when taken from jail by federal officials. "I could see the buildup of the crowd outside and I knew what the situation was and I specifically requested an armored vest. They said they'd work on it. And of course you've seen the picture coming out of the courthouse — they're all standing at arm's length away from me."

The *Newsweek* interviewer asks, "Did your memory bank spin up visions of Oswald?"

"Yes, yes," McVeigh responds.

Straightforwardly asked, "Did you do it?", McVeigh stated, "The only way we can really answer that is that we are going to plead not guilty."

A close study of the gloss that *Newsweek* reporters appended to the interview shows an attempt to subtly paint McVeigh as a guilty party, in essence to convict him for the crime of the Oklahoma City bombing before he had even been formally charged with it. *Newsweek* stated that McVeigh "seemed a lot more like a typical Gen-Xer than a deranged loner, much less a terrorist. His handshake was firm, and he looked his visitors right in the eye. He appeared a little nervous, maybe, but good-humored and self-aware. Normal." In the next paragraph, they sweepingly discount that apparent normalcy, saying that "is the image that Timothy McVeigh wants to project." [7]

In an article in the same issue of *Newsweek*, the interviewer, David Hackworth, a Militiary veteran, attempts to psychoanalyze McVeigh:

"What happened to McVeigh after Desert Storm? My hunch is that after the war, McVeigh slipped into what's known among vets as a post-war hangover. I've seen countless veterans, including myself, stumble home after the high-noon excitement of the killing fields, missing their battle buddies and the unique dangers and sense of purpose. Many lose themselves forever."

Hackworth makes the generous admission, "I'm no shrink," but then says, "but I've seen this failure to adapt many times before. The rules change on you. You're used to order — having a clear objective, knowing just how to get the job done. Then you're on your own in a different world, with no structure and little exact sense of what you're supposed to do. Does this excuse the horrible crimes of which McVeigh stands accused? No. It doesn't even begin to explain them. All anyone can surmise is that McVeigh had lost his anchor."

That is, if he committed the crime, Hackworth neglects to say. It is obvious that McVeigh's image is being carefully tailored to fit into the role of the guilty party in the public mind. [8]

NOTES:

1. *Facts on File*, April 27, 1995
2. "McVeigh reportedly confesses," *Associated Press,* May 17, 1995
3. "Lawyer disputes McVeigh confession," *Associated Press,* May 18, 1995
4. Myers, Lawrence. "OKC Update," *Media Bypass*, October 1995
5. Janofsky, Michael. "Militia plotted assault on Militiary base," *San Francisco Examiner*, June 25, 1995
6. Johnson, Kevin. "McVeigh: Blast 'very tragic', *USA Today*, June 26, 1995; "Defense tries to bolster image," *Associated Press,* June 26, 1995
7. Hackworth, David H. and Annin, Peter. "The Suspect Speaks Out," *Newsweek*, July 3, 1995
8. Hackworth, David H. "Talking 'Soldier to Soldier' Behind Bars," *Newsweek*, July 3, 1995

11

Indictments

On August 10, 1995, Timothy McVeigh and Terry Nichols were charged with 11 criminal counts in the Oklahoma City bombing by a federal grand jury. Three charges are for conspiring to use a "weapon of mass destruction" for murder, for the use of the Ryder truck as a bomb, and for the malicious destruction of federal property resulting in death. The remaining eight charges are for the killing of eight federal law enforcement officials who died in the blast. The charges carry a possible death penalty for both men. Michael Fortier, who had cut a deal with prosecutors, was charged with four lesser offenses. Fortier's crimes carried a possible 23-year prison term. A grand jury consisting of 23 Oklahoma residents delivered the indictments in a courthouse located directly across the street from the bombing site.

In the indictments, Timothy McVeigh and Terry Nichols are accused of formulating a plan in September 1994, and of stockpiling ingredients for explosives in two states. McVeigh and Nichols are said to have travelled from Kingman, Arizona; to Kansas; Arkansas; Nevada; to Oklahoma City; and back to Kingman. In Hot Springs, Arkansas, the duo are alleged to have carried out the robbing of an Arkansas gun dealer, in order to finance the venture, with Fortier selling some of the stolen weapons. McVeigh and Fortier are alleged to have cased the Oklahoma City federal building on December 16. McVeigh and Nichols are charged with using Junction City as a "final staging ground" and with building the bomb together at Geary Lake State Fishing Park. McVeigh is charged with parking the Ryder truck in front of the federal building, and setting off the bomb. Michael Fortier is charged with having knowledge of the alleged plot and not telling authorities, and with transporting firearms illegally across state lines.

Ninety minutes after the grand jury charges were announced, Michael Fortier entered a guilty plea before U.S. District Judge David Russell. When Fortier was asked whether he knew about plans for the bombing he answered, "Yes sir, I did."

Joseph Hartzler, the lead prosecutor in the case, commented that "The grand jury found probable cause to believe that there are others involved. We will continue our investigation." [1]

After the issuing of the indictments against McVeigh, Nichols, and Fortier, a member of the grand jury that had indicted McVeigh, Nichols, and Fortier risked prosecution by violating the secrecy oath he had taken. Hoppy Heidelberg talked to reporters from the Daily Oklahoman newspaper, and *Media Bypass*, a magazine popular in patriot or populist circles. The *Daily Oklahoman* declined to publish any of Heidelberg's statements, but *Media Bypass* went public in November 1995 with what Heidelberg had to say.

Heidelberg, who is the president of the Oklahoma Thoroughbred Breeders Association, expressed concern over the way the grand jury hearings had been held, and stated that a number of jurors were suspicious of the government's case, believing that they suspected there were other conspirators, and also thought that the government had been withholding information vital to the case. "Prosecutors treated us like idiots," Heidelberg said. "It was like a programming sort of thing. They wanted to make sure he looked like the man in the black hat... It was silly."

Heidelberg also complained that the jurors had been advised by an assistant U.S. attorney that they could not question witnesses directly, and that instead they must raise their hands when they had a question, and then the witness would be sent from the room while the question was asked of the prosecutors. The witness would then return to the courtroom and the prosectors would ask the question. Heidelberg stated that he disagreed with the prosecution's stipulation, based upon his understanding of the rights of grand juries, and that he had asked questions of witnesses directly, incurring the anger of the prosecutors. Some legal experts have offered the opinion that government interference with the grand jury's questioning of witnesses might jeopardize the federal indictments.

Heidelberg also asked if the jurors could interview a person who had helped create the composite drawing of John Doe 2, but that U.S. Attorney Patrick Ryan had said that it was "too late" due to the August 11 deadline for indicting McVeigh. Heidelberg stated that he and other jurors were unhappy with this "fast track" approach to indictment.

Heidelberg indicated that an issue troublesome to the jurors was that the media had reported that surveillance cameras had videotaped the Ryder truck and two occupants immediately before the bombing. "All they showed us were a series of video still photographs showing the Ryder truck," but no photos showing occupants or persons near the truck. Heidelberg voted against indicting Terry Nichols on certain of the 11 counts, and explained that, "He may be plenty guilty of assisting and other such things, but he didn't deliver the damn bomb to the building and he didn't control the timing of the explosion." He also stated that some members of the grand jury felt that Nichols had tried to prevent the bombing. "Nichols got charged with everything McVeigh did, and he shouldn't have," Heidelberg said. He characterized Nichols as "an unwilling accomplice in the end... He backed out. He didn't want to do it. He refused at one point to help McVeigh build the bomb..."

Heidelberg also said that one grand juror had felt "intimidated" when, after accidentally taking his court notebook home, it was retrieved at his home by an FBI agent with drawn gun. [2]

An important area of suspicion in the jurors' minds, according to Heidelberg, was the government's insistence that John Doe 2 was actually Private Bunting, a soldier at Fort Riley. *Media Bypass* quotes one juror as saying, "The story did not fit. When the media ran photographs comparing the soldier to the composite drawing of John Doe 2, it was a huge red flag that something wrong was going on." Heidelberg stated, "The media was a lot more inquisitive and concerned about the John Doe 2 angle than the prosecution. It was never brought up by the government." Heidelberg also believes that he is "satisfied that the government" knows who John Doe 2 is, and that he "was either a government agent or a government informant. Either way they had... prior knowledge to the bombing and that's what they can't afford to come out." [3]

After making his statements to the media, Heidelberg was removed from the grand jury.

NOTES:

1. "Trio indicted in terror attack," *Associated Press,* August 11, 1995; Meddis, Sam Vincent; and Johnson, Kevin. "3 indicted in Okla. blast," *USA Today*, August 11-13; Johnson, Kevin. "Indictment: Hatred fueled blast," *USA Today*, August 11, 1995; "3 named in Oklahoma indictment," Bee News Services, August 11, 1995
2. Myers, Lawrence. "OKC Bombing Grand Jurors Claim 'Cover-

Up'," *Media Bypass*, November 1995; Blair, Mike. "McVeigh's Lawyers Claim Bombing Cover-up," *The Spotlight*, October 30, 1995

3. Johnson, Kevin. "A 'terrible' turn in bomb case," *USA Today*, October 19, 1995; "Prosecutor denies allegations of government cover-up in bombing," *Associated Press*

12

Advance Warning

A lthough the FBI has said that there was no prior knowledge of a bombing taking place in Oklahoma City, that does not seem to have been the case.

Harvey Weathers of the Oklahoma City Fire Department told *USA Today* that dispatchers had received a report on Friday from the FBI that there would be "some people entering the city over the weekend." Weathers did not elaborate on this understatement, and his remarks have not been explained by the FBI, but this clearly points to foreknowledge of the bombing. It also suggests the possibility of a cover-up of the involvement of an FBI informant or agent provocateur in the bomb plot. Naturally remarks made by Weathers have been ignored by the mainstream media. They reveal loose threads that threaten to unravel further, and they possibly point to guilty parties lurking in wings other than the right. [1]

Judge Wayne Alley, who has an office across from the Oklahoma City federal building, was warned several days before the blast by "security specialists" to take "special precautions." This information is noted in the April 20 Portland *Oregonian* newspaper, but has never been touched again by the mainstream media. Judge Alley's warning may have stemmed from his possible special status in the intelligence community. Alley was an Army general and, as journalist Adam Parfrey noted, "Bo Gritz told me two years before the bombing that Judge Alley of Oklahoma City was instructed by U.S. intelligence to throw Gritz's associate Scott Weekly in jail for carrying false i.d. on one of his M.I.A. rescues in Vietnam." [2]

The information of Judge Alley's warning and of his possible intelligence connections would be of great interest, even omitting the most important fact: Judge Alley at this time is scheduled to preside in the trials of both Timothy McVeigh and Terry Nichols. [3]

David Hall, general manager of KPOC-TV in Oklahoma, has stated that he has videotape of eight workers in the federal building who say that they were warned that a bombing was going to take place on April 19. Hall also states that a secretary to a state senator also received information about the blast two days before it occurred, and that after she aired her claims she was contacted by the ATF and FBI and resigned her job due to "pressure." [4]

Oklahoma State Representative Charles Key, who I spoke with during the writing of this book, has said that he knows of two witnesses who heard ATF employees mention that they had been warned not to come to work on the day of the bombing. Key has also stated that at 7:15 a.m. on the day of the bombing, bomb squad employees were observed in front of the courthouse near the federal building. Key, after requesting a Congressional investigation of the bombing and being denied, has requested an independent investigation by an Oklahoma state task force. [5]

Further confirmation of foreknowledge comes from Edye Smith, the mother of two children who died in the bombing. She has spoken of an investigator, Malisa Moore, who contacted her shortly after the bombing. Ms. Moore told Ms. Smith, "You're right about the advance warning for ATF," and stated that she had received information of ATF agent Konop's son Mike telling his college class that his father was "conveniently" late to arrive at the federal building the morning of the bombing. Smith was uncertain of the credibility of the information until she found out that Konop was indeed one of the agents from the ATF who had arrived late to the Murrah Building the morning of the bombing, and that he has a son named Mike. [6]

Edye Smith's father, Glen Wilburn, said in an interview that,

"There was a lady in the building who, immediately after the explosion, her husband and his supervisor ran to the building — and we're talking about within minutes — and this story has been confirmed to me by a local investigative reporter who has spoken directly to the gentleman... And the first thing the gentleman did, the husband of the woman who was in the building, the first person he ran into was an agent of the ATF down on the street. And he asked him... what was happening, and the quote from the agent was 'It was either a natural gas explosion or it was a bomb. We had a bomb threat yesterday, and some of us were called and were told that we didn't have to come in if we didn't want to.'" [7]

Mr. Wilburn also informs us of another bomb threat that had been received in the week prior to the federal building bombing:

"I heard a rumor that a gentleman whose wife was in the building and had fallen three or four stories into the basement area, had ran up to an ATF agent the morning of the bombing. He was looking for his wife frantically and he found an agent, and he grabbed this agent and asked him, 'What's going on here? Can you help me? I need to find an agent who knows my wife, and can find her for me.' And the agent told him, 'That's going to be difficult to do, because they received a call this morning... that something was going on today and they didn't need to come in...'"

Mr. Wilburn relates that, "We've also been told by two different witnesses... that the bomb squad was in front of the federal courthouse that morning at 7:30 [a.m.] and they had already cleared the Murrah Building." [8]

On April 10, 1995, nine days before the bombing, Ken Stern of the American Jewish Committee sent a fax to "members of the press, AJCers, legislators, prosecutors, attorneys general, federal officials," about a terrorist strike scheduled to take place on "April 19... the anniversary of Waco... THE KEY event for the militias, and for the hard core April 20 is Hitler's birthday." The fax was received by Federal Judge Redden of Portland, Oregon. [9]

Michael Hinton, who lives near the federal building in Oklahoma City, has stated that on the afternoon of April 12th about 300 persons quickly evacuated the Murrah Building for unknown reasons. Speculations include a fire drill and a bomb scare. [10]

Oklahoma investigator Pat Briley offers additional startling information:

"There is evidence both the FBI and the BATF may have had foreknowledge. There was a meeting about seven weeks ago in Washington between President Clinton, Attorney General Reno, the FBI and the BATF to discuss the Oklahoma City bombing.

"We have a witness who was in the meeting who reports FBI and BATF representatives got into an argument during the meeting, blaming each other for the fact that each knew about the impending bombing, but didn't do enough to stop it. A reporter here in Oklahoma City talked to the person who was in this meeting. He got a first-hand description of what happened.

"We have other sources that indicate the FBI received specific warnings two months before the boming and the BATF at least nine days before the bombing. When I say warnings, I mean official warnings, from our own intelligence and from foreign intelligence. At this point we're not at liberty to give out specifics, but I can tell you the information we have is solid.

"The BATF had two distinct warnings about McVeigh months before the bombing. Individuals had called the BATF and left their names and phone number and told the BATF that McVeigh was trying to buy explosive fuels to make a bomb... Not only that, but there were also people in Michigan who called the BATF and complained about McVeigh and Nichols. So they were known to the BATF.

"However, we also have information that the BATF met with McVeigh the night before the Oklahoma bombing. We have sources that indicated he was paid to deliver that truck to Oklahoma City." [11]

There are allegations that Branch Davidian sympathizers met at the Brazos Lounge at the Holiday Inn in Waco, Texas the day before the Oklahoma City bombing. One individual in the group is quoted as saying, "Tomorrow God will have his vengeance on the ATF," with another member quoted as saying that a "mighty blow of vengeance" would be struck on the following day. Branch Davidians deny any foreknowledge, or that the bombing had any connection to their group. Rick Sherrow, a reporter for *Soldier of Fortune* who was present at the Brazos Lounge that evening, denies this report. [12]

Media Bypass magazine has stated that "low-ranking ATF employees [are] claiming that a 'rumor' going around the agency suggests that agents at the OKC federal building 'got into a vehicle and left the area about ten minutes before the explosion,' and that this departure was filmed by the video camera in front of the building..." [13]

Concerns about American government complicity in the Oklahoma bombing were fueled by reports such as the following, published in an underground Patriot publication:

"It was reported directly to the Militia of Montana (M.O.M.) by a secretary employed at the federal building in Oklahoma City, Oklahoma... that on Tuesday night, the night before the explosion, that all the 'top personnel' of the ATF and other federal agencies were moved out of the building. This same secretary was personally involved in the management move of federal personnel from that federal building." [14]

Others offered similar reports about the ATF having had an advance warning about the bombing. Edye Smith and others interviewed at the bombing site stated that minutes after the explosion or explosions, there were at least 10 ATF agents wearing ATF jackets wandering through the wreckage of the building, searching for evidence. An ATF spokesman has said that they "probably" had come from the federal courthouse across the street. Ms. Smith said in a Cable News Network television interview on or about May 23, 1995, that "it seems more than a coincidence to me that the ATF on the ninth floor had zero casualties."

Ms. Smith had other interesting things to add:

Interviewer Gary Tuchman: "Edye, at this point you're very busy. You've been talking to people like us, you've been talking to police officials, you've been with your family. But in the next couple of months when things start to get quieter here in Oklahoma City, do you think it will begin getting tougher for you?"

Edye Smith: "Yeah, but I don't think things are going to start getting very quiet, you know? There's a — there are a lot of questions that have been left unanswered, a lot of questions we don't have answers for, we're being told to keep our mouths shut, not talk about it, don't ask those questions, and I think things are going to get a lot busier."

Gary Tuchman: "What kind of questions have people been telling you to keep your mouth shut about?"

Edye Smith: "Well, we've — just from the very beginning, we, along with hundreds and thousands of other people, want to know just — and we just innocently ask questions, you know — where was ATF? All 15 or 17 of their employees survived, and they live — they're on the ninth floor. They were the target of this explosion, and where were they? Did they have a warning sign? I mean, did they think it might be a bad day to go in the office? They had an option to not go to work that day, and my kids didn't get that option, nobody else in the building got that option. And we're just asking questions, we're not making accusations. We just want to know, and they're telling us 'Keep your mouth shut, don't talk about it.'" [15]

The day following Ms. Smith's interview she was visited by ATF agents Luke Frainey from Oklahoma City, Steve Kyler from Dallas, U.S. Attorney Pat Ryan, a person from the Department of Justice, and someone from the IRS. According to these officials, five out of fifteen ATF agents were in the Murrah Building at the time of the bombing. These were Valerie Rodin, a secretary; Vernon Buster, a compliance officer; Jim Scaggs, another compliance officer; Luke Frainey, an undercover agent; and Alex McCully, the office manager. There have been other reports that Scaggs and Buster were, in fact, not ATF agents.

After the meeting, Ted Burton of KJRH-TV reported, "[Edye's mother] Kathy Wilburn and Edye Smith now believe that their [the ATF's] survival was the will of God, not a hunch that something was going to happen." Edye Smith denies this, and was upset when the statement by the television commentator was read to her. [16]

As of June 19, 1995, David Hall reported that Edye Smith had her compensation checks from the government cut off. [17]

David Hall addresses allegations that there were no ATF agents in the building at the time of the blast:

"A lot of people have heard these stories. The ATF has sent out a disclaimer saying that they had five agents who were dead. However, there's a bad problem with that because two days prior to that, one agent told us that there were no ATF agents in the office that day. He even told us where they were. He told us that he was in Oklahoma City in court with a fellow named Fuzzy Warren. Then, he said, there were three agents in Newkirk, Oklahoma on an arson case and a couple others were involved in cases around the country. He said that five agents were up all night because they were involved in surveillance until about 6:30 in the morning at which time they went home and went to bed. What he told us was that no agents were killed, but that there was a secretary in the office and she did not get hurt.

"According to him they were all out doing their jobs. I will tell you this much: We're going to have a real problem with those five agents who were up all night and went home and went to bed."

Les Martz, head of the Oklahoma BATF office, denied the claims of an agency bail-out prior to the bombing. He claimed that five of the 13 BATF employees in the Murrah Building had, in fact, been present at the time of the bombing, and that all five had been injured in the blast. The other employees, according to Martz, had been on assignment or in court at the time.

According to printed statistics in the *New York Times* on April 30, with the information sourced to "Federal agencies" and "Oklahoma City medical examiner's office," there were 15 BATF agents assigned to the federal building, with 15 present at the time of the blast. Zero were killed, zero were missing, and four were injured. [18]

Other reports disagree, such as one published in the *Jubilee*, a small-circulation Christian newspaper:

"Another good quesion being asked is: Where were the top officials from other agencies that day? KWTV reported that Chiefs of the DEA, Secret Service, and Marshall's Service were on annual leave playing in a

Special Olympics benefit golf tournament that morning. The report said, 'all had offices in the Murrah Building. FBI Chief Bob Ricks was also in the tournament.' " [19]

After the bombing, the ATF apparently engaged in covering up the small number of their personnel who had been present in the Murrah Building at the time of the bombing. ATF bulletins reported that agent-in-charge Alex McCulley had been in an elevator in the building when the blast took place, and that he and an unidentified agent of the DEA had fallen in the elevator from the eighth floor to the third floor. The story does not seem to hold water, as pointed out by investigator J.D. Cash in an interview. Cash reports that there were two elevator repairmen on the premises that day, and that within ten minutes there were as many as ten men checking on the elevators. Cash has interviewed the repairmen and they have stated that no elevators went into free fall and that, in fact, there is no way to accomplish that with a modern elevator, except by cutting the cable, which did not happen in the blast. All of the elevators, the repairmen stated, had to be accessed from the ceiling.

"Why is Alex McCulley telling this lie?" Cash wonders. "I suspect it's because he's been told that somebody has to be in that building from ATF that day because it looks pretty suspicious when the whole staff is gone." [20]

Prior to the Oklahoma City bombing, a reduction in security personnel at the Murrah Federal Building had taken place, despite a government report which had, the *Kansas City Star* reports, "warned of massive loss of life in a disaster strikingly similar to the blast that rocked Oklahoma City." At the time of the bombing security at the federal building consisted of one rent-a-cop who was not in the lobby at the time of the bombing. [21]

NOTES:

1. Keen, Judy. "'Justice will be swift, certain and severe'," *USA Today*, April 20, 1995
2. Parfrey, Adam. "Finding Our Way Out Of Oklahoma," *Cult Rapture*, Feral House, Portland, Oregon, 1995; "The Bomb... in Oklahoma," video by *Star Investigative Reports,* 1995
3. Johnson, Kevin. "20 years later, same lawyer, same argument," *USA Today*, August 18, 1995
4. Broward, Horne. Internet computer posting, May 28, 1995, in the possession of the author

5. Rappoport, John. *Oklahoma City Bombing, The Suppressed Truth,* Blue Press, Los Angeles, 1995
6. Hall, Paul. "So Where Was the ATF That Day?", *The Jubilee,* May/June 1995
7. Harder, Chuck. "Oklahoma City... A Closer Look," video, *For the People,* 1995
8. "Oklahoma City... What Really Happened?", video, Charles Allen, 1995
9. Parfrey
10. Rappoport
11. Briley, Pat. "Federals Know Identity of Oklahoma's John Doe No. 2," *The Spotlight,* October 2, 1995
12. Blosser, John, et al. "The Waco Connection, Terror plot revealed in bar hours before killer blast," *National Enquirer,* May 9, 1995
13. "20 Questions About the Oklahoma City Bombing," *Media Bypass,* July 1995
14. Wickstrom, James P., "Intelligence Report," April 22, 1995
15. Cable News Network, Inc. interview by Gary Tuchman, copy received from *American Patriot Fax Network.* Copy in the author's possession
16. Hall, Paul. "So Where Was the ATF That Day?", *The Jubilee,* May/June 1995
17. Hall, David. Interview by Tom Valentine on *Radio Free America,* WCCR radio, June 19, 1995
18. Lll, Jane H. "For Searchers, Exhaustion Grows as Hope Fades," *New York Times,* April 30, 1995
19. Hall, Paul
20. "Oklahoma City: What Really Happened?", Charles Allen, video, 1995
21. Pate, James L. "Bloody April," *Soldier of Fortune,* August 1995

13

Under Observation

Authorities may have known about Timothy McVeigh and his partners long before the bombing at Oklahoma City. According to Cable News Network, McVeigh had been under surveillance by "undercover operatives" at an Arizona gun show as much as two years prior to the bombing. [1] This surveillance possibly stemmed from an incident reported by the Mesa, Arizona *Tribune*, which stated that the FBI, the BATF, and the Arizona Department of Public Safety were warned about McVeigh in 1993, because of an alleged remark at a gun show about how a flare gun he was selling could be used to shoot down "an ATF helicopter." [2]

McVeigh was also reported to the BATF during the fall of 1994, when he is said to have attempted to buy large quantities of ni-tromethane, a fuel used in racing dragsters, and hydrozene, a fuel additive. [3] Yet again, according to the David Brinkley television program of Sunday, April 23, the Michigan Militia had informed the BATF and FBI of McVeigh's allegedly violent tendencies several months before the bombing took place.

An additional report on McVeigh was made when he and a man conforming to the description of John Doe 2 were in Tulsa, Oklahoma, on April 1, 1995. McVeigh allegedly made a casual remark to a gun dealer that he was not going to register some pistols he was buying with the BATF, a remark which was reported to the FBI.

There is evidence that the Anti-Defamation League of the B'nai B'rith may have been on to Timothy McVeigh prior to the bombing, and possibly as early as the summer of 1993. Perhaps this group was the source of information relayed by Ken Stern of the American Jewish

Committee when he faxed his warning about an April 19 terrorist attack to members of the press, government officials, and others on April 10. An April 27 press release of the ADL offered information about McVeigh's ad in *The Spotlight* newspaper, under the alias T. Tuttle, and also recounted information about his gun sales at a Phoenix, Arizona gun show.

Lacking police credentials, how would ADL investigators have gotten this information so quickly? The ADL has long maintained a private database on American citizens, has fielded an investigative force, and is also alleged to employ agent provocateurs among various factions of the populist right wing, among other groups. These proclivities toward clandestine activities by the ADL resulted in a scandal in December 1992, when the San Francisco Police Department probed League spying and the acquisition of classified police information from active police officers around the country. The ADL was let off with a fine.

Among organizations that have allegedly been infiltrated by agents of the ADL are the White Aryan Resistance group (WAR) and the Ku Klux Klan. It is alleged that ADL agent provocateur Jimmy Rosenberg infiltrated the Klan office in Trenton, N.J. and attempted to get Klansmen to bomb the local offices of the National Association for the Advancement of Colored People (NAACP). [4]

In all probability Terry Nichols had been under FBI surveillance since 1993 when, in an attempt to discharge a $17,000 credit card debt he sent Chase Manhattan Bank a personally, crafted "sight draft" he had composed. His claim was that he was paying off his credit cards "with like kind of money," logic not likely to appeal to Chase Manhattan or a judge, regardless of its essential truth. [5]

NOTES:

1. "CNN Confirms Suspicions," *The Spotlight*, June 19, 1995
2. Sniffen, Michael J. "More arrests likely in bombing," *Associated Press*, June 2, 1995
3. Johnson, Kevin. "No racing fuel in Okla. bomb," *USA Today*, August 3, 1995
4. Thompson, Scott. "Did the ADL have a Connection to Accused Bomber Timothy McVeigh?", *New Federalist*, July 10, 1995
5. Sharn, Lori. *USA Today*, June 16, 1995

14

Advance Testing

I f the government was quick to determine that the bomb that destroyed the federal building was of the ammonium nitrate type, they did have some experience with this type of explosive. A "comprehensive vehicle-bomb study" was done by the ATF and other federal agencies in the Interagency Counter-Terrorist Research Group, the study commencing after the 1993 World Trade Center bombing. The program was termed "Dipole Might" and $2 million in funding was invested in surplus cars that were exploded in White Sands, New Mexico, using bombs which "ranged from 50 to 1,000 pounds of ANFO and C-4."

Ralph Ostrowski, head of the ATF's Arson and Explosives Division in Washington, D.C., stated at the time that, "We feel that the data we're collecting on blast pressure, temperature, crater size and meteorological-type information will give us a very good idea of what the blast effect will be, whether it's a vehicle sitting at White Sands Missile Range or in downtown Manhattan." [1]

Cable News Network, announced on June 7, 1995 that the ATF had done a test explosion in October 1994 on a van "similar to the Ryder truck allegedly used in the OK bombing." According to CNN, 1,000 pounds of ammonium nitrate and fuel oil were used in the explosion, and the results were "invaluable" because one of the agents who had participated in the testing "happened to be across the street" from the Oklahoma City federal building when it was blown up on April 19. "It gave us, very quickly, an idea of what had occurred," ATF explosives chief Ostrowski said. [2]

Further information about the BATF's testing was provided by demolitions expert Charles Young in an interview with the author:

"After the Oklahoma City bombing *Newsweek* magazine reported that the ATF had conducted a series of tests to determine the explosion dynamics of vehicle-transported bombs. This series of tests was called 'Dipole Might' and was reportedly conducted at White Sands Missile Range in New Mexico several months prior to the bombing at Oklahoma City.

"Curiously enough I had an office next to the principle researcher who, while chatting in the hall, informed me in late October or early November 1994 that his research group had been given a contract from the government (no agency mentioned) to purchase twelve vehicles so they could be used in testing the effects of explosion on vehicles. He further informed me that after the test the vehicles were to be wrapped entirely in plastic and shipped to the FBI crime lab for analysis. Because of the proximity of these tests in time and location to those mentioned as being part of 'Dipole Might,' I believe that these tests were the same series.

"Fundamentally, the *Newsweek* story appears correct (in that the government did sponsor a series of tests) except for several points:

"1. The series of tests were conducted by the Department of Chemistry, New Mexico Institute of Mining and Technology.

"2. The tests were not conducted at the White Sands Missile Range but instead 40 miles north at the Energetic Materials Research and Technology Center — EMRTC (formerly known as the Terminal Effects Research and Analysis, for military projects, and the Center for Explosives Technology and Research, for civilian projects) located west of the town of Socorro, New Mexico.

"EMRTC is a large, secluded explosives test range that is owned and operated by the New Mexico Institute of Mining and Technology, a state-owned institution which specializes in the chemistry, physical properties and both military and civilian application. The terminal effects research involves the testing of ordnance and their effects on military hardware. The entire facility is littered with the blown up remains of MIGs, tanks (both U.S. and Soviet), a section of destroyer hull, etc...." [3]

NOTES:

1. Sandlin, Scott. "White Sands A Car Bomb Laboratory," *Albuquerque Journal*, July 16, 1995
2. "ATF Rehearsed Ryder Explosion 7 Months Before," *Newswatch*, September/October 1995
3. Young, Charles. Interview conducted by Jim Keith, July 20, 1995

15

The Dual Event

There is a matter of tremendous significance that remains virtually unreported in the national press. The Oklahoma City explosion was recorded on seismographs at the University of Oklahoma, 20 miles from the blast, and at the Omniplex Science Center in Oklahoma City, and both seismic records show an "event" at 9:02:13, but also a second event of apparently equal or even greater magnitude at 9:02:23, ten seconds later. These facts have been explained by a seismographic "echo" being recorded, but it is hard to comprehend how the second event could seemingly register as being of the same or slightly greater magnitude, if it is in fact an "echo." The evidence shows, confirmed by a number of seismograph experts, that at least two explosions took place.

Dr. Ken Louzza of the University of Oklahoma Geology Department stated on the day of the blast, "This indicates two detonations occurred in Oklahoma City at the precise time recorded by the seismograph." [1]

In a memo, Dr. Charles Mankin, Director of the University of Oklahoma Geological Survey, confirmed Louzza's statement:

"The seismograph picked up two events shortly after 9:00 AM that seem to be related to the bombing of the federal building in Oklahoma. The first surface wave arrived at 9:02 and 13 seconds, and the second arrived at 9:02 and 23 seconds. Given the time of the travel for the surface waves, that would make the time of the first blast at 9:02 and 4 seconds and the second blast 10 seconds later. If the report that two bombs were detonated at about 9:00 AM is correct, then these are the likely signals from those blasts." [2]

In a later press conference, Dr. Mankin responded to questions relating to the dual event:

Interviewer: "Does the fact there is a second wave on the seismograph #ID: 4053257069 positively mean that there was a second blast?"

Dr. Mankin: "Because there are two seismograph recordings, there would have had to have been two explosions, or two bombs. The news media itself even reported two bomb blasts initially, but later changed their story. There were two surface waves with very similar amplitude, duration and wave form, indicating a low frequency, or long wave, typical of what we might expect to see at that kind of short distance from a bomb blast."

Interviewer: "Could the second wave have been an 'air blast' or the building falling?"

Dr. Mankin: "It's certainly not an air blast, or the building collapsing. No air blast could have registered to the south, given the proximity of the seismograph in Norman [Oklahoma], about 20 miles to the south of the undamaged side of the federal building. In fact, no one felt an air blast to the south, but they did to the north, similar to a sound echoing off of a reflective surface, in this case, reflecting off of the back wall of the federal building. When you look at the two seismic recordings, they are nearly the same magnitude and energy. It was a fairly large event for surface phenomena; they were large explosions and both are comparable."

Interviewer: "Could the second wave have been an earthquake?"

Dr. Mankin: "No, and the reason I say that, our seismic equipment that's located in Leonard, Oklahoma, south of Tulsa about 130 miles to the south of Oklahoma City, didn't pick up anything. And that equipment is digital as opposed to our analog equipment here in Norman. In addition, the sensing instruments are located at the bottom of a 100-meter bore hole, so if it had been an earthquake, that equipment would have recorded it. The second wave indication is definitely not an earthquake, it is definitely a second [explosive] event, given the broad oscillations, amplitude, duration, and wave form." [3]

The original seismographic records were later confiscated from Dr. Mankin by the FBI. [4]

Many witnesses also describe two explosions. One man who heard two blasts is Charles Watts, an Army veteran who states that he has "been around demolitions and munitions for many years." Watts was in bankruptcy court in downtown Oklahoma City, approximately 50 yards away from the federal building. He says that, "It was 9:00, or just very, very shortly thereafter. Several lawyers were standing there talking and there was a large explosion. It threw several of the people close to me to the floor. I don't think it threw me to the floor, but it did move me significantly, and I threw myself to the floor, and got down, and about that time, a huge blast, unlike anything I've ever experienced, hit." Queried about what he experienced, Watts says, "A second blast. There were two explosions. The second blast made me think that the whole building was coming in." [5]

Another credible witness to two detonations was Michael Hinton, who had just gotten aboard a bus in Oklahoma City when the explosion went off. Hinton says, "I got on bus #18, and I climb aboard and just had sat down, when I heard this very violent rumble under the bus. It was a pushing-type motion. It actually raised that bus up on its side. About six or seven seconds later, another one which was more violent than the first pushed the bus again, and I felt that second the bus was going to turn over." [6]

One possible explanation of the dual explosion which has been fielded is that the bomb may have not been ANFO, but instead a sophisticated fuel-air explosive type with a double detonation, of the type depicted in the recent motion picture "Outbreak." Certainly, this type of bomb could not be manufactured by individuals lacking highly technical knowledge and facilities. No reliable corroboration of this possibility has been noted, although this does not rule out the possibility that the technology was used.

The Spotlight newspaper reported the views of ex-FBI man Ted Gunderson, who I spoke with during the course of researching this book:

"According to Gunderson, the bomb was an electrohydrodynamic gaseous fuel device (barometric bomb), which could not have been built by former Persian Gulf War Army veteran Timothy McVeigh and his rural Michigan farming friends, brothers James and Terry Nichols — at least not without the aid of persons, as yet unknown... Gunderson has obtained from an expert who has knowledge of the device an abstract description, including a diagram, of the bomb, described in the abstract as 'top secret due to the ease in which the device can be created.'

"'Technically,' according to the abstract, 'it is considered an "A-neutronic" device, hence the designated "Q" clearance is required for information.'... From sources familiar with U.S. government classification methods, "Q" clearance is required to obtain access to, among other things, nuclear weapons components, including small — easily transportable by a single person — portable nuclear bombs.

"Vastly more sophisticated than the fuel oil-fertilizer bomb now being described by federal agents as weighing up to 5,000 pounds, the

A-neutronic device may have been 'the size of a small pineapple,' according to the abstract... In any case, it was the two-explosion reports that led Gunderson to rule out the fertilizer bomb and to zero in on the more sophisticated A-neutronic device. Although the abstract provided to Gunderson is relatively technical in nature, it basically states that the bomb consists of a cylinder of just '64 ounces or more of ammonium nitrate,' which surrounds a shaft of aluminum silicate that has at its center another shaft of an explosive known as PETN, described... as a 'low-volume explosive.'

"The abstract states that when the PETN is detonated the top of the canister or tank containing the bomb 'flies upwards and the bottom of the tank opens up into a flower petal shape. Immediately the ammonium nitrate mixes with the shattered micro-encapsulated aluminum silicate to create an even more devastating explosive fuel cloud. This is then energized with a high potential electrostatic field resulting in the creation of millions of microfronts.'

"The abstract further indicates that the 'cold cloud' is then detonated by a charge that 'is cushioned from the first blast due to a shock absorbing cavity. This time the cold cloud ignites, creating a shock wave which surpasses the traditional effect of TNT. The most astounding effects of this type of detonation is the immediate atmospheric overpressure which has a tendency to blow out windows of any structure within the vicinity of the blast.'"

Corroborating the possibility that the Oklahoma City bomb was of the "A-neutronic" type was information which came out during a hearing before Federal Magistrate Ronald Howland on April 28. Again quoting from *The Spotlight*:

"*USA Today* of April 28 reported on its page 3A that final clue. The paper's editors do not realize that they had inserted in their newspaper the final piece of the bomb's mosaic.

"The article stated: 'The decision came after hours of testimony from [FBI] Special Agent John Hersley, who said a shirt McVeigh was wearing when he was arrested by an Oklahoma state trooper during his alleged get-away] had traces of the explosive PDTN...' The explosive PDTN, Gunderson had been told, is the substance used to detonate the second explosion, which in turn detonates the electrified cloud mixture of ammonium nitrate and aluminum silicate, causing the major devastating blast that virtually wiped out nearly two-thirds of the federal building.

"Completing the picture of the A-neutronic device even further, the Arkansas *Democrat Gazette*, published in Little Rock, in describing the

FBI's contention in its April 30 edition stated that the 'fertilizer' bomb concoction was detonated by using explosive cord wrapped around the barrels. It stated: 'The barrels were somehow tied together with high-explosive detonator cord, a rope-like device that contains the explosive PETN, an official told the *Dallas Morning News*.'

"While it is true that the explosive PETN may be used in explosive cord, as described, it is also, according to the A-neutronic bomb designers, the explosive used in the initial phase of detonating the A-neutronic device — the release and dispersal of the ammonium nitrate and aluminum silicate combination. There is no evidence that has surfaced, or [has been] claimed by FBI agents, that both explosive substances — PDTN and PETN — were used in their 'fertilizer' bomb story."

Ted Gunderson primarily attributes his information to the self-described designer of the A-neutronic bomb, Michael Riconisciuto, who is currently incarcerated on charges of drug manufacturing, and who was one of deceased journalist Danny Casolaro's primary sources during his research on the Inslaw software thievery case. [7] In an interview with Steve Quayle, Riconisciuto provides further information on the A-neutronic device:

"It doesn't quite achieve the conversion efficiencies of matter to energy that a nuclear detonation is, but it does convert a certain amount of matter to energy — and it is A-neutronic. In other words, there are electrons and positrons involved; the nucleus is not involved in the conversion of mass to energy. There is a considerable amount of energy, much more so than is available from a simple oxidation reaction of the chemical components or thermal decomposition of chemical components. Explosives work either on deflagration [fast burning] or when it burns faster, it reaches a point where it is called a detonation. This can be done either through oxidation (which is what regular combustion is) or through thermal decomposition. When certain chemical compounds are formed, they are formed with a certain amount of heat-of-formation. Chemical compounds with negative heat-of-formation are highly thermally unstable, and if you bump them (like with nitroglycerine) mechanically or physically you can detonate them. It depends upon what category of initiator is used. Initiators such as blasting caps contain fulminates which are very sensitive to mechanical shock, and which can initiate their explosive decomposition. Booster initiators are less sensitive, but more is required in setting them off. The main explosive charge actually requires another explosion to detonate it. Dynamite is a secondary explosive; a blasting cap is the primary. Blasting caps are very sensitive, while dynamite is not. The main explosive material is desensitized so that large quantities of dynamite can be shipped without worrying about mechanical shocks. Dynamite requires a 'kick' to set it off.''

Commenting on the 'shear-and-drop' effects of the explosive on the concrete columns of the federal building at Oklahoma City, Riconisciuto says, "A shear-and-drop effect is really out of the question — unless the building was also rigged with demolition charges. If the building was rigged with demolition charges on the inside, it would have required a pretty involved procedure. The people inside the building would have seen that something was amiss. You have to actually drill into the structure to set the charges. You can use military demolition unit charges externally and have what is known as a 'Monroe Effect,' which produces a shockwave cone, but that stuff is impossible to hide from the people inside the building. Those public buildings are built to an architectural standard known as 'Seismic Zone 1 or better' ratings, and the flexural strength of the supporting beams and the floors are such that they can withstand a massive upheaval and then drop without structural failure. Modern buildings, especially public buildings, have to be designed to certain seismic standards... It is very unlikely that the drop-and-shear effect would cause such castrophic structural failure." [8]

Demolitions expert General Benton K. Partin, while believing that charges were detonated inside the building, doubts Riconisciuto's analysis. Partin states of the Gunderson/Riconisciuto theory, that an A-neutronic bomb was used in the Oklahoma City bombing:

"In my opinion [that] is part nonsense and part a fuel air explosive (FAE) device. Some large FAE devices were made to clear helicopter landing spaces in Vietnam jungles. It appears to be an obfuscation capitalizing on gullibility. The big explosion in Japan recently was an 'accidental' fuel air explosion. The 'ping' in your car engine is a fuel air explosion." Partin responds that the idea that the Oklahoma bombing was accomplished entirely by a bomb placed outside the building is "presposterous." [9]

Demolitions expert Rick Sherrow also takes apart the Gunderson/Riconisciuto hypothesis in an article for *Soldier of Fortune* magazine. Sherrow says,

"As for the 'device' itself, the diagram looks like a cross between a flashlight battery and a funky Fuel-Air Explosive (FAE) bomb. The description of how the Gunderson device functions is somewhat reminiscent of the principle behind the FAE bomb. A highly volatile liquid (in the case of the FAE device it is normally propylene oxide) is released from its container by an initial explosion allowing the fuel to mix with air thus forming a fuel-air vapor cloud. This cloud is initiated milliseconds later by explosive cloud initiators. The resulting explosion forms a massive shock/pressure wave which effectively destroys the target. An interesting signature of a FAE bomb is that it leaves no crater such as is commonly associated with a conventional surface blast. In Oklahoma City I observed a rather large crater, approximately 20 feet in diameter and 8 feet deep. So much for 'explosive clouds'." [10]

Whatever the nature of the actual bomb used, there is more than adequate reason to suggest that the government's story of a single ANFO bomb carried in a Ryder truck does not explain the damage inflicted on the Murrah Federal Building in Oklahoma City, nor the dual seismographic accounts. It is not surprising, however, that discussion of the nature of the bomb, the seismographic evidence, and other evidence relating to the bombing event itself is a totally "hands-off" proposition in the national press.

NOTES:

1. Gunderson, Ted. "The Gunderson Bomb Report," 1995
2. McAlvany, Donald S. "The Oklahoma City Tragedy: Implications for Free Speech, Political Dissent, and Liberty in America (A Clear and Present Danger)," *The McAlvany Intelligence Advisor*, May/June 1995
3. McAlvany
4. Granse, Karl. "Anguish in Oklahoma City," A. Sgarlatti Productions, Hopkins, Minnesota, 1995
5. "Report from Ground Zero," *Media Bypass* magazine, June 1995
6. "Oklahoma City: What Really Happened?", Charles Allen, video, 1995
7. Gunderson; Blair, Mike. "Feds 'Fib' On Oklahoma City Bomb Says Ex-High Level FBI Official," *The Spotlight*, undated clipping
8. Riconisciuto, Michael. Interviewed by Steve Quayle, *USA Patriot Magazine*, June 1995
9. Katson, Trisha. "Ex-Military Explosives Expert Doubts FBI Blast Story," *The Spotlight*, July 10, 1995
10. Sherrow, Rick. "Oklahoma City Bombing: Supersecret Government Conspiracy? or Conspiracy Theory Con Job?", pre-publication manuscript for *Soldier of Fortune*, copy in the author's possession

16

The Partin Analysis

B rigadier General Benton Partin, a retired United States Air Force officer and one of the most qualified demolitions experts in the world, has come forward with the most well-reasoned analysis of the logistics of the bombing to date, and his conclusions are startling. Partin discussed the Oklahoma City bombing in *The McAlvany Intelligence Advisor*. General Partin said:

"When I first saw the picture of the truck bomb's assymetrical damage to the federal building in Oklahoma, my immediate reaction was that the pattern of damage would have been technically impossible without supplementary demolition charges at some of the reinforced concrete column bases (inside the building) — a standard demolition technique.

"First, a blast through the air is a very inefficient energy coupling mechanism against heavy reinforced concrete beams and columns. Second, blast damage potential falls off more rapidly than an inverse function of the distance cubed. That is why in conventional weapons development, one seeks accuracy over yield for hard targets. Reinforced concrete targets in large buildings are hard targets to blast.

"The entire building could have been collapsed with relatively small charges against the base of the columns and with even less explosives if linear activity cutting charges had been used. I know of no way possible to reproduce the apparent building damage without well-placed demolition charges complementing the truck bomb damage." As an aside, the use of a truck bomb also conceals the usage of explosives that would not be available outside of the military.

General Partin also stated, "The gross asymmetry in the federal building damage pattern is ipso facto evidence that there was an inside bomb effort and a truck bomb effort. They need not have known each other, but it would have had to have been coordinated at some level. That coordination could have been accomplished from almost any location in the world.

"Efforts of this magnitude and criticality are generally orchestrated by an outside team sent in for this limited purpose. In such cases, the usefulness of FBI infiltration of domestic organizations is totally circumvented." General Partin speculated that a special ops team from an unknown Eastern country might have been responsible for the bombing. [1]

On May 17, 1995 a letter was hand-delivered by General Partin to Oklahoma Senator Don Nickles, with copies delivered to other senators. In this letter, General Partin said that:

"I am concerned that vital evidence will soon be destroyed with the pending demolition of the federal building in Oklahoma City. From all the evidence I have seen in the published material, I can say with a high level of confidence that the damage pattern on the reinforced concrete superstructure could not possibly have been attained from the single truck bomb without supplementing demolition charges at some of the reinforced column bases. The total incompatibility with a single truck bomb lies in the fact that either some of the columns collapsed that should not have collapsed or some of the columns are still standing that should have collapsed and did not.

"An oversimplified analogy will help you see this point. It would be irrational or as impossible as having a 150 pound man sit in a flimsy chair and the chair collapses: then a man weighing 1,500 pounds sits in an identical flimsy chair and it does not collapse — impossible. To produce the resulting damage pattern on the building, there would have to have been an effort with demolition charges at the bases to complement or supplement the truck bomb damage. A careful examination of the collapsed column bases would readily reveal a failure mode produced by a demolition charge. This evidence would be so critical, a separate and independent assessment should be made before a building demolition team destroys the evidence forever...[2]

Later, General Partin was able to travel to Oklahoma, although not in time to view the Murrah Building before it was demolished in the supposed interest of public safety and feelings. Partin expanded upon his earlier remarks in an interview with Chuck Harder, on his *For the People* television and radio broadcast:

"When I first looked at the reports coming out of Oklahoma, I knew that the truth was not coming out. The media was very much confused, passing out disinformation, and I think some of the officials down there were putting out disinformation, and what was going on down there was totally at odds from what I had 25 years of experience of knowing. So I got all of the information that I could together, and took a look at it, and ran some analyses, put the damage profiles on the building. And I concluded there was a very high probability and a high level of confidence that there were demolition charges in the building. And I wrote, I felt it was very important, that the Senate and the House move to have an independent investigation in Oklahoma City because it needed to be established without question whether and how many demolition charges were in that building, because it's an entirely different story if you had a bunch of demolition charges in the building in contradistinction to a truckload out in front of the building."

Partin was asked whether the damage that was done to the Murrah Building could have been accomplished with an ANFO bomb, and responded: "Absolutely not." General Partin expanded on the evaluation by talking about an "ideal" ANFO bomb, stating that it would do "Very light damage. An analysis that I did, I considered that 4,800 pounds of ammonium nitrate was highly compressed, it was in a sphere which would have been about 4 1/2 feet in diameter, and it was detonated from the inside out to give the maximum energy release and the maximum effectiveness..."

Partin stated that a bomb that was not constructed to these state-of-the-art specifications "would have been less than that. If the maximum is insufficient, then something less than the maximum would have been even less sufficient. Ammonium nitrate in that condition, you'll get about 1/2 million pounds per square inch in the internal volume of the ammonium nitrate. Now, because the pressure falls off inversely proportional to one over the distance cubed, then one over the distance cubed the pressure is down by the time it reaches the first column to less than about 2,000 pounds per square inch. Now the yield strength of concrete is about 3,500 pounds per square inch, so the maximum pressure that reaches the building is far less than the yield strength of the concrete... I'll even say if you had used a high order of military explosive — Comp-B or C-4 — your pressure would have been a little more, but not significantly enough to change that conclusion. When you're using high brissance explosives it makes a big difference if you have the explosive in contact with the column, but when you're pushing a blast wave... See, air is a very inefficient means of coupling energy from the explosive into the building. Very inefficient. The pressure falls off and you don't go very far before you're below the yield strength of the target you're trying to destroy. That's why much of my military career I worked on precision guided weapons, for the simple reason [that] I knew that you can't kill hard targets with bombs unless they're guided with high precision and you hit them." Partin went so far as to say that the destruction of the Murrah Building, "...wouldn't have happened if you had used 4,800 pounds of Comp-B."

Partin's analysis is precise, and seems to reveal the exact nature of the bombing. Partin stated:

"Last week I went down and, as I said, I went through literally hundreds and hundreds of pictures — they were covering the removal of the debris from the building site. And I was looking for those specific locations and the columns at those specific locations where my analysis said that you would have had to have a demolition charge at, and I was going through those as they were clearing the site. All those demolition charge positions were clearly revealed."

Partin continued: "Around the perimeter from that failure line it goes all the way down to the ground. You have the same failure line everywhere across the face of the building, which tells you one thing — the failure — everthing dropped straight down, the break points along that line, all of the rebar [or iron structural bar] is bent over and pointing straight down, so that what happened... You had the bottom of the columns cut out from under the building and the building just went straight down, the front row of columns went straight down... and that's all there was to it. It wasn't blown in — the big header across the front that probably received the biggest impulse of anything, it went straight down — it did not get blown in or blown out."

His conclusion is simple:

"There had to have been four demolition charges within the building... Now, when I wrote the letter to the House [of Representatives] I said it was perfectly possible for that [exterior demolition] to have been done, because those columns were available to people from the street, and I expected when I looked at it if it had been some outside job that the demolition charges would have been at the base... But they weren't. They were up at the third floor level, which says those charges were on the third floor. You look at the end of the columns... and you can see at the top... that you have more destruction than you do at the bottom...

"We don't know who did the damage down there, but I know who's covering it up. They not only brought the building down, they cleared out the site, they've covered the site with dirt, they've carted the 200 tons of the building over to a site, and I was under the impression it was laid out for the possible inspection, but we went over to that site and there were guards at the gate, you were not permitted to enter, and we were told by the people at the site that all the material was buried... It's a classic coverup." [3]

Dr. Rodger Raubach, with a Ph.D. in physical chemistry, and working on the staff at Stanford University, agrees on Partin's analysis of the bombing:

"General Partin's assessment is absolutely correct. I don't care if they pulled up a semi-trailer truck with 20 tons of ammonium nitrate; it wouldn't do the damage we saw there." Raubach explains that, "the detonation velocity of the shock wave from an ANFO explosion is on the order of 3,500 meters per second. In comparison, military explosives generally have detonation velocities that hit 7,000 to 8,000-plus meters per second. Things like TNT have a detonation velocity of about 7,100 meters per second. The most energetic single-component explosive of this type, C-4 — which is also known as Cyclonite or RDX — is about 8,000 meters per second and above. You don't start doing big-time damage to heavy structures until you get into those ranges, which is why the military uses those explosives." [4]

NOTES:

1. McAlvany, Donald S. "The Oklahoma City Tragedy: Implications for Free Speech, Political Dissent, and Liberty in America (A Clear and Present Danger)," *The McAlvany Intelligence Advisor*, May/June 1995
2. Gibson, S. Internet posting, May 21, 1995, copy in the author's possession
3. Partin, Brigadier General Benton. Interview by Chuck Harder, "Oklahoma City... a Closer Look," *For the People* video production, 1995
4. Jasper, William F. "OKC Bombing: Expert Analysis," *The New American*, June 26, 1995

17

More Dissenting Opinions

F rom the beginning, there were many who doubted that the whole truth was being told about the bombing. Discrepancies in the record were noted in the *Veritas* newspaper:

"Initial examinations of the bomb scene show that a minimum of two bombs were needed to inflict the damage that was presented. The steel reinforced concrete pillars that held up the building were sheared off at ground level clear back to the third pillar throughout the building. Explosives experts have confirmed that this is impossible with the one bomb scenario being presented by the government and the media. The reports of the survivors who were blown out of the front of the building into the street and the front of the building blown outward across the street support their findings." [1]

According to an NBC news commentator, reporting live from Oklahoma City on April 19, "The blast worked its way outward through the front of the building." On the same broadcast, the commentator noted, "all of that glass exploding out of the building..." [2] As proof of an explosion outward from within the building, chunks of concrete from the exploded building may be noted in photos on the rooftops of buildings in front of the federal building.

An outward directed blast would also neatly explain the behavior of the Ryder truck's axle after the explosion, whose trajectory seems to violate all of the laws of physics. With the explosives situated above the axle in the truck, and with the bomb blowing a crater an estimated eight feet deep into the roadway underneath the truck, it would seem to dictate that the axle would have been propelled to the bottom of the crater, but with another blast coming from within the building the location of the recovered axle becomes theoretically possible. The only other solution that suggests itself is that the Ryder truck might have been positioned above explosives planted underneath the ground, perhaps in the sewer system.

Another observer from the underground press noted that:

"Reviewing the newspaper and television pictures from Oklahoma City, the truck bomb could never have caused the pattern of damage that was evident from those photos. A truck bomb charge immense enough to break, from a distance, those reinforced concrete columns would certainly blow out the exterior curtain wall at ground level on the opposite and undamaged side of the building. There is no damage on the opposite side exterior wall, which is intact.

"The pattern of blown columns is not close to being circular as would be expected if the blast emanated from one origin. As we know, the power of a detonation diminishes proportionately as the distance (in all directions, i.e., circular) is increased. However, this pattern of destruction is essentially linear, except for one indentation that should have been, but is not directly opposite of the crater. Unbelievably, the truck bomb was parked in the wrong spot. Most incredibly, there are intact window frames closer to the center of the ground crater than are the missing reinforced concrete columns. (At the World Trade Center bombing in New York, the truck bomb was much larger than this one, while parked in the garage right next to a support column, failed to take it out.)

"The debris of the A.P. Murrah Federal Building is blown out of the building as one would expect from an interior blast. An exterior blast would blow debris into the still standing interior of the building. In summary, this linear pattern is totally indicative of high brissance charges placed directly on the columns. The 1,200 pounds of ammonium nitrate (a slow burn explosive) reported in the press could not have caused this kind of massive damage to support columns from that distance, no way." [3]

Sam Gronning, a demolitions expert with 30 years of experience with explosives, also doubts the official explanation of the bombing. He stated, "what everyone in this business knows: No truck bomb of ANFO out in the open is going to cause the kind of damage we had there [in Oklahoma City]. In 30 years of blasting, using everything from 100 percent nitrogel to ANFO, I've not seen anything to support that story." Gronning recently set off an ANFO charge three times the size of the Oklahoma bomb, and commented: "I set off 16,000 pounds of ANFO and was standing upright just 1,000 feet away from the blast." [4]

Gary McClenny, an Army veteran experienced in the detonation of ammonium nitrate-fuel oil combinations, also weighed in on the side of a hoax being perpetrated on the American public. In a letter sent to Judge Louis Freeh, the director of the FBI, McClenny stated:

"At the tail end of the Vietnam War, I volunteered for military service and was deployed as a Combat Engineer, Explosives and Demolitions specialist, from 1972-1976 in the regular army and continued in that position from 1976-1979 in the active army reserve. My background in explosives is extensive; I was qualified for proficiency pay based upon my Military Occupational Specialty (MOS) test scores. I was cleared Secret BI (background investigation) to work with atomic explosive devices and did so for a nine month period prior to being rotated overseas. As a Combat Engineer, I was trained extensively in the destruction of roads, airfields, bridges and abutments, and buildings as well as the construction of abatis and tank traps. I was trained in both conventional and atomic explosive devices, to include, but not limited to, ammonium nitrate, ammonium nitrate/fuel oil breaching charges, TNT, Dynamite, Dat-cord, and Plastics. After the military, and during and after college through the present, I have studied and been involved in commercial construction with heavy emphasis on high-rise construction. I am intimately familiar with the various methods of commercial concrete construction as well as steel construction. I have also been involved in some commercial building structure removal. Additionally, I served as a reserve police officer for the City of Irving [Texas] for five years and am currently registered as a reserve police officer in the State of Texas. Please keep this background information in mind as I offer my opinion.

"In watching the event unfold on national TV and then in various newspapers, I have become increasingly uneasy as the story has come out; in other words, I smell a rat! First, the media reported an ammonium nitrate bomb, then it was an ammonium nitrate/fuel oil bomb. First it was a 1,000 pound bomb, then 1,200, then 2,000, then 4,800 pounds! This information was supposed to come from federal experts. The media had a heyday with the fact that any farmer could purchase ammonium nitrate in the form of fertilizer and how we need to consider regulating fertilizer to prevent terrorism... Not once in all the distortion of truth did anyone mention that ammonium nitrate bombs require a kicker charge of conventional explosives to detonate them — a blasting cap will not set them off! In the army, we used a mixture ratio of 30 pounds of ammonium nitrate to 10 pounds of TNT in order to ensure detonation. Also, ammonium nitrate has a high affinity for water and when it gets wet, IT

WILL NOT DETONATE. It must be stored in airtight, watertight containers to ensure that it will be dry enough for detonation. Farm supplies and hardware stores are not concerned with moisture content and take no steps to ensure dryness of the fertilizer making commercially procured ammonium nitrate a poor choice for large-package explosive devices."

Although McClenny becomes somewhat technical in his analysis of the bombing, his conclusions should be carefully noted, because they are damning:

"Also bear in mind that ammonium nitrate is a poor choice for breaching reinforced concrete for two reasons: it is a low-level, low velocity (2700 m/sec by itself, 3400 m/sec when boosted by a 25% TNT charge) explosive primarily used to move dirt from drilled holes and even when mixed at a ratio of 25% TNT/75% ammonium nitrate it has a relative effectiveness of only 0.42 when compared with TNT standing alone! Simple calculation based on the formula $P = R$ cubed $\times K \times C$ where P=pounds of TNT, R=breaching radius in feet, K=material factor of material to be breached and C=tamping factor yield startling results. Follow me for a minute. Radius is the distance from the explosive device to the farthest point of breaching. Let's use 80 feet as a conservative estimate from the truck to the uppermost floor destroyed. The material factor is 1.76 for reinforced concrete which matches the building construction. The tamping factor is 3.6 for a ground placed device without tamping which would match this scenario. Applying this standard military formula yields P=3,244.032 Did you catch that? To breach concrete at 80 feet would require 3-1/4 million pounds of TNT!!! But, we're not through; to convert to ammonium nitrate we must multipy by the inverse of 0.42 which is 2.38. This yields 7,720,796 pounds of ammonium nitrate! Okay, that sounds a little outrageous because we're not really breaching 80 solid feet of concrete; but what about the crater? We were told the device left a crater 25 feet deep. Using the same formula but substituting 0.29 for the material factor for the earth below street level and leaving the concrete completely out of the equation even though the blast would have had to completely devastate a heavily steel-reinforced 6-12 inch thick concrete street before blasting into the dirt, let's calculate. 25x25x25x.29x3.6x2.38=38,823.75 pounds of ammonium nitrate! That is still a lot more explosive than we are told was used. These federal experts are at least as smart as I am — what gives? Here is another fact; explosive force is equal in all directions. The damage to the federal building should have been equal to the damage to all buildings in the same radius. How is it that the device that was supposed to have been in the street could devastate the federal building without destroying all the buildings around it? Also, based upon the damage to the upper floors and roof and keeping in mind that force decreases as the inverse square of the distance, the bottom floors of the federal building should have been completely destroyed, leaving no structure to support the upper floors. If the device was an ammonium nitrate device, what was used as the booster charge and where was it obtained? Dynamite, TNT & C4 are the main booster; all are tightly regulated; there should be a record of their purchase. Black powder and smokeless powder do not create enough shock to detonate ammonium nitrate based devices." [5]

Independent investigator Devvy Kidd was at the bombing site one month after the blast. She reports that:

"The government continues to spew bilge about a 'fertilizer bomb.' One source with the local fire department told me that there was no fertilizer found and this is what I should be investigating. The odor immediately following the blast was chemical, not a manure smell but more like toxic chemicals. This was reinforced by the local businessmen I interviewed who lived through this horror.

"Many experts have stepped forward, including one engineer I spoke with in downtown OKC, and explained that it is mathematically impossible to fit 4,800 pounds of fertilizer in a 24-foot truck. The media has continued to increase the size of the 'bomb' from 1,000 to 1,500, to a ton, to 4,800 pounds, and the *Chicago Tribune* last week declared the bomb to be 5,000 pounds. Why? Because fertilizer is a low-yield, low-frequency bomb that simply can't do the magnitude of damage that was done to that building." [6]

Although I disagree with certain aspects of Ted Gunderson's published analysis of the Oklahoma City bombing, I concur with him in his belief that the bomb was probably not of the ANFO type. According to his published material:

"Gunderson has been contacted indirectly by a federal criminal investigator who is involved in the investigation. He stated the Oklahoma City bombing on April 19, 1995 was with a dual charge. Had it been ammonium nitrate (fertilizer bomb) the workers would not have been allowed in the area without breathing apparatus due to the presence of Nitric Acid vapors. He advised that John Doe 2 was vaporized by design. McVeigh is also a 'throwaway.' He stated that the debris was collapsed toward the crater. There was something inside the building, probably another bomb. It was a shear and drop charge. The investigators have looked for signs of un-oxidised ammonium nitrate pellets left over after the explosion, but none were found. This fact alone serves as a crucial indication that something is terribly wrong with the government's version of the type of explosives used in this bombing." [7]

When interviewed by the author of this book, demolitions expert Charles Young also agreed with the unlikelihood of the bomb being of the ANFO variety. Young stated, "There should have been lots of residue. Large amounts of undetonated material and carbon residue, as well as clouds of noxious gas." Young explained that the only way this residue might have been avoided would be with "a multi-point detonation — or a higher order brissance of material, meaning a greater degree of sophistication by the bomb-builders. If it was 'homebrew' there would have been so much evidence..." When asked straightforwardly as to whether the bomb was of the ANFO type, Young stated: "It doesn't appear to be."

Doubts about the Oklahoma City bomb being of the ANFO type gain additional credibility when we consider the explosion of a fertilizer plant that took place in Salix, Iowa, on December 13, 1994. Four workers were killed, along with 15 injured, and a huge cloud of ammonia gas was emitted, causing the evacuation of hundreds of persons. According to the *New York Times*, "At the explosion site, the cloud of ammonia was almost crippling." Firefighter Dick Braun was quoted as saying that the smell was so strong, it "stopped me in my tracks... You couldn't see. You couldn't breathe."

Salix Assistant Fire Chief Dave Huot said of the ammonia cloud, "It was difficult to drive through. We poured a fog of water on the cloud, trying to break it up, but nothing worked. Then we pulled our guys out of there. It was scary. It was staying close to the ground."

Jack McGeorge, an explosives expert interviewed on CBS television on the day of the bombing stated that the determination of the Oklahoma bomb as being of the ANFO type was only a "logical guess," and that the signature of such a bomb was a "fine residue" of nitrates. So far, information on this residue is entirely lacking in media and in-person accounts of the bombing. [8]

So where was the ammonia cloud at Oklahoma? Where was the residue? Admittedly, lacking an in-depth study of chemical residues and other factors at the bombing site we can only speculate on much of the information about the bomb, but why hasn't the government released the results of their investigation, which supposedly proves that the bomb was ANFO? Even if there is a thorough study of chemical residues done, it may not be conclusive, especially since an area-specific evaluation of ammonium nitrate residues is no longer possible. That there are minute amounts of ammonium nitrate in the area does not prove that the bomb was of the ANFO type. Car exhaust leaves nitrates. Fire extinguishers and other innocuous things leave ammonium nitrate residue. [9]

Michael Riconisciuto also doubts the ANFO analysis, and believes that it is probably based upon data gathered in the government's "Dipole Might" testing. Riconisciuto stated in an interview that:

The BATF has claimed that through a 'modern computer program' the evidence has been analyzed; and in their conclusions they have characterized the blast in Oklahoma City as that of an 'improvised ammonium nitrate fuel oil sensitized explosive device.' To begin with, the BATF program (known as 'Dipole Might') is a mathematical simulation program. In order to be effective in technically analyzing the bomb, it would have to be a computer simulation program capable of the analysis of a general class of engineering problems known as 'boundary value problems.' These are all technical terms, but I know of no other way to describe it. Furthermore, to be effective in formulating a realistic blast scenario, 'Dipole Might' would have to be able to merge non-integrated data types such as chemical kinetic data from explosives analysis, and architectural data from a structural engineering analysis program, with technical and non-technical forensic data in matrix and link analysis second-order factor analysis programs from criminal investigations. This is all high tech stuff and a very tall order. I really wonder whether such a program exists, and if the BATF is really using it. What probably does exist is a watered-down version of it."

Riconisciuto says, "I challenge the BATF to demonstrate the efficacy and the accuracy of the computational methods using their their 'Dipole Might' program, the program they say that they have used to identify 'positively' that a fuel oil sensitized ammonium nitrate bomb did all that damage." Riconisciuto continues by saying, "I challenge the BATF to publicly perform a structural engineering analysis of the building with an off-the-shelf recognized structural design engineering computer program that is based on boundary element methods, which is the latest state of the art. They should base the parameter section on standard engineering practice. They should model multiple blast scenarios, using an explosive engineering analysis program that is based on boundary element methods. Then they should use as examples of possible scenarios the closest approximation of an improvised device, as described in the book *The Turner Diaries*; use that as a baseline. Next, take a high performance ammonium nitrate-based military explosive device such as BLU-82, which contains approximately 6 tons of ammonium nitrate explosive, in an engineered and optimized configuration known as 'DBA-22M.' This is a high performance, large-scale military device. My position is that even an optimized, fine-tuned high performance device like that would not do the damage that this so-called 'improvised' device did." [10]

Admittedly, there are those among the community of demolitions experts who believe that it is possible that an ANFO bomb could have done the damage which was sustained at the federal building, but there are enough qualified experts who disagree to demand a thorough investigation, even though such an investigation will be greatly hampered by subsequent events which took place at the Murrah Federal Building, and which we shall describe.

So far, evidence of the probable double explosion at Oklahoma has been virtually ignored by the mainstream media, except for an occasional slighting reference to "conspiracy theory." The reason for this is apparently that the dual nature of the explosion opens up possibilities which the government would apparently prefer to not have explored.

It is possible that the dual-event and the extreme amount of destruction was the result of the detonation of the truck bomb augmented by charges placed on the support columns in the interior of the building. In order for explosives to be placed inside the building, the perpetrators would have had to have access to the interior, suggesting that individuals connected to one or more of the agencies at the federal building may have been among the guilty. I stress that there is no proof of this at the moment, but given the convincing evidence of a double explosion, the improbability that the bomb was of the ANFO type, and the fact that the government has soft-pedaled and even suppressed this and other information, the possibility of an inside job should not be overlooked.

As a final word on the subject, it should be mentioned that even the U.S. government's own manuals seem to put the lie to the Oklahoma City bombing being done by an ANFO bomb. The U.S. Government Technical Manual No. 9-1910 obtained from the Departments of the Army and Air Force, titled Military Explosives, states that an ANFO bomb must be of a greater than 99% purity of the ammonium nitrate, and requires a specific dryness probably not obtainable from commercial fertilizer. The manual also makes clear that 4,800 pounds of ANFO could not create the devastating effects on the building observed in Oklahoma City, and that it would not leave a crater anything near the size that the OKBomb did. [11]

NOTES:

1. Cooper, William. "Oklahoma City Bombing, Truth among casualties, buried under mountain of lies," *Veritas*, May 9, 1995
2. ABC Television news broadcast, April 19, 1995
3. Prukop, John R. "News Release, Oklahoma City Bombing Was An Inside Job," *Citizens For A Constitutional Washington*, April 22, 1995
4. Jasper, William F. "OKC Bombing: Expert Analysis," *The New American*, June 26, 1995
5. McClenny, Gary. Letter to Judge Louis Freeh, Director of the FBI, May 16, 1995. Copy in the author's possession
6. Kidd, Devvy. "A Quest for the Truth: My Visit to Oklahoma City, May 18th & 19th, 1995," May 21, 1995, copy obtained from *American Patriot Fax Network*, copy in author's possession
7. Gunderson, Ted. "The Gunderson Bomb Report," 1995
8. CBS Television News, April 19, 1995
9. Dwyer, Jim; Kocieniewski, David; Murphy, Deidre; and Tyre, Peg. *Two Seconds Under the World*, Ballentine Books, New York City, New York, 1995
10. Riconisciuto, Michael. Interviewed by Steve Quayle, *USA Patriot Magazine*, June 1995
11. Parfrey, Adam. "Finding Our Way Out Of Oklahoma," *Cult Rapture*, Feral House, Portland, Oregon, 1995

18

Cover-ups and Altered Evidence

On May 4, attempts to rescue victims from the rubble of the Oklahoma City federal building were concluded. [1] Despite a request filed in court, McVeigh's federal court-appointed attorney Stephen Jones was given only two and one half hours to inspect the federal building for evidence for the defense, with the destruction ostensibly performed "for safety reasons." This contradicts statements of the architect of the Murrah Building, Ed Kirkpatrick, who said:

"I thought they were much too hasty in bringing it down. I think technologically we could have removed the damaged part of the building and rebuilt it, and I was for that." [2]

Attorney Stephen Jones said the inspection was "mainly for preservation and understanding the dynamics of the bomb. I doubt there's anything left in the building of evidentiary value. All we can get from this is to understand the physics of the explosion: Where did it come from? How far did the damage go?" [3]

If the federal building had been a sabotaged jetliner, all of the scattered fragments would have been picked up and reconstructed for evidence, but the authorities in the case of the Oklahoma City bombing seemed to be in a hurry to put the event behind them, regardless — or perhaps because of — the kind of evidence the building might contain.

On May 23, 150 pounds of dynamite were detonated at key points in the building, turning the scene of the crime into a 27-foot high pile of rubble and rendering impossible potentially important on-site investigation work about the bombing. Gary McClenny, the demolitions expert whose letter to the director of the FBI is quoted earlier in this book, was one among many voices who objected to the quick destruction of the federal building:

"Are we being steered away from the truth? Could it be that someone placed charges inside the building, in between floors, as booster charges to augment the charge on the outside? From the photographs, it appears that someone attached high-velocity breaching charges to the bottom side of each floor, above the ceiling tiles. These charges could have been triggered by the outside blast using pressure switches set at about three atmospheres (approximately 45 psi) so as not to detonate prematurely by ventilation systems or the slamming of doors, etc.; they would be sensitive enough to be triggered by the blast from the street and would detonate in such a way that it appeared to be one explosion! An examination of the concrete would give conclusive evidence." [4]

After the demolition of the building, the area was excavated, with recovered material carried to BFI Waste Systems, a fenced landfill outside of town, and buried. Employees and security guards at the landfill denied access by investigators to the area, stating that they had been given orders to do so by the FBI. [5]

The destruction of the federal building was a literal and figurative cover-up by the government, only one of many in the OKBomb case, and provides a strong indication that there may have been a government connection in the bombing, or that the government was trying to cover up other matters.

Was the demolition done to hide evidence proving that the bombing could never have been accomplished with a single truck bomb? Was there proof that the explosives were of a sophistication that could not have been matched by ex-Army men making homebrew bombs in their backyard? Was the evidence destroyed because of proof that charges had been placed inside the building, thus suggesting that the perpetrators had access to the interior, and possible connections with the government agencies located in the building? [6]

Of great interest is the fact that the final demolition of the Murrah Building did not register on the same seismographs which reported two explosive events on April 19.

NOTES:

1. *Facts on File,* May 4, 1995

2. Jasper, William F. "Explosive Evidence of a Cover-up," *The New American*, August 7, 1995
3. "Defense inspects rubble," *Associated Press*, May 21, 1995
4. McClenny, Gary. Letter to Judge Louis Freeh, Director of the FBI, May 16, 1995. Copy in the author's possession
5. "The Bomb... in Oklahoma," video by *Star Investigative Reports*, 1995; Jasper
6. Prodis, Julia. "Site of terror blown to bits," *San Francisco Examiner*, May 24, 1995; Blair, Mike. "Feds Blow Away Evidence in Oklahoma City Blast," *The Spotlight*, June 5, 1995

19

The Continuing Cover-up

After the physical evidence of the Oklahoma bombing had been criminally destroyed, the cover-up continued. The government conducted its prosecution of the case at least in part through leaks to the media, downright lies, coerced testimony, and innuendo.

On June 15, 1995 the attorneys for Terry Nichols asked for a hearings on allegations that Justice Department investigators had leaked information and had withheld information from the defense. Defense attorney Mike Tigar, specifically cited the furnishing of sealed documents to the *Detroit Free Press,* without notification to Nichols or his defense, and the leak of information obtained by federal prosecutors before a federal grand jury.

The motion submitted by the defense stated, "The pattern of leaks must raise serious concern about any potential trial. The leaks are timed and spaced to poison the well of justice in every potential venue, from Michigan, to Kansas, to Nevada, to Oklahoma."

According to attorney Tigar, "In this case, one abuse has bred another — the government claims the right to inquire at leisure and leak at will." [1]

On June 22, McVeigh defense team lawyer Robert Nigh sought a hearing on the charges that the government was denying access to key witnesses. Nigh stated that the Junction City, Kansas rental agency where the alleged bombing truck had been rented was under guard, and that government employees had instructed witnesses not to talk and were "discouraging defense access." Nigh also indicated that the state trooper who arrested McVeigh would not talk to the defense, even after complaints had been filed in federal court.

"As it stands now," Nigh said, "they are very important witnesses in the case. The government has relied on statements from these people at the preliminary hearing and a judge considered that information as sufficient to hold our client." [2]

Other lawyers agreed that the government was doing everything it could to paint Nichols and McVeigh as guilty in the public's mind prior to going to court. "It's like [the judges] are writing rave book reviews for a novel that hasn't been written yet," said Ronald Kuby, a New York lawyer. "It seems very clear that the tone of these remarks would make it much more difficult for these defendants to get a fair trail."

Gerald Goldstein, president of the National Association of Criminal Defense Lawyers, stated, "There is a danger in these kinds of high-profile cases that potential jurors will be predisposed toward guilt before they come to court." [3]

In September 1995 allegations of the alteration of forensic evidence by the FBI scientific crime lab was presented on the *Prime Time Live* television show, in an episode titled "Crime Lab Crimes." FBI agent Fred Whitehurst, the former senior agent at the bomb residue analysis section in the FBI, came forward to whistleblow on what he perceived as a pattern of perjury, fraud and fabricated evidence by members of the FBI crime lab. Agent Whitehurst stated that when he had been in charge of analyzing bomb residue in the World Trade Center bombing case he had been threatened by other agents to reach conclusions that he felt the evidence did not warrant, and that he had been under pressure by other members of the lab to prove the defendants guilty in the case even though no official conclusions were ever reached about the nature of the bomb used. Relevant to Whitehurst's statement may be the testimony of James T. Thurman, who testified in the trial of the alleged World Trade Center bombers that the bomb they had been mixing could never have exploded because the amount of ammonium in the fertilizer was insufficient.

Of tremendous relevance to the fate of Timothy McVeigh and Terry Nichols is that Agent Whitehurst pointed at FBI agent Tom Thurmond as one of those guilty of altering evidence in the World Trade Center case. Agent Thurmond is currently one of the lead agents involved in investigating the Oklahoma City bombing. [4]

In October 1995, information was released suggesting that defense investigators would advise McVeigh's attorneys of a necessity to examine original forensic records from the Oklahoma City coroner's office. The reason for this was that lab technicians and other employees at the state medical examiner's office had privately voiced their objection to the official reports being "altered by the government in a number of substantive ways prior to release to the defense team or the public." These persons advised that FBI agents had been present at every autopsy and analysis done by the medical examiner's office, and that they believed the FBI was altering or "influencing" the documentation. [5]

Also in October, Sheriff Jerry R. Cook of Noble County, Oklahoma publicly protested that the FBI had confiscated film from the booking camera, mug shots, McVeigh's fingerprint card, booking receipts, McVeigh's clothing and property, and the mattress cover he had slept on at the Perry jail, and had not returned the items, despite their agreement to. The sheriff indicated that aside from a single booking card, there was no other record of McVeigh's presence in the jail. Sheriff Cook said, "We have other suspects on the roll of film they took. The FBI agents were only here for a brief time, and, for the most part, they did what they said they would do... But I need the original photos back for our court records." [6]

NOTES:

1. Reuter news release, June 15, 1995
2. Johnson, Kevin. "McVeigh lawyer says prosecutors hinder defense," *USA Today*, June 23, 1995
3. Johnson, Kevin. "Delay sought in bombing indictments," *USA Today*, June 9, 1995
4. *Prime Time Live* television show, "Crime Lab Crimes," September 13, 1995; "Expert says alleged bomb materials wouldn't work," Statesman wire services, August 25, 1995
5. Myers, Lawrence. "OKC Update," *Media Bypass*, October 1995
6. Ibid.

20

An Arsenal Full of Secrets

After the demolition of the Murrah Building, information began to come to light which may explain many facets of the Oklahoma City bombing case that have so far remained mysteries. Representative Charles Key of Oklahoma was the first person to make public the existence of an Oklahoma County Sheriff's Department film indicating the existence of an "arsenal room" within the Murrah Building, where explosive devices had been stored at the time of the April 19 bombing. Key also revealed that U.S. Army bomb squads had been summoned from local military bases shortly after the bombing. Now there was hard evidence which potentially explained the dual nature of the seismographic record of the bombing, as well as the two explosions heard by many witnesses. Now there was a single, simple explanation for the numerous bomb scares that took place on the day of the bombing, and there was a credible explanation why officials had been in such a hurry to demolish the Murrah Building.

Key reported that the Sheriff's Department film, "establishes, beyond a doubt, that the BATF was maintaining an arsenal room in the Murrah Building the day of the bombing and that [the] arsenal room was ruptured by the initial blast from a truck bomb. Considering the fact that the remains of that arsenal room [were] scattered about an area of the crippled federal building where death and destruction were most greatly realized, it is entirely reasonable to investigate whether or not this arsenal room contained improperly and illegally stored high explosives.

"Additionally, an investigation should occur to determine if some of those explosives may have been secondarily detonated by the truck bomb. These possibilities should be carefully and full explored for the most obvious reasons. Since the bombing, I have been told repeatedly by explosives experts that a 5,000 pound fertilizer bomb detonated near the center of the federal structure could not have caused the incredible loss of life and destruction to the remote southeast quadrant of the building. Consequently, now that we have absolute proof that an arsenal room was being maintained in that precise location of the structure, it is incumbent upon and would behoove us to investigate whether or not this played a role in contributing to the enormous death toll in that area which is more commonly referred to as the 'pit.'

"In addition," Key continued, "and since this arsenal room was being maintained by the very federal agency charged with prohibiting the possession and introduction of high explosives into a public building, it is necessary and proper, I believe, for the formation of an independent state committee to address these and related matters. The state legislator, who has questioned since the blast various aspects of the federal investigation of the bombing, pointed out at a press conference in Oklahoma City on September 15 that 'it should be noted that a fire in 1987 detonated improperly stored explosives at the FBI headquarters in Washington, D.C.' I feel, therefore, that it is not improper to question another federal agency [ATF] about similar, more catastrophic conduct. So, I would ask that those who have in the past tried to discredit, even obstruct, an independent state investigation to now swallow their pride and get behind this effort. With the discovery of this critical new evidence, I believe now, more strongly than ever, that we owe this effort to those families directly affected by this tragedy, to both justice and to history." [1]

Other Oklahoma City investigators supplied additional information on the arsenal room or rooms in the Murrah Building. Pat Briley stated that the arsenal room "was ruptured during the bombing. We have interviewed three General Services Administration employees who removed boxes of unexploded explosives from this vault. There were percussion cap boxes and at least one or two TOW missiles. We're not sure if the missiles were armed or not." [2]

In an interview with Chuck Harder, Oklahoma investigator J.D. Cash stated that, "We have an eyewitness account, this is from a civilian that the GSA had retained to help clean up the building leading up to the May 23 implosion. He helped the ATF agents unload an arsenal room, a magazine room that they were maintaining up on the ninth floor in the southeast corner [of the Murrah Building]. Among the items removed were the usual things, your firearms, your machine guns, lots of stuff, cases of ammunition, but among those items were boxes marked explosives and a TOW missile — a tank killer. Now, we had one of those which caused one of the bomb scares the morning of the disaster. The experts come in, they load that thing up, and they're on the way to the range to detonate it. And now they're saying, 'Well, we got a phone call on the way to detonate that missile, and they won't tell me from who, but we were told that thing was all right, and now the FBI has been in, and they've said, yeah, that thing is all right. It's now become a training device, and people down here are being told that all those boxes of explosives and stuff that these rescuers shut down the rescue effort so that the bomb squad could come in, and people are dying and bleeding to death while this is going on, we're now supposed to be believing that these are training devices. And, of course, training devices are marked as such so that there cannot be any confusion, and we know that, but now we have a fellow who says 'I helped them do the deal'." [3]

Cash also noted that he had spoken to Dick Miller, the Oklahoma City Assistant Fire Marshal, who admitted that there had been explosives removed from the Murrah Building on the morning of the blast, and that it had been the removal of those explosives which had caused at least three evacuations of personnel and had impeded rescue efforts.

Cash stated that Miller had told him that the bomb scare at 10:30 a.m. on April 19 had been caused by a two by two foot box which had been clearly marked "high explosives," and that the box had been filled with percussion caps for C-4 explosive. Cash also mentioned that he had videotaped four witnesses who observed the ATF unloading their arsenal room two weeks after the initial blast, and that the contents of the room had contained "every firearm known to man, hundreds of thousands of rounds of ammunition, explosives, boxes marked explosives, TOW missiles, hand grenades, about everything short of a T-72 Russian tank."

Cash pointed out that, "In discovering where the ATF room is located, sure enough it turns out that that room was up on the 9th floor and it runs from north to south on the furthest east side. That room was ruptured, the photographs clearly show that the room was ruptured and the area that is ruptured is directly over what we now know or call as the pit area. And the pit area is that large coned-in area on the southeast section of the Murrah Building [where assymetrical damage can be seen]. Now, what is important about that is that's the area where far more than 50 percent of the fatalities that day occurred."

Cash also said that, "the truck that was parked out in front of the building brought the front of the building down. If you know that that is a cantilevered building, it's a perfect structure for a truck bomb to do the maximum amount of damage to, and if it did and the explosion, if it did bring down that facia area and rupture the ATF arsenal room — and since the ATF was keeping the propellant caps or percussion caps for C-4, it is reasonable to assume that they also were keeping C-4 there — if a case of C-4 fell out of that room during that initial blast, then demolition people... and you can check with anybody who is familiar with C-4, they will tell you that C-4 is extremely safe to handle, but you can set it off with 3,500 pounds of pressure per square inch. And so, if a case of C-4 came out of that room, or if C-4 was stored in another area of that building, in that southeast area, and if that facia came down from the explosion outside, which I think we all agree it did, then it builds up on top of... 3,500 pounds is nothing when you look at the facia of the building... then that would explain that huge amount of destruction on the southeast side. So what we may have had is the government's ineptitude, the ATF overlooking and not following procedure. They may have killed most of the people in that building that day, and certainly they're not going to be the first ones to admit it." [4]

NOTES:

1. Blair, Mike. "Secret BATF 'Arsenal Room' Killed Kids in Oklahoma,' *The Spotlight*, October 2, 1995
2. Briley, Pat. "Federals Know Identity of Oklahoma's John Doe No. 2," *The Spotlight*, October 2, 1995
3. Cash, J.D. Interview by Chuck Harder, "Oklahoma City... A Closer Look," *For the People*, 1995
4. "Oklahoma City: What Really Happened?", video, Charles Allen, 1995

21

Unproven Theories

D uring the Oklahoma City bomb investigation a number of unproven, although not disproven, theories have been presented about who was responsible for the crime. Information theoretically linking the bombing to Japan and to American intelligence agencies was released by Norman E. Olson and Ray Southwell, officers in the Michigan Militia, on April 28, 1995. Amid the heat of media coverage about Oklahoma City, they faxed a press release to news organizations about CIA and FBI involvement in the bombing — with the ultimately responsible party being the Japanese government, according to them.

At any other time, it is unlikely that the press release would have gained any mainstream notice, given media disdain for "conspiracy theories," not to mention the truth. But, with so much attention riveted on citizen militias after the bombing — particularly the Michigan Militia, which some had alleged McVeigh had been associated with — Olson and Southwell's revelations did receive a good deal of media attention. [1]

Gaining still more attention in the press were the subsequent resignations of Olson and Southwell from the Michigan Militia. In a subsequent press release, Olson and Southwell stated that they had released the information on the Japanese/CIA connection to the OKBomb "against the majority vote of the staff" of the Michigan Militia, and that this was the reason that they were resigning. [2]

Southwell and Olson attributed the information of a Japanese connection to the bombing to Debra von Trapp, of Trapp Technologies, based in Irvine, California. In subsequent interviews and press releases von Trapp stated that Japan was acting in retaliation for a recent gas attack on a subway there — which von Trapp believes the CIA was responsible for

— allegedly as a payback for the Japanese electronic bugging of the Clinton White House.

The von Trapp theory creates a problem for researchers, and most investigators have simply rejected her material out of hand, some even going so far as to call her theories disinformation, and to label her as a "CIA agent." The main difficulty in accepting the von Trapp theory is that her statements are unsubstantiated while not utterly implausible, although suggesting through a number of details that she does have an inside view of espionage activities.

Debra von Trapp has worked in the computer field and, according to her, she was an outside consultant to Xerox Corporation. She reportedly was in charge of selecting foreign management for a division of Xerox called Shugart in the early 1980s, during which time she found out that hard disk drives were being illegally shipped and diverted to a company called Isotempex, alleged to be a front organization for the Soviet KGB. This was during the tenure of Soviet mole Aldrich "Rick" Ames as Russian counterintelligence chief for the CIA. Von Trapp states that Ames and a director of operations at Xerox were reaping the rewards for the illegally-shipped hard drives. She also states that the Xerox Corporation was "conducting CIA training camp at its Leesburg, Virginia facility." Von Trapp states that, "I am outside this. I owned a consulting firm that was taken over by the FBI and CIA, without any choice on my part. Because I had crossed Aldrich Ames and [a Xerox official, name deleted] early on in my career. And then they had come back and tried to take everything from me, including my house. Then they threatened to kill myself and my child."

Von Trapp alleges that some of the persons involved in the alleged Xerox/Aldrich Ames scam "transitioned" into the era of the Japanese/American trade wars, and struck a bargain where FBI, CIA, and DEA agents allegedly became double agents for Japan, hired by individuals at the Japanese Embassy to wiretap the offices of President Clinton, and paid through the Japanese-owned MCA/Universal. Von Trapp says of Clinton, "from the very moment that he was president, he was spied on by the Japanese government, and all of his communications were compromised."

Von Trapp indicates that these individuals in American intelligence had been the recipients of large amounts of funding under the Bush administration, but that with the advent of President Clinton the funding had dried up.

One nexus of this alleged spy web was a base in Alabama, which housed a "national network surveillance project," which researcher Sherman Skolnick has speculated is Gunther Air Force Base. Von Trapp relates that a military Lear Jet which crashed in Alabama on April 17th, 1995 carried officials involved in the plot. She states that the same "Special Ops team" that was responsible for downing the aircraft was also responsible for the Oklahoma City bombing. Von Trapp says, "And April 19th is not the significant date on this. It was April 20th in Japan — it was one month to the day of the subway attack, which was March 20th."

According to von Trapp, Walter Mondale (the current ambassador to Japan) learned of the bugging operation on September 27, 1994, and attempted to get an investigation going. In the meantime, the U.S. had gassed Japanese citizens in the subway ("to discredit the government," the Southwell/Olson press release says). The Japanese at least publicly blamed a religious cult, and played turnabout by bombing the federal building in Oklahoma City with an Arab copycat bomb.

According to the von Trapp theory, at least one Secret Service agent, Alan Whicher, was involved in the Japanese spying operation. Whicher, "cooperated entirely. And that Secret Service agent was bounced out of the White House. He'd been there under Bush, and then with Clinton. And he was sent back to the Secret Service office at Oklahoma City." Von Trapp alleges that the actual target of the Oklahoma City bombing was Secret Service agent Whicher, who she alleges was "in the loop" with the CIA/FBI conspirators.

Von Trapp also calls the Vince Foster death a "CIA hit," and a "reminder of who really runs the roost." She states that the head CIA conspirator "called me the night that Vince Foster died — excited, screaming over the phone, 'We did him! We did him!' And I said, 'Did who?' And he said, 'Vince Foster.' And I said, 'What do you mean?' And he said, 'We did him!' And I said, 'Well, where did you do him?' And he said, 'Well, we did him somewhere else, but we dumped him in a queer park to send Clinton and his queer wife a message!'" [3]

In an interview with researcher Brian Francis Redman, von Trapp stated, "I've been on-record since the morning of April 19th: there was no Ryder truck in front of that building. Tim McVeigh had nothing to do with this operation. There was no 'fertilizer bomb.' There were three devices, to the best information that I have been given first hand, there were three devices inside that building. I don't know how many were detonated." [4]

Von Trapp was interviewed on the *Dateline* television show, in an episode luridly titled "Suspicious Minds," but feels that the television show set her up to be discredited. After viewing the show, I have to agree. She says, "They didn't accurately represent what I'd said at all! They took a few moments of the [videotape] clip of me, out of about a two-and-a-half hour interview, and completely misrepresented what I said to them.

"They contacted me. I never contacted them. They came to me and told me that they were doing a piece on the Oklahoma bombing and were interviewing people that had factual information to offer regarding it. They never suggested that they were doing a theory piece. They never suggested that they were going to cover this in any way that they did. And, in fact, there are a couple of things that they totally misrepresented. They said I said the Japanese did it. That's not what I said. I said the Japanese government, through Matsushita and MCA Universal, provided the money to a team of U.S. federal employees, that were acting outside the U.S. government's authority, that contracted that bombing on behalf of the Japanese government."

Von Trapp states that her interview was edited to make her appear crazy. The *Dateline* segment closes with an audiotape of a voice mail message which she had supposedly left. Von Trapp says of the audio clip, "No. In fact, you know what that was? If anyone has that recorded, and they listen to it carefully, and... they did a very clever thing. They took two dash marks, on the screen, and two messages. And the second part of that alleged statement [i.e., the voice mail] is actually a question. And that voice mail was left in response to an NBC affiliate, in Ponca City, Oklahoma, putting out an erroneous report, on air, that Edye Smith had in fact stated that she was fully satisfied that the investigation was complete, that she knew everything she had to know from the ATF, that no one had not shown up to work [at the federal building], that she and her mother believed that the fact that they [ATF personnel] had survived was 'the will of God' — when, in fact, Edye never said any of those things, and, in fact, Edye emphatically denies those things...

"And so, I followed up with a phone message to Benno Schmidt, at *Dateline*, and left him a voice mail. And I said, 'How could Ted Phillips, the producer of your affiliate, NBC in Ponca City, put this out and then not give a retraction? Because of what it does is, it leaves the impression that NBC could be the front for...' And that is the rest of that message. 'The CIA' — it was a question! And they completely mis-represented the quote, and spliced two voice mail messages together. And if you listen to them, you can hear the intonation is different.'" [5]

According to the Southwell/Olson press release, the impending Japanese attack was reported by Ms. von Trapp to veteran journalist Sarah McLendon of the *McLendon News Agency* on April 18. When I spoke to Ms. McLendon on the telephone she denied this. She said that von Trapp had left a message on her answering machine, about some unspecified "trouble," but that she had not been able to talk to her until the following day, after the bombing. McLendon's view is that von Trapp is sincere, but incorrect in her evaluation of responsibility for the Oklahoma City bombing. [6]

Thus far the von Trapp theory has received only a curt dismissal from both the mainstream and underground media. I personally do not have enough information to prove or disprove these allegations, and am also not of a mindset to name everyone who argues or disagrees as being an agent of the "secret government" or CIA. It is, however, possible to substantiate American government concern about terrorist attacks emanating from Japan immediately prior to the Oklahoma City bombing with the following news story, titled "Military Prepares For Poison Gas," from the *Spotlight* newspaper, published in the April 10, 1995 issue:

"The U.S. government is concerned terrorists may be planning an attack with poison gas, similar to that which killed 10 and injured 5,500 when released in five subway trains in Tokyo during the morning rush hour on March 20.

"It was apparently no coincidence that just 10 days prior to the attack in Tokyo, which is believed to have been perpetrated by an extremist religious sect, U.S. authorities completed a three day exercise at the Midland International Airport, located between the cities of Midland and Odessa in western Texas. The principal part of the exercise, named Operation Crisis Look 1995, was a simulated poison gas attack on the civilian airport by mock terrorists.

"The *Spotlight* has received reports the government has been deeply concerned about potential terrorist activity in the United States — in particular some type of attack utilizing poison gas — for months.

"In Tokyo, the terrorists released a nerve gas similar to sarin, an agent that was formulated while scientists were working on new types of insecticides.

"During Operation Crisis Look 1995, more than a dozen Air Force planes few into the Midland airport, including giant C-141 Starlifter transports and KC-135 re-fueling tankers. Just before landing, pilots of the C-141s were advised the Midland airport was under chemical attack. After the aircraft had landed they remained on the runways, or tarmac, while hundreds of troops on board donned chemical warfare protective gear before exiting the planes...

"It is believed the Midland International Airport, which is located in the Pernian Basin region of western Texas, where some of the nation's most productive oil and natural gas fields are located, was chosen for the exercise due to its close proximity to the Mexican border. U.S. government officials, according to *Spotlight* sources, are concerned about some type of terrorist activity taking place near the border, perpetrated by terrorists who have entered the United States from Mexico. This is due no doubt to the relative ease in which illegal aliens routinely breach security along the border and enter the country." [7]

Although no one in the press, either above or underground, was taking the Japanese connection to the Oklahoma City bombing seriously, the government may have. According to an Internet computer posting by David Feustel:

"Seven plain-clothes federal agents with hand-held radios arrived in four cars and surrounded the home of Debra von Trapp Friday for 3 hours yesterday. This apparently was an attempt to take DVT into custody for the duration of the holiday weekend. The reason for the attempted apprehension was not clear, but it is probably related to the increasing attention being paid to alternative theories concerning U.S. and Japanese government involvement in the Oklahoma City bombing. The U.S. government appears to be making a concerted effort to suppress any and all information concerning the bombing that does not square with the FBI's 'official' version." [8] Later reports, although sketchy, suggested that von Trapp had not been taken into custody, and that she was unharmed, although not providing interviews.

Another unproven theory about the Oklahoma City bombing has been presented by Ron Jackson, currently incarcerated in a prison in Nevada. On April 29, 1995 Jackson was interviewed by Mark Boswell, on the Citizen's Rights Forum on *American Patriot Network* radio. During the interview, Jackson stated:

"Last week, after the explosion in Oklahoma City, two members [of his fax network] contacted a very prominent attorney in the East, and for obvious reasons I'm not going to be very specific, but they came forward and told quite an astounding story. They were part and parcel of the planning stage of the explosion in Oklahoma City. And they are also current members, or were until a few days ago, of the Justice Department. In other words, what I'm saying to you is, they admitted, in the form of affidavits, that they, as being part of our government, created the situation and are responsible for the explosion in Oklahoma City... As I understand, what they have said to me in the form of the affidavits, one of the gentlemen was in a 10-member group within the Justice Department that planned the bombing in Oklahoma City." Jackson states that all of the government's records on the attack on the Branch Davidians at Waco were in the building, and that in one of the affidavits, "...it states that the explosion was originally scheduled for 6 a.m. In other words, they wanted to try to just make a point."

Jackson stated, "We specifically know what the government's intent was. Their primary intent was to exploit the date, April 19th. That coincides with the Waco incident and it also coincides with the situation in Idaho [the attack on Randy Weaver, in which his son and wife were murdered by federal agents]... And also, government needs justification to implement Presidential Directive 12919. That gives the president the authority to suspend the Bill of Rights, and the Constitution, for a period of up to 90 days and there can be no interference or anything from Congress done after it's initiated."

Jackson also stated:

"Furthermore, in line with the same thing, we've had a Secret Service agent come forward and state that the day prior to the bombing he overheard conversation in the White House that confirms this and he did not know the meaning of the conversation until the explosion was announced on television."

Jackson also indicated that he had been contacted by an attorney from Oklahoma City, and reported:

"When I spoke to the attorney, he had in his presence a BATF agent who was part of the class on explosives in the basement of the federal building in Oklahoma City. He certified that the day prior to the explosion, he and others in the class were told to not come to work on the day of the explosion, April 19th, because the building was coming down."

Here is one of the affidavits that Jackson alludes to:

I hereby certify that I make the following statement of my own free will and do so under the penalty of perjury.

I am an attorney employed by the UNITED STATES JUSTICE DEPARTMENT, my place of employment is Constitution Avenue & 20th, Washington, D.C. I am a seven (7) year employee of the United States government.

On February 20, 1995, I was asked to be part of a team that was to prosecute a group of terrorists who had blown-up a government facility. This group was represented as being a training exercise that would develop into an autonomous branch of the Justice Department. The information provided was as follows:

The United States government was notified by Israeli intelligence that the "Mossad" terrorists from Syria and Italy had gathered in this country in the past year and were planning several explosions in several cities. Also, an informant who had been very reliable in the past told an agent of the "FBI" that the first attack was to take place in Washington, D.C., on the Federal Courthouse, other targets were to be the IRS service center in Ogden, Utah; the Federal Courthouse in Portland, Oregon; the federal building in Oklahoma City, Oklahoma; the NCYC facility in MacLean, Virginia and others. The first explosion had occurred on 2-19-95 on a Sunday and several deaths had been reported mostly from motorists passing by the building. Five (5) arrests had been made and 3 others were sought.

This department was being formed for future anticipated needs by the government against acts of terrorism in this country, and we were led to believe that those acts were being perpetrated by Foreign Groups.

In the ensuing weeks, the group met in various locations such as the "FBI" labs in Quantico, the Virginia Hotel in Tyson Corners, Virginia, the "CIA" building in Langley, Virginia, and several military locations in the Greater D.C. area.

Many people, all experts, were brought in to speak to us. Explosive experts from all over the country were brought in and the scenario as originally put before us changed.

On or about 4-5-95 or 4-6-95, myself and another of the group were directed to write a synopsis of the class and to have it ready for review by 4-11-95. The actual day is not known, but during the class a 5" x 3" photograph was introduced to us as being the typical government building and no mention of its location was made to us.

During the approximately six (6) weeks of the class, Attorney General Janet Reno was present twice, however she only greeted a couple of people she knew and she did not participate in any way in the class. When I first heard of the explosion, my reaction was that of shock and did not make any connection to the class which we had just completed. The first realization I had of what had happened was when I saw the pictures on the evening news, the building was the same one as the photograph we had in class. As other details came in the point that made me realize what I had just participated in was the mention of the type of explosive that was being reported by the press. We had changed the original scenario from plastic explosives to one that was composed of ordinary farm fertilizer. The synopsis written by myself and the second party was the exact same duplicate of what had occurred in Oklahoma City, with the only variation being the time the blasts on paper were scheduled to go at 6:00 a.m.

I have placed with the recipients of the Affidavit, a copy of the synopsis written...

I have requested that I be given safe haven as a result of this disclosure, and it has been granted. I am and have terminated my employment with the Justice Department.

I further state that these words on this document are my own and it was prepared by myself and that I am responsible for its content.

DATED THIS 21ST DAY OF APRIL, 1995 WITNESSES: Attorney at Law Member, U.S. House of Representatives; Attorney at Law Lt. Col. U.S. Army Retired Private Business Owner and Citizen [9]

While I am in no way ruling out the idea that the American government was involved in the OKBomb, my initial response to the Jackson-presented material is that the unprofessional character of the affidavit, which includes several misspellings in the original document, suggests that it was not prepared by a Justice Department attorney, but is in fact a hoax. Another factor militating against the affidavit being factual is that the idea of Israeli intelligence alerting U.S. intelligence to the fact that "Mossad" agents from Syria and Italy had entered the country and were planning terrorist acts is extremely unlikely — "Mossad" being the name of the Israeli intelligence organization.

There are, however, other avenues in the investigation of responsibility for the Oklahoma City bombing which offer up verifiable evidence...

NOTES:

1. "Key pair in Michigan militia resign," *Associated Press*, April 30, 1995
2. Ibid.
3. Von Trapp, Debra. Interview with Sherman Skolnick, May 5th, 1995, transcribed by Brian Francis Redman. Copy in the author's possession
4. Ibid.
5. Ibid.
6. McLendon, Sarah. Conversation with Jim Keith, September 13, 1995
7. Blair, Mike. "Military Prepares For Poison Gas," *The Spotlight*, April 10, 1995
8. Feustel, David. "Subject: Federal Agents Attempt to Kidnap Debra von Trapp!", copy in author's possession
9. *The Omega Report*, April-May 1995

22

Oklahoma City,
Turn Right

J ames D. Ellison, the founder of an Aryan supremacist group The Covenant, the Sword and the Arm of the Lord, spoke to a prosecuting attorney prior to a 1988 trial in which he testified against 14 other rightist militants accused of attempting to overthrow the government. The trial resulted in the acquittal of all the defendants, but it was during this discussion that Ellison mentioned a multiple-group meeting which had taken place at the Aryan Nations' Hayden Lake, Idaho headquarters in July 1983.

According to prosecuting attorney Stephen Snyder's account of the conversation, Ellison said that late night sessions were held at Hayden Lake in which discussions about the overthrow of the government — or rather, what some term ZOG, the Zionist Occupation Government — took place. *The Turner Diaries*, a futuristic, Aryan supremacist fiction by Andrew McDonald (nee William Pierce), was at the time projected as a blueprint by which this goal might be accomplished. According to Snyder, during these meetings plans were hatched for the destruction of federal buildings nationwide, and for blowing up the Dallas office of the Jewish Defense League.

The *New York Times* has recorded that *The Turner Diaries* was Timothy McVeigh's "favorite book," which he "pressed... on friends and acquaintances." James Nichols has also said that McVeigh had spoken of the book to him, and that Terry Nichols, while in prison, recommended that he read it. [1]

An examination of *The Turner Diaries* makes one wonder, in fact, if the book was not the inspiration for the bombing of the Oklahoma City federal building, and if there is not a larger battle plan of which the Oklahoma City bombing was in effect the "first shot fired." Relevant quotes from *The Turner Diaries* follow:

"September 16, 1991. Today it finally began! After all these years of talking — and nothing but talking — we have finally taken our first action. We are at war with the System, and it is no longer a war of words...

"As carefully as we could, we calculated that we should have at least 10,000 pounds of TNT or an equivalent explosive to destroy a substantial portion of the [FBI national headquarters] building... Instead, what we have is a little under 5,000 pounds, and nearly all of that is ammonium nitrate fertilizer, which is much less effective than TNT for our purpose...

"We can wreak havoc in all the offices with windows opening on the courtyard, but we cannot hope to blow away the inner facade of the building or to punch through the sub-basement where the computers are. Several hundred people will be killed, but the machine will probably keep running...

"October 13, 1991. At 9:15 yesterday morning our bomb went off in the FBI's national headquarters building. Our worries about the relatively small size of the bomb were unfounded; the damage was immense...

"My day's work started a little before five o'clock yesterday, when I began helping Ed Sanders mix heating oil with the ammonium nitrate fertilizer...

"Meanwhile, George and Henry were out stealing a truck. With only two-and-a-half tons of explosives, we didn't need a big tractor-trailer rig, so we had decided to grab a delivery truck belonging to an office-supply firm...

"We were still two blocks away when the pavement shuddered violently under our feet. An instant later the blast wave hit us — a deafening 'ka-whoomp,' followed by an enormous roaring, crashing sound, accentuated by the higher-pitched noise of shattering glass all around us...

"We ran the final two blocks and were dismayed to see what, at first glance, appeared to be an entirely intact FBI headquarters — except, of course, that most of the windows were missing... Dense, choking smoke was pouring from the ramp leading to the basement...

"Dozens of people were scurrying around the freight entrance to the central courtyard, some going in and some coming out. Many were bleeding profusely from cuts, and all had expressions of shock or dazed disbelief on their faces..." [2]

Evidence linking Timothy McVeigh and the bombing that actually took place at Oklahoma City with the group that met at Hayden Lake, Idaho exists, although it is discussed almost not at all in the mainstream media. Ellison's CSA had "built a relationship" with Reverend Robert Millar of Elohim City, an Adair, Oklahoma Christian Identity conclave which houses about 100 members, and with other rightist groups such as the Silent Brotherhood of Robert Matthews. [3] Reverend Millar visited the Aryan Nations community, has met James Ellison, and was in close touch with convicted murderer and CSA member Richard Wayne Snell, who apparently had advance information that the Oklahoma City bombing was going to take place. [4] Ellison, released from parole on April 20, 1995, coincidentally or not the day after the bombing, was last seen that day in Jasper, Florida, in the company of two women, driving a car with Oklahoma license plates. [5]

According to Snyder, James Ellison stated, "on one of the trips when I was with Wayne [Richard Wayne Snell], he took me to some of the buildings and asked me to go in the building and check the building out. That kind of thing." Snyder says that Ellison had told him that at the request of Snell he had gone into the federal building in Oklahoma City to see what it would take to destroy the building.

Snell bore a grudge against persons in the Oklahoma City federal building, according to Snyder. "Ellison said that Snell was bitter toward the government because of the IRS, and I think these were agents from the Oklahoma City office, and they had taken him to court, and his property had been seized by the FBI and other agents in a raid." [6]

Snell reportedly took part in a number of illegal activities in tandem with other individuals in the Aryan Nations/CSA/Silent Brotherhood orbit. He and CSA elder William Thomas are said to have been involved in bombing a natural gas pipeline near Fulton, Arkansas on November 2, 1983. They mistakenly believed that the pipeline was a major conduit from Gulf of Mexico gas fields to Chicago. Later in the same month they attempted to bomb a major electrical transmission line.

On November 11, 1983 Snell, Thomas, and CSA member Steve Scott held up a pawnshop in Texarkana, Arkansas. It is alleged that Snell, believing the owner of the shop, William Stumpp, to be Jewish, murdered him by pistol shot. Snell, according to published reports, was mistaken about the man's ethnicity.

On June 30, 1984, Snell was stopped, reportedly in a routine traffic stop, by a state trooper outside De Queen, Arkansas. Snell emerged from the car, in the manner that one might reasonably have expected Timothy McVeigh to have done in Perry, Oklahoma, and shot the trooper dead. Later that day Snell was captured in Broken Bow, Oklahoma, and a gun was found in his car, alleged to have been the same one used in the murder of William Stumpp. I find it quite curious that Snell would have held on to this incriminating weapon and carried it around with him, a fact that lends credence to Snell's protestations that he was framed by the police. After his capture, Snell is alleged to have maintained that, like the statement attributed to Timothy McVeigh, he was a "prisoner of war." [7]

Snell's defense of the killing of the state trooper was that, "we were justified in doing so, as we feared for our life, and self-defense is an inalienable right. Right?... Needless to say, I failed to convince the jury and was convicted of Capital Murder. This successfully made this writer a victim, as you will see. Not dead — yet. Just live in a Tomb.

"Never have we felt animosity toward those men and women who sat in judgment. They were un-informed and too naive to relate to the evil described. (Calling one 'naive' is not derogatory, as it is one of the traits of honest people.) Time does pass, people do learn, and in light of what has transpired the past decade, I would be happy to have these same people sit in judgment again. This time I feel they would relate to evidence presented and return a verdict of 'Not Guilty.'" [8]

Governor Jim Guy Tucker of Arkansas determined the date of Snell's execution on March 9, 1995, and Snell was put to death by lethal injection on April 19, 1995, coincidentally or not, the day of the Oklahoma City bombing. The patriarch of Elohim City, Reverend Robert Millar, stayed with Snell for the last three hours prior to his execution, observed the execution, and brought Snell's body back to Elohim City to be buried there.

Although Reverend Millar denies ever meeting Timothy McVeigh, the accused bomber was aware of Elohim City and, according to sources in the government quoted by the *New York Times* and *Reuters*, had visited the compound about two weeks before the bombing, on April 5. [9] McVeigh was also stopped for a traffic violation about 20 miles from Elohim City and, according to federal officials, telephone records show that the accused bomber called the compound on April 16, as well as four minutes after reserving the Ryder truck allegedly employed in the bombing. It is not plain to me how officials know that it was McVeigh

who made the telephone call. Was the Ryder truck agency under sur-
veilance at the time of the renting of the truck? Certainly, a convenient
phone call to Elohim City would be perfect if someone was attempting to
link McVeigh to the right wing, while phoning collaborators or even
allies would seemingly be the last thing that one would do if one was
intent on the commission of a crime. [10]

Based upon statements that Snell made to prison guards and fellow
prisoners, he apparently knew that the bombing was going to take place.
Alan Ables, a spokesman for the Arkansas Department of Corrections,
says that Snell repeatedly told prison guards as well as Reverend Millar
about an imminent bombing.

"He said there was going to be a huge bombing, and not much more
than that," Ables has stated. "He didn't give any impression that it
would be a domestic bombing or something overseas. Just that there
would be some confusion as to who did it and the United States was
going to blame someone in the Mideast." Ables also remembered that,
"He commented at least once (in his last week) that he wished he wasn't
leaving; he'd like to stick around a few more weeks because he wanted
to watch what was going to happen" in regards to the bombing. Guards
observed that Snell was "smiling and chuckling" on the day of his execution as he viewed television news about the Oklahoma City bombing. [11]

Snell's last words were, "Governor Tucker, look over your shoulder. Justice is on the way. I wouldn't trade places with you or any of
your political cronies. Hell has victory. I am at peace." [12]

The Silent Brotherhood, a group closely connected with the CSA,
and with members present at Hayden Lake in 1983, was infiltrated by
FBI informant Thomas Martinez, who later testified against members of
the group.

There were rumors within the Aryan Nations and affiliated groups
that Bob Matthews, the leader of the Silent Brotherhood, was an agent
provocateur for the FBI. Those rumors have never been substantiated,
although it is known that Matthews did have a cousin who worked for
the FBI in Washington. [13]

It is suspicious that Terry Noble, the "second in command" in The
Covenant, the Sword and the Arm of the Lord, served only a two-year
prison sentence. According to the *Miami Herald*, "After getting busted,
he underwent profound changes in attitude, renouncing extremism and
cooperating with his prosecutors." But the most remarkable thing is that
after his release from prison, Noble was hired by the FBI. [14]

Members of the Silent Brotherhood are reported to be living in

southern Missouri, on a 160-acre parcel allegedly purchased with funds stolen by armored car robberies. Although the physical location of the camp is suggestive, it is not known whether Terry Nichols or Timothy McVeigh were in contact with members of the group. [15]
If the idea of the FBI actually fostering violent right wing groups is alien, reflect on the following. In July 1993, there were reports of an FBI agent using the name Reverend Joe Allen through whose activities as an agent provocateur 100 persons had been convicted since 1977, and who most recently had infiltrated the skinhead movement in Los Angeles. Allen opened a gymnasium in Los Angeles which he decorated with Nazi paraphernalia and, according to the *L.A. Times*, provided skinheads free admittance to the gym as well as funding for White supremacist activities. In the meantime, Allen was videotaping skinheads making pipe-bombs at his gym, and their buying of illegal weaponry. Allen reportedly encouraged the skinheads to plot assassinations against Blacks and Jews, but was in fact setting the conspirators up for an FBI raid in which eight arrests were made. The skinheads were arrested on charges of weapons violations and the plot to kill L.A. ethnic leaders. [16]
Another case of government intelligence agency funding of a right wing group was recently revealed in Canada. A government watchdog agency released information that they were investigating the Canadian Secret Intelligence Service (the CSIS) for having funded and controlled the main Nazi organization in the country, the Heritage Front. Grant Bristow, while receiving $50,000 a year from the CSIS, had allegedly run a dirty-tricks unit of the Heritage Front which infiltrated groups opposed to the Nazi cause. [17]
And one wonders just what the ATF is up to these days, especially after their murderous conduct at Ruby Ridge and Waco. According to journalist Jim Martin, Jonathan Preston Hayes, a Bureau of Alcohol, Tobacco & Firearms chemist until March 1993, was charged with the murder of a plastic surgeon near Chicago. Hayes told police that his motive was a campaign to execute people "feeding off Aryan beauty." Hayes also admitted to a 1987 murder of a San Francisco hairdresser, because he changed the color of people's hair. "I condemn fake Aryan cosmetics," Hayes told the judge. "I condemn bleached blond hair, tinted blue eyes and fake facial features brought by plastic surgery. This is the time that we face up to it and stop feeding off Aryan beauty... like a horde of locusts." [18]
More unfavorable attention has been recently drawn to the ATF due to revelations about the annual "Good Ol' Boys Round-up" organized by

present and former officers of the ATF and attended by ATF and other law enforcement officers.

The following is the notarized affidavit of a woman who attended at least one "Round-up" in Alabama:

"I, [deleted], being duly sworn states the following:

"1. I have personal knowledge of the facts set forth below.

"2. On May, 1990: I attended a party at Ocoee Outdoors at their bar, Grumpy's that the 'Good Ol' Boys' were throwing. Understand that after midnite the bar is closed to the public and those left are by invitation only. Anyway, I was curious to [see] how law enforcement behaved at this roundup, so I went to see. At the dance I was approached by a man who identified himself as being a Drug Enforcement officer. He asked me to step outside. I asked why. He says he 'has the best drugs available' and we'd do some. I informed him I didn't do drugs and asked him how he could do that since he had said he was with Drug Enforcement. He laughed and said that's why he had the best.

"I left him standing on the dance floor and angry. Here was a person that was paid to uphold the law — sworn to do so and he is making fun of that fact.

"After this, I decided I wanted nothing to do with this party and I left. I did not like anything that I saw at this party which was the obvious intent of the officers there to break any law they wanted. Their attitude was, 'we are the law. Who is going to arrest us or call us to account?'

"There was no respect for any woman there. We were 'open game.' I was told it was unsafe to go into the campground because if I did I was subject to rape or anything else that the 'Good Ol' Boys' wanted to do to me. Needless to say, I did not go into the campground. I have been troubled about this, time and everytime the round-up is held since.

"I had no idea that this type of thing and things could happen and be going on involving the very people that are sworn to uphold the law.

"Some things I mean are: At one round-up, 25 officers got a very attractive young woman drunk. She passed out and they placed her on a picnic table in the campground and took turns having sex with her. She didn't have sex. She was passed out. They gathered around her and urinated on her. Now I ask you, what kind of statement was that making? Think about it. Really think about it.

"At another round-up, the 'Good Ol' Boys' purchased a goat to commit beastiality on. If the ones involved didn't want to do the goat, they had to drink a quart of motor oil. How sick are these people?

"They gather around and expose themselves to see who is the biggest. At this year's round-up (May 1995) they performed public sex on the makeshift stage that the band played on and some had oral sex performed on them on the dance floor.

"Are these truly our best and finest? I sincerely hope and pray not.

"I believe they are about as sick and inclined to commit crime as any criminal they arrest. You've got a lot of cleaning up to do.

"These things I've related sounds like fiction. I wish they were. The nightmare is they are all too true.

"Affiant further sayeth not. Name of affiant [deleted]. Subscribed and sworn to before me this 20th day of July, 1995."

Reprinted next is the notarized affidavit of another woman who attended several "Good Ol' Boy Round-ups":

"I, [deleted], being duly sworn state the following:

"1. I have personal knowledge of the facts set forth below.

"2. On 1995-May: Party in campground had gotten so bad over the years I stayed away — heard about drugs and men at the bar dropping pants and flashing.

"1994-May: I saw a female stripped on a table in the campground. This was in the presence of both men and women. The men in attendance were tipping her by inserting paper currency into her [deleted in photocopied document]. During this show, a friend of mine and myself were offered $1,000 each if we would do the same. I was offended by the conduct of the men present and was extremely disturbed that I was approached and asked to perform.

"1993-May: I saw men running around flashing themselves (their penis). I was told by friends of drugs.

"I can't remember the year but I do know I was working at

Grumpy's. After work I went to the campground for dinner. My breasts were grabbed at and someone tried to flip up my skirt. One of the men (from Canada) came to my aid and watched over me so no one else would try anything. I was in the campground when a girl was 'gang-banged' by many officers. She was drunk enough to pass out. After they were finished, they all stood around her and [deleted in photocopy] on her.

"Many made the statement that this was one week out of the year they could do as they pleased. I also heard of one very upset because he got pulled over and put in jail for drinking and driving.

"A friend told me of four rapes. He [the friend] knew nothing was ever done.

"Affiant further sayeth not. Name of affiant, [deleted]. Subscribed and sworn to before me this 20th day of July, 1995."

In August 1995, the U.S. Justice Department served a civil subpoena on members of an Alabama citizen's militia group who had infiltrated and videotaped activities at the 1995 "Good Ol' Boys Roundup" in Polk County, Alabama. According to Mike Kemp, a spokesperson for the Gadsden, Alabama Minutemen, video and photos had been taken at a "Roundup" of the distribution of hunting licenses for Afro-Americans, officers wearing T-shirts with the face of Martin Luther King on a target, O.J. Simpson in a hangman's noose, and a picture of a black man spread on a car hood, captioned "Boyz on the Hood." The Minutemen issued a statement that they were willing to supply certified copies of the materials documenting their allegations, but would not hand over the originals.

According to the Gadsden, Alabama *Times:*

"As of this date, the joint militia operation known as 'Achilles Heel' has identified 91 Treasury Department agents and 29 Justice Department agents involved with the 'Good Ol' Boys Roundup.' A source has reported to me that Mr. Gene Rightmyer (retired BATF and organizer of the Good Ol' Boys) is facing criminal charges for obstruction of justice; the source also stated that further criminal charges pertaining to other agents are being pursued. One charge being the misuse of government property during the event, other charges pertain to gang rape and illegal drugs and alcohol. The ATF officers who consumed illegal homemade 'moonshine' while at the event were caught on camera." [19]

Given the above information, it becomes more credible that ATF and other law enforcement agencies might harbor members who would be willing to bend and break the law. Members of law enforcement agencies should not be utterly ruled out as possible conspirators in the Oklahoma City bombing, but should be given the same scrutiny as any other individuals or groups.

Untangling intentions and plans whose effects spread out from the Hayden Lake, Idaho meeting, as I have done in this chapter, is complicated and speculative, but the above facts show that Timothy McVeigh and Terry Nichols may have been moved by the violent currents that originated there, and possibly collaborated with their creators, through discussion or more, in the commission of the bombing.

So, the answer is perfectly apparent. It was a group of right-wing radicals who were responsible for the bombing of the federal building, and they may have had controllers in the FBI, in the ATF, or in some other domestic intelligence group.

If only the answer was so simple.

NOTES:

1. Kifner, John. "Prosecutors say Oklahoma bomb plot was limited to a few bitter ex-GIs," *New York Times* Service, August 7, 1995; Nichols, James. Interview by Chris Hansen, "His Brother's Keeper," *Dateline*
2. McDonald, Andrew (William Pierce). *The Turner Diaries*, National Vanguard Books, Hillsboro, West Virginia, 1993
3. Flynn, Kevin, and Gerhardt, Gary. The Silent Brotherhood, *The Free Press*, New York, New York, 1989
4. Potok, Mark. "Group denies any role in blast," *USA Today*, May 25, 1995
5. Thomas, Jo, and Smothers, Ronald. "Oklahoma City Building Was Target Of Plot as Early as '83, Official Says," *New York Times*, May 20, 1995
6. "Oklahoma City had been target of previous bomb plot," *New York Times* News Service, May 21, 1995
7. Flynn, Thomas.
8. Snell, Richard Wayne. "The Seekers," undated newsletter in author's possession
9. Weinraub, Bernard. "Leader of sect denies having ties to McVeigh," *New York Times* News Service, May 25, 1995; "More Arrests Reported Soon In Bombing," *Reuters* News Service, May 22, 1995

10. Potok
11. "Prisoner predicted big blast," *Detroit News*, July 2, 1995
12. "State Police On Alert," *Corrections Digest*, April 28, 1995
13. Flynn
14. "New guy in the FBI: an ex-extremist," *Miami Herald*, August 7, 1995
15. Coates, James. *Armed and Dangerous, the Rise of the Survivalist Right*, Hill and Wang, New York, New York 1987
16. "FBI, BATF Continue Their Dirty Work in U.S.," *New Dawn*, Number 21, September/October 1993
17. "Canadian Neo-Nazi Group Created by Britain's MI5?", *Nexus*, December 1994/January 1995
18. Martin, Jim. "BATF Agent Charged With Murder," *Flatland* #10
19. *Patriot Report,* September 1995 Info Packet, Present Truth Ministry

Timothy McVeigh is escorted from the Noble County Courthouse in Perry, Oklahoma, Friday, April 21, 1995. (Photo: AP/Wide World Photos)

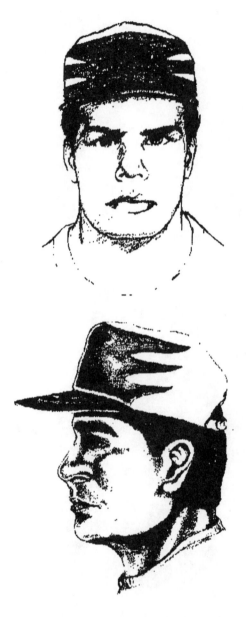

FBI sketches of Oklahoma bombing suspect #2.

FBI sketch of Oklahoma bombing suspect #1, updated April 26, 1995 after the arrest of Timothy McVeigh.

April 26, 1995 CNN video image of Michael Fortier of Kingman, Arizona. Fortier pleaded guilty in August to charges of not telling authorities of his knowledge of plans to bomb the Alfred P. Murrah Federal Building in Oklahoma City. (AP/Wide World Photos)

Terry Nichols is led by U.S. Marshals from the United States Courthouse in Wichita, Kansas, Wednesday, May 10, 1995. (AP/Wide World Photos)

Alfred P. Murrah Federal Building after the April 19, 1995 bombing.
(Photos: R. L. Sherrow)

Rescue units at the Alfred P. Murrah Federal Building after the April 19, 1995 bombing. (Photo: R. L. Sherrow)

Collapsed garage located three blocks northwest of Murrah Building (top); Alfred P. Murrah Building after bombing. (Photos: R. L. Sherrow)

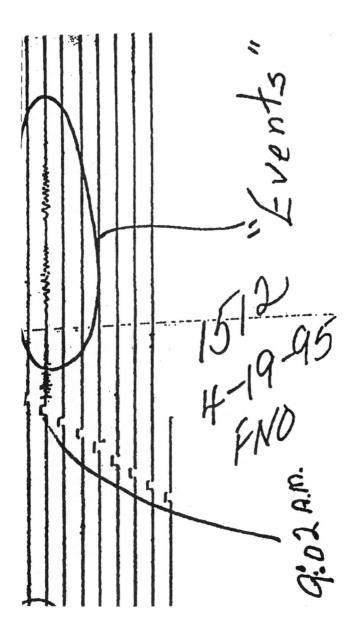

Seismograph from the Oklahoma Geological Survey Energy Center; University of Oklahoma at Norman, Oklahoma. The seismograph picked up two events on the morning of April 19, 1996, the first at approximately 9:02 a.m., followed by a blast 10 seconds later, corroborating reports of a second blast.

TINA ROWE, U.S. MARSHAL

APRIL 1 1995

DEAR MS ROWE:

AFTER LEAVING DENVER FOR WHAT I THOUGHT WOULD
BE FOR A LONG TIME, I RETURNED HERE LAST NIGHT
BECAUSE I HAVE SPECIFIC INFORMATION THAT
WITHIN TWO WEEKS A FEDERAL BUILDING (S) IS TO
BE BOMBED IN THIS AREA OR NEARBY.

THE PREVIOUS REQUESTS I MADE FOR YOU TO
CONTACT ME 27TH + 28TH OF APRIL '95 WERE
IGNORED BY YOU, MR. ALLISON AND MY FRIENDS
AT THE FBI.

I WOULD NOT IGNORE THIS SPECIFIC REQUEST
FOR YOU PERSONALLY TO CONTACT ME IMMEDI-
ATELY REGARDING A PLOT TO BLOW-UP A FEDERAL
BLDG. IF THE INFORMATION IS FALSE REQUEST
MR. ALLISON TO CHARGE ME ACCORDINGLY.

IF YOU AND/OR YOUR OFFICE DOES NOT CONTACT
ME AS I SO REQUEST HEREIN, I WILL NEVER
AGAIN CONTACT ANY LAW ENFORCEMENT AGENCY
FEDERAL OR STATE, REGARDING THOSE MATTERS SET
OUT IN THE LETTER OF IMMUNITY.

CALL 832-4091 (NOW)

Handwritten letter of informant Cary Gagan.

FACTUAL STATEMENT
IN SUPPORT OF PLEA PETITION

On December 15th and 16th I rode with Tim McVeigh from my home in Kingman, Az. to Kansas. There I was to receive weapons that Tim McVeigh told me had been stolen by Terry Nichols and himself. While in Kansas, McVeigh and I loaded about twenty-five weapons into a car that I had rented. On December 17th, 1994, I drove the rental car back to Arizona through Oklahoma and Oklahoma City. Later, after returning to Arizona and at the request of Tim McVeigh, I sold some of the weapons and again at the request of Tim McVeigh I gave him some money to give to Terry Nichols.

Prior to April 1995, McVeigh told me about the plans that he and Terry Nichols had to blow up the Federal Building in Oklahoma City, Oklahoma. I did not as soon as possible make known my knowledge of the McVeigh and Nichols plot to any judge or other persons in civil authority. When FBI agents questioned me later, about two days after the bombing and during the next three days, I lied about my knowledge and concealed information. For example, I falsely stated that I had no knowledge of plans to bomb the federal building. I also gave certain items that I had received from McVeigh, including a bag of ammonium nitrate fertilizer, to a neighbor of mine so the items would not be found by law enforcement officers in a search of my residence.

Michael Joseph Fortier

Handwritten statement of Michael Fortier.

Implantable Transponder

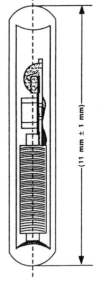

2.1 mm Dia Max

(11 mm ± 1 mm)

Product Description:

The Implantable Transponder is a passive radio-frequency identification tag, designed to work in conjunction with a compatible radio-frequency ID reading system. The transponder consists of an electromagnetic coil and microchip sealed in a tubular glass enclosure. The chip is preprogrammed with a unique ID code that cannot be altered; over 34 billion individual code numbers are available. When the transponder is activated by a low frequency radio signal, it transmits the ID code to the reading system. Independent testing has shown the transponder to be safe and easy to implant.

Although specifically designed for implanting in animals, this transponder can be used for other applications requiring a micro-sized identification tag.

Specifications:

DESTRON/IDI

23

The John Doe 2 Cover-up

As early as June 1995 possibly significant leads began to be received about new suspects in the Oklahoma City bombing. Witnesses and researchers were claiming that John Doe 2 and a possible accomplice in the bombing had been identified as residents of Oklahoma City, and that they were still walking the streets there. These new leads, apparently a major breakthrough in the investigation, inexplicably were not touched by the national news media, not even to the degree of being refuted.

On May 27, 1995 David Hall, the general manager of KPOC-TV in Ponca City, Oklahoma, announced that both he and the FBI knew the identity of John Doe 2, and that the FBI and independent investigators had the suspect under observation. Hall announced that his television station was investigating the matter, that they were employing three special investigators (two of them ex-FBI agents), and that he expected the case to be resolved within two to three weeks. Hall also indicated his feeling that McVeigh was guilty, but that the entire story of the bombing was not being told in the national press. Hall was unwilling, when questioned in an open forum, to say whether he knew if the U.S. government was involved in the bombing.

On June 6th, Hall was interviewed by Tom Valentine, on the *Radio Free America* radio show, and provided further information about his investigation of the alleged John Doe 2:

"I think the thing that really bothered us," Hall said over the air, "is that we were told on the afternoon of April 19, the day of the bombing, that they had videotape of a brown Ford pickup with McVeigh getting in it, leaving the truck that was supposed to be carrying the bomb, and that there was another suspect in that brown Ford pickup with McVeigh. They also stated that a female witness had been driving away from the scene as the bomb exploded. She had her front car window blown out. She also saw these two individuals...

"About two weeks ago, we and another television station confronted them on this and asked why they were not continuing to look for the brown Ford pickup and John Doe 2. That seemed to have fallen by the wayside.

"The authorities told us, though, that they had not put out an all-points bulletin for the brown pickup and that we were totally in error. We videotaped that interview, by the way, and so did the other television station.

"However, we then went to the police broadcast tapes that went out on April 19. We brought up the tape which indicated that there had been an all-points bulletin for a brown Ford pickup that had two occupants and that this bulletin was put out with the authority of the FBI. We replayed that tape for them and they said that they had 'no comment' on it." [1]

On June 7th, KFOR-TV, the NBC affiliate in Oklahoma City, began a televised series following these otherwise unexplored leads in the bombing case. Reporter Jayna Davis stated:

"Sources tell us the FBI canceled that all points bulletin for the brown pickup just hours after it was issued, refusing to say why and demanding that it not be rebroadcast. Little attention has been paid to the brown pickup, although the FBI has confirmed to us that the vehicle may still be connected to the April 19th attack. We've been investigating the mysterious brown pickup ourselves. The trail of that pickup has led us to direct connections to Timothy McVeigh in the very heart of Oklahoma City. Four sources have confirmed the truck which matches the FBI description was seen on several occasions in the days before the bombing in a northwest Oklahoma City business. An employee of that business is this man [video footage showing man with face blocked out] who law enforcement officers agree with us strongly resembles the FBI sketches of John Doe 2. We know who he is, but we can't show you his face at this time because he has not been arrested or charged. However, we have eyewitnesses who identified him in the company of Timothy McVeigh just days before the blast and just a few miles away from the Murrah Building."

Oklahoma City resident Mike Moroz came forward with more startling first-hand information. Moroz, an employee of Johnny's Tire Store, was at work the morning of the bombing when a yellow Ryder truck pulled up. According to Moroz, the driver of the truck was Timothy McVeigh, and there was another man with him. According to Moroz, McVeigh got out of the truck and asked him for directions to 5th and Harvey, the location of the federal building. Moroz says, "Then, he crawled back into the truck and sitting right next to McVeigh was a man wearing a ball-cap who, during the entire conversation, just sat staring straight ahead." Moroz watched the men for 10 minutes as they sat in the truck. After they had driven away, only a few minutes passed before he heard the blast that destroyed the Murrah Building.

Investigator J.D. Cash states that Moroz was shown a photo of a Middle Eastern-appearing suspect on August 8, and that the man said the photo "bore a strong resemblance to the individual he saw riding with McVeigh that morning." In another interview, Moroz stated that the man with McVeigh was "Caucasian, Middle Eastern, was not an African-American, he was not a real light complected, he was not real blonde hair, light skin... wearing a ball cap."

Moroz remarked of the demeanor of the men that, "they didn't seem that concerned, they didn't seem nervous, they really seemed lost..." Moroz told J.D. Cash that although he had been contacted by the FBI and identified McVeigh in a line-up prior to seeing a photo of the accused bomber, that they had never arranged for him to testify before the grand jury. [2]

Another witness, who chooses not to be identified, was going to the Sooner Post Office, just northwest of the federal building, on the morning of the bombing. He noticed that there was a Ryder truck parked across the street, and that two men were standing behind it. The witness identified Timothy McVeigh and another male who was shorter than McVeigh. He also noticed that there was a man sitting in the passenger seat of the Ryder truck, wearing a billed cap. Parked immediately in front of the truck was a yellow Mercury. According to the witness, "After I finished my business at the post office, the truck and car were gone, but when I pulled through the parking lot of the Murrah Building, I noticed the tall guy [McVeigh] strutting away from the truck... I don't know where the other guys were." This witness also told his story to the FBI but also was not summoned before the grand jury to testify. [3]

Investigator J.D. Cash presents information of another witness who, while interviewed by the FBI, was never called to testify. Gary Lewis was working as a pressman for the Oklahoma *Journal Record,* which is located only a few hundred feet from the Murrah Building. Shortly before the bombing Mr. Lewis stepped outside of the building for a smoke, when he noticed a yellow Mercury parked illegally next to the Athenian Restaurant, "75 steps to the north and west of the Murrah Building." Inside the car was a single man in the passenger seat. Lewis remembered that he needed to get his work clothes from his truck, and then went west to the parking lot where the vehicle was parked. As he walked back along the south side of the *Journal Record* Building he saw the yellow Mercury speeding directly at him, with two men in the car. The automobile made a sudden right turn a few feet in front of Lewis, jumping two curbs, and then raced east and out of the parking lot. Lewis identified the driver as Timothy McVeigh and recalled that the man with McVeigh looked just like the composite drawing of John Doe 2, although he was not able to match it to a suspect's photo when shown to him. "But," Lewis says, "the man I remember with the ball cap on, was also olive-skinned." Lewis also notes that the white Oklahoma license plate on the Mercury was "just swinging back and forth on one screw."

After the destruction of the federal building, Lewis left the *Journal Record* building with minor injuries. That was when he saw another man standing nearby, who was also Middle Eastern-appearing.

"This guy stood out to me," Lewis remembered, "because with all the chaos and injured people around me, this guy was just standing by himself — staring at the Murrah with a smile from ear to ear." [4]

Just as these discoveries about a possible identification of John Doe 2 began to come to light, efforts began to be made by agents of the FBI to discredit the whole notion that John Doe 2 even existed. On June 14, 1995, the *Associated Press* reported that a spokesperson for the FBI had said that the man who had been identified as John Doe 2 at the Junction City rental agency had been located, and completely ruled out as a collaborator in the bombing. The previous suspect, they said, was Army Private Todd Bunting of Fort Riley, Kansas. Employees at the Ryder rental agency, the FBI said, had been mistaken about Bunting being in the company of McVeigh.

This, however, does not correlate with statements of individuals at the Ryder agency. Owner Eldon Elliott and his employees, while not giving interviews, are confirmed by friends and employees as still being positive that John Doe 2 was with McVeigh at the time that the Ryder truck was rented, and they are also certain that Private Bunting is not the man whom they saw. According to Dave Nelson, President of the Junction City Chamber of Commerce, Eldon Elliott is "downright adamant about it. Eldon contends there were two men that day who rented the truck." [5]

Of highest importance in the Oklahoma City bombing case is other information suggesting that John Doe 2 may be a Middle Easterner. The Junction City, Kansas motel keeper who provided information for the composite drawing of John Doe 2 described the man as foreign, with a foreign name, and speaking in "broken English."

Connie and Donald Hood recall seeing a McVeigh "look-alike" and an apparent friend of McVeigh with a dark complexion staying next door at the Dreamland Motel in Junction City, Kansas on April 16 and 17. Donald Hood says:

"The first time I noted the foreigner was Sunday evening. He was staying next door to the other guy — the guy that I now understand to be McVeigh. This foreigner was about average height, maybe 180 pounds, dark hair. He stuck his head out of the room that evening and saw me, then shut the door." Hood says, "Sometime on Monday, those two — McVeigh and the foreigner — loaded up together, in a Ryder truck, and pulled out of the Dreamland parking lot together... that was the last I saw of them."

Other witnesses appeared in subsequent broadcasts on Oklahoma City's KFOR-TV. The owner of a restaurant located in an area where McVeigh was observed by others said that he had served the alleged bomber and a man who fit the appearance of John Doe 2. He stated that the Doe 2 look-alike seemed like he might be an employee of McVeigh, "like a contractor coming by and buying his [hired] hand a lunch or something. It's the impression I had."

Another witness interviewed by KFOR-TV said that she saw McVeigh buying drinks for a John Doe 2 look-alike in a bar in Oklahoma City. When photos of the person that KFOR-TV identified as a Doe 2 suspect were shown to the woman, she provided a positive identification, going so far as to say that she would testify to the man's identity before a grand jury. She also stated that the man spoke broken English that reminded her of the voice inflections of Iraqis that she had heard during the Gulf War.

Three other women interviewed by KFOR-TV said that McVeigh had entered the store they work in, located near the bar where the other observation took place, on April 14 and 17, and that he had been in the company of two other men. According to the women all three men had spoken to each other in a foreign language. One witness said, "They spoke in a foreign language. They huddled together and they all three spoke secretly to one another, and it was a foreign language." [6]

According to David Hall, Terry Nichols told him in an interview that Timothy McVeigh was at the McDonalds restaurant at Sheridan and Western in Oklahoma City on April 18, the day before the bombing, and that he had met with Middle Eastern men who had given him $2,000 as a pay-off for his role in the bombing. Another Oklahoma City investigator verified the meeting through the knowledge of a "Middle Eastern source" based in Oklahoma City, as well through the accounts of two other witnesses. [7]

After the bombing, Mrs. Joe Royer was walking her dog near her Oklahoma City apartment when she saw a very stocky man backing his yellow pickup into a parking area for tenants. When the man saw her looking at him, he gave her "a look that told me to forget I had ever seen him." Mrs. Royer told an interviewer, "So I got my dog and we went back into the apartment. It was about a week later that the FBI showed up, going from apartment to apartment, asking if anyone knew anything about that truck parked out back." When queried by Mrs. Royer's husband about why he wanted to know, the agent stated, "That truck was used in the bombing."

Mr. Royer asked, "I thought you were looking for a brown truck, not a yellow one?"

"If you look close," the FBI agent responded as a tow truck hooked up to the vehicle, "you can tell the truck over there has recently been painted yellow — there is over spray on the fenders and the VIN (identification) numbers have all been ground off."

Mrs. Royer was shown a photo of a stocky, Middle Eastern suspect in the case, and stated, "It sure does look like him. I would sure like to see a close-up of his eyes. Those eyes of his were frightening!"

On the 8th of June KFOR-TV stated over the air that they had identified an Oklahoma City resident as possibly being John Doe 2, and that he was an Iraqi national who had served in the elite Republican Guard in Iraq during the war. This person, KFOR-TV announced, had been seen with McVeigh at least four times in Oklahoma City prior to the bombing, on April 15 and 16. It was stated that the alleged John Doe 2 spoke in broken English, and owned a brown pickup with tinted glass, its appearance corresponding to early bulletins about the bombing. Another detail substantiating the suspect as John Doe 2, according to Jayna Davis, is that it has been "confirmed that this man has a tattoo on his upper left arm."

Another witness interviewed by KFOR-TV stated that they had seen a Middle Eastern-appearing man speeding from the bombing site in a brown pickup truck. This witness identified the Iraqi from photos taken by KFOR-TV as being the same man.

The Iraqi man tentatively identified as John Doe 2 went to KFOR-TV's competing television stations in Oklahoma, protesting that he was innocent of the allegations. Now, as of October 1995, I am told that the man has filed a legal suit against television station K-FOR for defamation of character.

Information of the possible identification by Oklahoma City investigators of John Doe 2, of the possible implication of other Middle Easterners, and of alleged associations of these men with McVeigh prior to the bombing, has been kept almost totally under wraps and has not been released through any of the major national news media, although virtually every other scrap, false trail, and questionable clue in the Oklahoma bombing case has been given air time. Why hasn't *Dateline* jumped on this story, if only to discredit it, like they did with von Trapp, Gunderson, and Jackson? The story would be significant even if the identification of John Doe 2 was conclusively disproven, yet it is not even glancingly touched upon in the national media.

Melissa Klinzing, the news director at KFOR-TV in Oklahoma City, has stated that NBC television claims they will not carry the John Doe 2 story nationally because they are unable to obtain the names of the witnesses who saw McVeigh and John Doe 2 together. These witnesses are understandably concerned about their safety, and many of them have requested anonymity, an accommodation that the media is not usually so reticent about. [8]

While independent investigators were for the most part intent on identifying John Doe 2 and on solving the Oklahoma City bombing, the FBI continued to make public statements doubting that John Doe 2 existed, this apparently in an attempt to limit the scope of the investigation. One FBI official quoted by *USA Today* stated that John Doe 2 could be a "red herring." If the FBI and the government was truly interested in solving the Oklahoma City bombing, why wouldn't they be doing everything they could to investigate these possible leads in the case; and if the Oklahoma City investigators were mistaken, why wouldn't information be released which proved that? [9]

There are two possible reasons that we know of.

NOTES:

1. Hall, David. Interview by Tom Valentine on *Radio Free America*, WCCR radio, June 6, 1995

2. Cash, J.D. "Why No John Doe II? III?", *The Jubilee*, September/October 1995; Parker, Charles. "Oklahoma City... What Really Happened?", video, 1995
3. Cash
4. Ibid.
5. Jasper, William F. "Searching for John Doe No. 2," *The New American*, September 4, 1995; Cash
6. Cash
7. Rappoport, John. *Oklahoma City Bombing, The Suppressed Truth,* Blue Press, Los Angeles, 1995
8. Watson; Rappoport
9. "Bombing mastermind still free, source says," *Associated Press*, June 14, 1995

24

The Middle East Connection

Within hours of the Oklahoma City bombing, *Radio Tehran* in Iraq had the answer to whodunnit. It was announced that, "the perpetrators were Christian extremist militias from Montana and Oklahoma observing the two-year anniversary of the U.S. government killing of 86 men, women, and children in the Branch Davidian Waco massacre." It was a simple, easy explanation — but where did Tehran get its inside information, and so quickly?

Whether the statement was true or not, it is quite understandable why Iraq was interested in promoting this solution. From the beginning, there were suspicions by the media, politicians, and populace of a Middle Eastern connection to the Oklahoma bombing, although after an initial flurry of speculation, finger-pointing, and expediency assessment, this line of inquiry was hushed up, and at least officially dropped.

Immediately following the bombing, Texas police were notified to apprehend "two men of Middle Eastern appearance" said to be heading for the Mexican border. An ABC television news broadcast announced that three Middle Eastern men had been observed leaving the crime scene driving a brown truck. Two Middle Eastern men were in fact taken into custody in Dallas, Texas, were interrogated for 16 hours, and later released. [1] On April 20, ABC news announced that there was information about three Middle Eastern men buying large quantities of fertilizer. [2]

Jordanian-American Abrahim Ahmad was detained in London, England after his flight there on April 20. An Oklahoma resident, Mr. Ahmad was questioned but was released and had departed from Oklahoma City airport shortly after the bomb blast. He was headed for Jordan, and wore a blue jogging suit similar to those described as worn by suspects

in the bombing, while his description matched a suspect profile issued by
the FBI. On April 21 Abrahim Ahmad, returned from London to the
U.S. in shackles by English authorities, was questioned and released. [3]
   Suspicions have been raised that Terry Nichols was used as a go-be-
tween in the Oklahoma City bombing plot by the Abu Sayyaf, implicated
in the World Trade Center bombing, which took place on February 26,
1993, or some other Islamic organization located in the Philippines.
These allegations came after the FBI interrogation of Nichols' ex-wife
Lana Padilla, although in her memoir nothing is mentioned of the matter.
During the four years preceding the bombing, Nichols had renounced his
American citizenship, and had become a resident nonalien. He had also
taken approximately 20 "lengthy" trips to the Philippines, where he met
with "potential business partners." Nichols only sometimes travelled with
his Philippine-born wife Marife, who he had met through a marriage
introduction service. Costs for tickets and expenses for these trips are
conservatively estimated by a travel agent I contacted at a minimum of
$60,000, this expense undertaken by a "partially employed" Nichols who
"hadn't worked steadily in a couple of years." Marife is stated by one
source to have returned from one trip to the Philippines carrying $4,000
in cash and ten gold coins. Nichols is also said to have had a minimum
of $30,000 in cash hidden away, and about $60,000 in precious metals,
to be retrieved by Padilla in case he died in the Philippines. Link these
facts to information that Tim McVeigh was only sporadically employed at
low-paying jobs, and possessed cash in excess of $10,000 at the time of
his capture, and one must wonder if these two men were being funded by
an outside source, perhaps one located in the Philippines. [4]
   Nichols' marriage to a Philippine suggests other intriguing possibilities. It is a longstanding procedure of intelligence agencies to use female
assets to compromise politicians and other targets. Obvious examples include Lee Harvey Oswald, who after defecting to the Soviet Union, married the daughter of a high-ranking KGB member, and Aldrich "Rick"
Ames, who married a Latin American scholar who assisted him in his
spying for the Mossad. Is it possible that foreign intelligence agencies
utilize companies arranging marriages with foreign women (such as the
one Terry Nichols contacted to obtain his Philippine bride) to compromise these husbands-to-be? Career military men in particular might have
difficulty establishing permanent relationships, and also might be prone to
using marriage brokers, and applications received from members of the
military might be culled for special attention at these agencies. One can
speculate about a Philippine woman being threatened with murder by the

KGB or some other group unless she acted as an informant on her husband in the military. One can also speculate that she might be induced to tell her husband of rich relations in the Philippines who would be happy to fund his fantasies about striking back against the Zionist Occupational Government.

As mentioned, the headquarters for the Islamic militant organization Abu Sayyaf is located in the Philippines. Members of the Abu Sayyaf group have been linked to the car bombing of U.S. Marines in Beirut in 1983, to the plot to assassinate Pope John Paul II during his recent trip to the Philippines, and to the bombing of the World Trade Center which, as also noted, bears a remarkably similar modus operandi to the Oklahoma City bombing.

Six of the conspirators in the World Trade Center bombing were members of Abu Sayyaf, as well as members of other Islamic militant groups, while at least 24 men were involved at some stage of the planning and execution of the attack. [5] After the bombing, six of the conspirators were caught in the Philippines and deported to the U.S. [6] The Abu Sayyaf is connected to a web of Islamic militant groups with partially interlocking memberships that are reportedly supervised from Iran and Syria, and which have collaborated with groups such as the Japanese Red Army, the KGB, and the PFLP (Popular Front for the Liberation of Palestine).

In August 1994 Ali Akbar Mohtashemi, one of the patriarchs of Iranian terrorism, made the intentions of the HizbAllah or Islamic militant movement quite clear. He said, "the HizbAllah should extend its defensive and aggressive lines all over the region, into Europe, and even into the United States." Mohtashemi stated his intention that, "actual blows should be dealt in Israel and its American supporters in places they cannot even imagine. This should be done in such a manner that the enemy's power to think and plan is constantly wrested from him as was done in the past."

In 1993, at a major conference of Islamic militants in Tehran, it was stated that the terrorist war against the United States would include "targeting buildings for bomb spectaculars." [7]

According to CBS news, the FBI has stated that eight claims of responsibility for the Oklahoma City bombing were initially made, and that seven had come from the Middle East. [8]

Oklahoma is, in fact, home to an estimated 5,000 Muslims, and Islamic fundamentalists held a conference in Tulsa, Oklahoma only days before the bombing. Oklahoma City has been the site of several Islamic conferences, and at one of these conferences in 1992, 6,000 fundamentalists applauded calls for a "Jihad against Jews." This, in itself, suggests a possible linkage of purpose between the Islamics and the ZOG-hating contingent of the right wing in America. A recent PBS television documentary, "Jihad in America" placed Oklahoma City as a significant link in a militant Islamic network centered in New Jersey, Texas, and Chicago. According to Bruce Hoffman, at the Centre for the Study of Terrorism and Political Violence at St. Andrew's University in England, there have been attempts to infiltrate Islamic terrorist teams in Oklahoma. [9]

Details of the World Trade Center bombing which correspond to the Oklahoma City bombing include the use of a truck bomb (a Ryder truck, rented near the World Trade Center), and explosives said to have been employed by the bombers in both instances: ANFO, with added containers of hydrogen and nitroglycerin in the case of the Islamic bombers, according to the FBI.

The Oklahoma City "bomb spectacular," to use the phrase coined in Tehran, was apparently not done by a simple ANFO charge, according to the evaluations of numerous demolitions experts. Some have indicated that in order to have had such destructive force, that the Oklahoma City bomb would have had to have been, at the very least, a "shaped" charge, directing the explosive force for maximum destruction. This, in fact, is a signature of Middle Eastern terrorist bombs, as opposed to backyard bombs from home-grown radicals of both the left and right wings. According to Middle Eastern terrorism expert Yossef Bodansky, "The car bomb itself [detonated at the World Trade Center] was built in accordance with the proven principles of shaped charges used by the Iranian- and Syrian-controlled terrorists since the bombings of the American and French installations in Beirut in 1983." [10]

Logistics of the World Trade Center bombing were apparently supervised from the topmost levels of international terrorist coordination. As early as 1990, conspirators El-Sayyid Abdulazziz Nossair, Mahmud Abouhalima, and Clement Rodney Hampton-El (an American Black Muslim, and member of the Black Muslim group Al-Fuqra) had met in New York City with Sheikh Abd-al-Aziz Awdah, who is alleged to have been a senior commander engaged in the coordination of terrorist operations with Iranian, Palestinian, and HizbAllah leaders.

Al-Fuqra, it is said, takes special pains to recruit disgruntled Afro-American members of the American military into its ranks. This is interesting in light of the fact that a supposedly rascist McVeigh is reported by a witness to have been seen in the company of an Afro-American man in the days prior to the bombing.

In 1989 and 1992 Al-Fuqra compounds were raided in Colorado Springs, Colorado, and explosives, bombs, guns, and photos of Sheikh Abdel-Rahman were discovered. Two members of Al-Fuqra were also arrested in 1992 in Colorado Springs, and charged with stealing $355,000 in government funds to finance training camps in Pakistan. [11]

It was at about the time of the meeting with Sheikh Abd-al-Aziz Awdah that the New York Islamic group responsible for the World Trade Center bombing, headed by El-Sayyid Nossair, began to operate within Iranian guidelines dictated for local cells, and began to gather information on bombing sites. El-Sayyid Nossair wrote that they "wanted to blow up their [Americans'] edifices." [12]

Conspirator Mahmud Abouhalima told Egyptian intelligence that the plan to blow up the World Trade Center had been approved by Iranian intelligence, and two Iranians had come to New York just before the bombing to work out the details. Money had been obtained through the Gama al-Islamiya organization from wealthy Iranian industrialists and Islamics living in Europe, and transferred through the important Islamic cell in Munich, Germany. Later, two Iraqis had arrived to oversee the bombing and to ensure technical details on the bomb, such as the placing of the blasting caps. This is interesting considering the fact that John Doe 2 has been tentatively identified by David Hall and KFOR-TV as being an Iraqi.

Emerson also states that,

"Evidence collected by federal investigators in the cases related to the February 26, 1993 World Trade Center bombing, for example, shows that leaders or representatives of at least five different groups — including the Palestinian-based Islamic Jihad, Hamas, the Sudanese National Islamic Front, the Pakistan-based al-Fuqra... and groups funded by Persian Gulf donors — were involved in the plot. Sudanese diplomats affiliated with the National Islamic Front aided conspirators with access and credentials. In addition, Sheikh Umar Abdel-Rahman, the blind Egyptian cleric accused of being the spiritual ringleader of the World Trade Center conspiracy, had been hosted or sponsored in the U.S. by at least half a dozen mosques and innocent-sounding Islamist 'charitable' and 'religious' organizations." [13]

Testing of the bomb used in the World Trade Center was carried out in February 1995, near New Bloomfield, Pennsylvania, not far from Harrisburg. Involved in the test run were Mahmud Abouhalima, Ramzi Ahmad Youssuf, Siddig Ibrahim Siddig Ali, Mohammed Salameh, Rodney

Hampton-El, and possibly others.

During planning sessions, the World Trade Center bombers were in close touch with members of Islamic cells in Houston and Mesquite, Texas, a suburb of Dallas. Initial Oklahoma City bombing reports mentioned a maroon mini-van which had been seen at the federal building just prior to the blast, and that portions of the vehicle were recovered which showed that it had been rented from an agency in Dallas. Initial reports on the VIN number alleged to have been on a car used in the bombing, reported by Cable News Network, were also linked to Dallas. The day of the bombing, three Arabic men were detained in Dallas as suspects in the bombing, then later released.

Allegedly a "supreme commander" for American and international Islamic forces, [14] controlling the shots in the World Trade Center bombing, was the blind Sheikh Umar Abdel-Rahman. Sheikh Abdel-Rahman is a CIA asset, if Egyptian President Hosni Mubarek is to be believed. [15] Beginning a collaboration with Iranian intelligence in 1986, by about 1988 Sheikh Abdel-Rahman had created an alliance with Afghan warlord Gulbadin Hekmatayar, who received approximately half of the arms that the CIA was providing to the Afghanistani mujahadeen resistance to the Soviets. Sheikh Umar moved in and began acting as a middleman for CIA arms shipments to the mujahadeen.

After the war in Afghanistan, in 1990, Sheikh Abdel-Rahman was able to repeatedly enter and leave the U.S. unhindered, despite the fact that he was on the U.S. State Department's terrorism watch list. This was based, according to one reporter, upon "astounding incompetence" by the Immigration and Naturalization Service, but one wonders if that was all that was involved. This "incompetence" included a U.S. Embassy employee forgetting to check a terrorism lookout list because, it is said, a computer was down. After that, the State Department delayed for four months in notifying the Immigration and Naturalization Service that the Sheikh was in town. Even though his name had been added to an updated list, the INS didn't bother to check on him as he entered, left, and re-entered the U.S. Finally, the State Department clarified these repeated cases of "incompetence." A CIA officer had given the Sheikh a clean bill of health and stamped his visa.

Sheikh Abdel-Rahman is reported to be the leader of other Islamic Jihad cells set up in Texas, California, Illinois, and Michigan. Within the Sheikh's Al Salaam mosque in Jersey City, there was at least one informant for the Mossad, who informed the Israeli Secret Service of attempts by members of the mosque to buy explosives.

The breakthrough lead in the World Trade Center case was, as in the Oklahoma City case, allegedly obtained through tracking the VIN number on a "piece of the frame" of the Ryder truck found by a member of the ATF, although this seems ridiculous, since the FBI had a paid informant within the bombing cell. The World Trade Center bombers were also thoughtful enough to write down their address and one of their actual names on the application for the Ryder truck, an accommodation similar to ones McVeigh performed in Junction City, Kansas. Again, similar to suspicions in the Oklahoma City bombing, one of the conspirators said that they had tried to bomb the World Trade Center early in the morning when there would be few people in the building, but "something went wrong."

Another of the many similarities to the Oklahoma City case is that the first of the bombers was captured through another act of remarkable stupidity, like McVeigh's forgetfulness about a license plate for his car. Mohammad Salameh, an illegal alien, appeared at the Ryder rental agency requesting that his deposit on the truck be returned, claiming that the truck had been stolen. Salameh continued to demand his deposit even after the media had reported the recovery of parts of the van, suggesting that they might be able to identify it as the bombing vehicle. Traces of ammonium nitrate were conveniently found dusted on the van rental documents, just as McVeigh's fingerprints were said to have been found on a receipt for ammonium nitrate fertilizer. Nidal Ayyad's business card was found in Salameh's possession, just as a business card with a nota-tion for the purchase of TNT was allegedly left by McVeigh in the police cruiser.

Although authorities described Salameh's capture as "a case of dumb luck," his demand for the rental deposit was assuredly an act done under orders, to offer up a "patsy" to defuse the incident and deflect attention from those who were actually responsible.

"He is either dumb or some kind of martyr," one law enforcement official stated of Salameh, while another noted with surprising candor that they "left him behind as a signature. Maybe it was their game plan all along to leave him behind." Similar speculations could be voiced of Timothy McVeigh. [16]

In a briefcase at Mohammad Salameh's apartment was a photo of him standing next to El Sayyid Nosair, a militant accused of assassinating Rabbi Meir Kahane. There was another photo which harkened to the famous, incriminating *Life* magazine photo of Lee Harvey Oswald hold-ing a rifle and a clutch of Communist newspapers: one of the bombers,

Nidal Ayyad, is photographed holding a hand grenade, with a Palestinian flag displayed behind him.

El Sayyid Nosair, when he wasn't engaged in terrorist bombings, held down a job at the New York City Health Department, building pipebombs in the basement of the Health Department in his spare time. He had been under FBI surveillance since 1989.

Islamic terrorism expert Yossef Bodansky specifically notes Ayyad and Ibrahim A. Elgabrowny (al-Jabaruni) as patsies in the bombing; he calls them "expendables." Bodansky states, "As a chemical engineer, Ayyad could appear to have provided the know-how to mix the chemicals to make the explosives. Just to ensure that Ayyad was incriminated, Salameh repeatedly called him from the storage company site where the chemicals used in making the bomb were stored." This harkens to Colbern's explosives expertise, and to McVeigh's phone calls to Nichols and Elohim City.

Of Elgabrowny, Bodansky says, "He was the stay-behind commander, intentionally left in place to go to jail, where he might ensure that the captured expendables continue to perform their preassigned roles, i.e., to attract attention to themselves (thereby diverting it from others) and transform their trial into a show of Islamist defiance." [17]

The World Trade Center bombing resulted in the conviction of more than a dozen Arabs, with the prosecution assisted in its efforts by one Emad Salem, an Egyptian Army officer who offered his services to the FBI for a price, in excess of $1.5 million, and who was the lead witness in the government's case. Salem was known to play the covert ops field, hawking information to Egyptian army intelligence, to the CIA, and to the Immigration and Naturalization Service, at least. He had reportedly even tried to sell information to Kahane Chai, the organization of the murdered Jewish leader Rabbi Kahane.

Salem was a mole in Sheikh Abdel-Rahman's inner circle, recruited as an FBI agent after the assassination of Rabbi Meir Kahane in 1991. Kahane was the founder of the Jewish Defense League, and had been under contract to the CIA and the Israeli Mossad. His alleged murderer, Mahmud Abouhalima, one of the World Trade Center bombers, had also been the recipient of CIA funds.

Salem reportedly began informing for the FBI in 1993, tape recording conversations of the conspirators and videotaping them in the safe house he had conveniently provided, but unbeknownst to his FBI handlers he was also recording the conversations that he had with them.

What has not been noted, and which will be little noted in the mainstream press because of its possibly devastating import, is that the FBI shares responsibility with the Islamic militants — and is possibly ultimately responsible — for the bombing of the World Trade Center, which as pointed out is a terrorist attack eerily close in numerous details to the Oklahoma City bombing.

A number of observers of the World Trade Center case have, after hearing some of the tapes between Salem and his FBI controllers, wondered just who was actually in charge of the bombing. Was it the men who were subsequently convicted of the bombing, or was it Salem himself? Many of Salem's statements to the FBI suggest that the plot would have never come off if he had not encouraged and goaded the conspirators at every step of the way, and certainly the FBI could have stepped in at any time to prevent the bombing.

At one point, when talking to an FBI handler, Salem states in broken English, "...we was start already building the bomb which is went off in the World Trade Center. It was built by the supervising supervision from the Bureau and the DA and we was all informed about it and we know that the bomb start to be built. By who? By your confidential informant. What a wonderful great case!" [18] Here Salem is stating that the bomb which was used at the World Trade Center was built under the supervision of the FBI and the New York District Attorney's office.

On August 2 and 3, 1993, ABC-TV ran secretly taped conversations with the FBI informant, Emad Salem, and individuals implicated in the World Trade Center bombing, including the infamous blind Sheikh Umar Abdel-Rahman. These tapes were published by the *New York Times*. In these conversations we find one of the conspirators, Siddig Ali, protesting that he "wanted to stop planning the New York City action, and instead go to the Philippines..." Salem, the FBI informant, convinced Siddig Ali to remain in New York and to go on with the bomb plot.

We also find this same FBI informant, according to court documents filed in May 1993, teaching the driver of the bomb truck, Mohammed Salameh, how to drive two days prior to the explosion, furnishing the conspirators with explosives and a house to be used for bomb-making, teaching them how to build bombs, and making suggestions as to possible targets, including the World Trade Center.

Salem's handlers in the FBI have an interesting idea of the rules that govern them. FBI agent John Anticev told Salem at one point, in a conversation that Salem tape recorded, "Terrorism is a hybrid. It's half counterintelligence rules, half criminal. And how to apply one from the other is still a gray area in the government... Things can happen when you're doing an intelligence case. All of a sudden it turns immediately into a criminal case... and it could jeopardize people like yourself."

The escape route for conspirators in the World Trade Center bombing led from New York to Toronto, Canada, to Sweden, and then to the Middle East. [19] Recent press releases have related that the search for clues in the Oklahoma City bombing has migrated in focus to Canada and Spain, and Canada is known to be a major deployment point for Islamic militants.

After the World Trade Center bombing, a second, related Islamic cell was activated in New York, with leadership provided by Muhammad Rezah Shalchian Tabrizi, a senior officer of the IRGC (Islamic Revolutionary Guard Corps), and the financial comptroller of the Iranian U.N. mission, and Sarag al-Din Hamid Youssuf, the Counselor of the Sudanese U.N. mission. The plot included active cooperation by both the Iranian and Sudanese U.N. missions. Siddig Ibrahim Siddig Ali was the representative of Sheikh Umar Abdel-Rahman in the plot, and was in overall charge of the cell, while Emad Salem, the FBI informant, oversaw the support team for the cell. In charge of technical aspects was Ramzi Ahmad Youssuf, who was later replaced by Fadil Abdelghani (Abd-al-Ghani), when Ramzi had to flee the United States. Also involved were at least six "expendables" recruited from Sudanese, Palestinian, Egyptian, and Afro-American militants. Coded instructions (reportedly intercepted by Egyptian and Israeli intelligence, and forwarded to the U.S.) were sent to Sheikh Abdel-Rahman from Khartoum and Tehran, the messages continuing until the indictment of the Sheikh and his group in August 1993.

One of the plans of this second cell was to destroy the U.N building, the federal building in New York, and the Holland Tunnel or the Lincoln Tunnel (or both) on July 4, 1993. The date is suggestive of the thinking processes of the conspirators. Were these bombings intended to be linked by planted evidence to the radical right, to be presented as patriotically motivated, as the April 19, 1995 Oklahoma City bombing was immediately linked to the destruction of the Branch Davidian compound because of the significance of the date?

Members of the militant Islamist cell were arrested on June 24, 1993, as they mixed ANFO in a "safe house" that had been rented by Salem, the FBI informant.

Two men allegedly connected to the World Trade Center bombing were members of the Fifth Battalion of the Liberation Army, based in Pakistan. They were engaged in a third plot, termed Bojinka, or "the explosion," a plot to blow up 11 American jetliners over the Pacific Ocean in a single day. Five Islamic militants were going to plant bombs aboard the planes. Accused as the leader of the plot is Ramzi Ahmed Yousef, a Pakistani who was one of the guiding forces behind the New York World Trade Center bombing. Yousef and his alleged partner, Abdul Hakim Murad, have also been accused in the Philippines of planning to assassinate Pope John Paul II. Yousef apparently carried out a practice run for Bojinka, planting a bomb on Philippine Airlines Flight 434, headed for Tokyo on December 11, 1994. One tourist was killed with 10 others wounded, and the flight made an emergency landing in Guam. Murad has fingered Yousef as the man who called the *Associated Press* after the bombing, claiming that it was carried out by Abu Sayyaf.

According to the *L.A. Times:*

"Philippine and Western intelligence experts said in interviews that the investigation into the Bojinka plot has also provided disturbing evidence of the existence of a worldwide network of terrorists who received weapons training and firebrand religious indoctrination during the decade-long international effort to defeat the Soviet Union in Afghanistan.

"The international brigades of Afghan 'mujahedeen,' or resistance fighters, were recruited throughout the Islamic world as part of a covert, $4 billion effort in the 1970s and '80s by the U.S. Central Intelligence Agency and Saudi Arabia to drive the Soviets from Afghanistan. Since the Soviet-installed government fell in 1992, many of the fighters have returned to their home countries as converts to radical Islam determined to overthrow secular regimes and attack the 'Satan' United States for its support of Israel." Mujahadeen have assumed what have been called "commanding roles" in dozens of militant groups worldwide.

In March 1995 the *Star-Ledger* of Newark, New Jersey ran the following story, under the heading "Lawmen get warning of plot on U.S. targets":

"U.S. law enforcement authorities have obtained information that Islamic terrorists may be planning suicide attacks against federal courthouses and government installations in the United States.

"The attacks, it is feared, would be designed to attract worldwide press attention through the murder of innocent victims.

"The *Star-Ledger* has learned that U.S. law enforcement officials have received a warning that a 'fatwa,' a religious ruling similar to the death sentence targeting author Salman Rushdie, has been issued against federal authorities as a result of an incident during the trial last year of four persons in the bombing on the World Trade Center in New York.

"The disclosure was made in a confidential memorandum issued by the U.S. Marshals Service in Washington calling for stepped-up security at federal facilities throughout the nation.

"The 'fatwa' was allegedly sanctioned by an unidentified Islamic Iman, or holy man, in retaliation for what was perceived as a religious 'insult' against Islamic fundamentalists by federal law enforcement officers.

"According to the memo, the information about the threat was obtained from an unidentified 'informed source' who said the death sentence was specifically directed against U.S. Marshals Service personnel.

"The informant reported that the threat was issued because deputy U.S. Marshals allegedly 'insulted' Islam 'by stepping on a copy of the Koran,' the Islamic holy book, during a scuffle with several prisoners convicted in the World Trade Center bombing...

"The Marshals Service memo said the agency believes that 'there is sufficient threat potential to request that a heightened level of security awareness and caution be implemented at all Marshals Service-protected facilities nationwide...'

"The memo, issued by Eduardo Gonzalez, director of the U.S. Marshals Service, warns that attacks may be designed to 'target as many victims as possible and draw as much media coverage as possible' to the fundamentalist cause..." [20]

On April 19, 1995, the day of the Oklahoma City bombing, a warning was issued by the U.S. Embassy in the Philippines to Americans. The announcement warned U.S. citizens of possible attacks taking place in public areas in the Philippines. An additional Consular Information Sheet dated April 28 advised, "The recent extradition to the U.S. of a Muslim extremist suspected of complicity in the New York World Trade Center bombing could possibly trigger retaliatory responses from extremist supporters in Metropolitan Manila. Such retaliatory acts would likely be directed toward U.S. government and/or American business personnel and facilities. The regional security office recommends additional caution in the utilization of public establishments such as churches, restaurants and shopping areas known to be frequented by large numbers of Americans." [21]

The financing of individuals connected (even if marginally) to American rightist causes by Islamic or other militants might benefit those groups in a number of ways. The placing of blame for the Oklahoma City bombing upon citizen militias would conceal actual responsibility. It would also deepen the rift between liberal and conservative factions in the United States, increasing political chaos, and furthering the psychological demoralization of the American "Satan" through an increased atmosphere of violence and possible armed confrontation. It would instill a "payback" attitude in the police and government agencies that would further enflame the conflict.

Is there any evidence that this sort of funding, of Middle Eastern money to the right wing, goes on? According to a statement of Bob Matthews, the now-deceased leader of the American radical rightist Silent Brotherhood — who met at the Hayden Lake, Idaho conclave in 1983 where the initial OKBomb plot may have been hatched — arrangements had been made for him to meet with a representative of the Syrian government, with the purpose being to obtain financing for their operations. Syria has been a central coordinating point for international terrorism since the late 1960s, although it is not known whether Matthews obtained the desired funding.

A case that bears numerous parallels to the Oklahoma City bombing, and which employs both Japanese and Islamic militant factions, was initiated in 1987, when Iran and Syria were first beginning a major terrorist mobilization against the United States. Again, the staging base of Canada was used, when the SSNP (Syrian Socialist National Party), working in tandem with the KGB, and trained by the PFLP (Popular Front for the Liberation of Palestine), sent Walid Kabbani, a Lebanese, across the border to Rockford, Vermont. Kabbani transferred a backpack with bomb components to Georges Younan and Walid Mourad, both Burlington, Vermont merchants. The official account says they were waiting for the bomb ingredients in an illegally parked van, and that the operation was foiled by local police who just happened to act on the parking violation. This is a story with a familiar ring.

In early 1988, the PFLP liased with the Japanese Red Army to send Yu Kikumura on a tour of Europe and finally to Paris, where he obtained a visa to enter the U.S. On March 8 he arrived in New York and rented an apartment, then on March 17, he embarked on a seventeen-state tour of the U.S. in which he gathered bomb components for an ANFO/gunpowder bomb. On April 12, Kikumura was returning to New York when he was arrested on the New Jersey Turnpike where, for no reason that the New Jersey state trooper could give, he was pulled over and the bombs (disguised as fire extinguishers) were discovered. Kikumura had planned to blow up the Manhattan Army recruiting station "on or around April 15," the second anniversary of the American bombing of Libya. [22]

Apparently the American government, while playing down any possible connections of the Middle East to the Oklahoma City bombing, does not underestimate the threat posed by these factions. Less than two weeks after the bombing at Oklahoma City, President Clinton attended the American Jewish Congress where he spoke on behalf of liquor magnate Edgar Bronfman. Clinton had nothing but praise for the Mafia-connected figure, and announced that in order to combat terrorism he was going to place economic sanctions on Iran. Clinton called Iran "inspiration and paymaster to terrorists," and said, "To do nothing more as Iran continues its pursuit of nuclear weapons would be disastrous, and to stand pat in the face of overwhelming evidence of Tehran's support for terrorists would threaten to darken the dawn of peace between Israel and her neighbors." Does Clinton know something that he is not telling the American people?

Despite connections suggesting the possibility that the Oklahoma City bombing may be linked to militant Islamic factions, and that these factions may be in contact with the American right wing, this information, like so much else in the Oklahoma City bombing case, is completely suppressed by the mainstream media. It has been suggested that the reason for this is that the press is trying to prevent a backlash against innocent Middle Easterners resident in the U.S. Yet, the media does not seem quite so concerned about so connecting and demonizing everything connected to the politically right, and to those who would suggest that sometimes history is dictated by deepest conspiracy.

There are other possible reasons that the American government would not want to pursue leads suggesting that the Oklahoma City bombing was done by Middle Easterners. Enough public furor might be created by the announcement of a Middle East connection that it might jeopardize the Middle East peace talks and might conceivably cause the U.S. to go to war.

There is another less obvious reason. Middle Eastern sources might be blackmailing President Clinton with information connecting the Oklahoma City bombing conspirators not only with the Middle East but with the American government.

NOTES:

1. Keen, Judy. "'Justice will be swift, certain and severe,'" *USA Today*, April 20, 1995
2. ABC Television news broadcast, April 20, 1995
3. *Facts on File*, April 27, 1995

4. Kifner, John. "Prosecutors say Oklahoma bomb plot was limited to a few bitter ex-GIs," *New York Times* Service, August 7, 1995; Padilla, Lana and Delpit, Ron. *By Blood Betrayed,* Harper Paperback, New York, 1995
5. Bodansky, Yossef. *Terror! The Inside Story of the Terrorist Conspiracy in America,* SPI Books, New York, New York, 1994
6. "Call to Arms," *MacLean's,* April 17, 1995
7. Bodansky
8. CBS Television News, April 19, 1995
9. MacIntyre, Ben. *London Times,* April 21, 1995
10. Bodansky
11. Ibid.
12. Ibid.
13. Emerson, Steven. "The Other Fundamentalists," *The New Republic,* June 12, 1995
14. Bodansky
15. *"Time* Magazine Targets Islam," *New Dawn,* September-October 1993
16. Bodansky
17. Ibid.
18. DeRienzo, Paul; Morales, Frank, and Flash, Chris. "Who Bombed the World Trade Center? FBI Bomb Builders Exposed!!", *The Shadow,* October 1994/January 1995; Dwyer, Jim, et al. *Two Seconds Under the World,* Ballentine Books, New York City, New York, 1995
19. Bodansky
20. Rudolph, Robert. "Lawmen get warning of plot on U.S. targets," *Star-Ledger,* Newark, New Jersey, March 22, 1995
21. Kuncl, Tom, "Oklahoma bomb was paid for by Arab Assassins," *National Enquirer,* May 16, 1995
22. Bodansky

25

Government Complicity?

From the beginning, horrific rumors had been flying about responsibility for the Oklahoma City bombing. One common theory was that the American government or some faction of it was guilty of the crime, sacrificing its own in order to gain justification for a nationwide crackdown on civil liberties and an increase in its own dictatorial powers. Although mainstream news commentators declare that it is paranoid to think that there might have been government involvement in the OKBomb, there are ample reasons to give these speculations a second look.

As indicated earlier in this book, there have been repeated allegations that there were no ATF agents in the building at the time of the blast. Until the government gives a solid accounting of who was present, and the whereabouts of those who were not present, such suspicions will persist.

Two witnesses are reported to have seen a black helicopter hovering above the Murrah Building "for some time prior to the explosions, only to fly away minutes before the explosions took place, and not return." When contacted, NORAD (North American Radar Air Defense) would neither confirm nor deny the black chopper's existence above the federal building immediately prior to the bombing.

A caller to the radio Citizen's Rights Forum, who identified himself only as "Frank," stated:

"Well, I can verify some of the seismographs with the two explosions, 'cause up here at the house we felt two explosions... I was part of the Red Cross team that went in right after the explosion. They set up a trauma team next... one block away. While we was down there, we started talking to people who had eye-witnessed, we had two black heli-copters flying about the building, fifteen minutes before the explosion, loading people up to take them out of the building."

The interviewer, Mark Boswell, asked incredulously: "You have a confirmed eyewitness to that?"

"Frank" replied: "We've had two or three people that's told me this week... Yes, just fifteen minutes before the blast, we had a friend who was working down the street from there, kept on seeing the helicopters hovering over the building. We had also two secretaries who work down there who had noticed that, and these ladies survived it, and they was told that all the top-level officers, and the FBI, ATF, and all the DEA was transferred prior to the explosion, so we knew that the ATF was not, anyone in the building when this happened, and the FBI was told to get out of the building."

There is a possibility that Timothy McVeigh was in contact with a government agent provocateur prior to the bombing. This fact emerges in the statements of Eric Maloney, who was allegedly present at meetings of the Michigan Militia Corps with McVeigh in January 1995. Maloney says that there were calls for an attack on a northern Michigan National Guard base, and that McVeigh volunteered to be involved in the attack. Others, however, remember the meetings differently, and say that it was Maloney who came up with the plan for the National Guard assault. After the meeting, Maloney reportedly contacted the ATF about McVeigh and the alleged plans to attack a National Guard base. [1]

There is one very important reason that the American government may not want to probe the reality of John Doe 2 as being an Iraqi living in Oklahoma City. Sources at KFOR-TV in Oklahoma City state that the man identified as being John Doe 2 has been reported by witnesses as being an ATF informant. [2]

The *New York Times* elaborated on the above in an article broadly debunking conspiracy theories about the Oklahoma City bombing:

"David G. Hall... said he believes the explosion was the result of a setup by the Bureau of Alcohol, Tobacco and Firearms that went awry. The ATF had been monitoring McVeigh and Nichols because of their right-wing affiliations and had informants approach them about blowing up the federal building, a plot that agents had planned all along to thwart in a moment of public glory, he said."

The *Times* quotes Hall as saying, "The ATF wanted to look like the great people who headed off a terrorist attack because they fouled up Waco and the Weaver case in Ruby Ridge."

Again, according to the *Times*, "McVeigh was supposed to pull up to the building in the truck that contained the bomb at 3 a.m. on April 19, when nobody was working inside. But for some reason he showed up six hours later, long after the agents had grown tired of waiting and left."

The *Times* quotes Hall again: "I don't think there was any intent on the part of the ATF for that building to blow up." [3]

If, in fact, the ATF or some other faction of the government was involved in the Oklahoma bombing, what would have been the motive for such an act?

As David Hall mentions, the image of the ATF has become severely tarnished in recent years because of their "jackbooted" tactics and operations they have engaged in such as the bloody Waco and Ruby Ridge confrontations. The above scenario in which ATF agents plot a publicity stunt of a bombing in order to heroically thwart it, given those concerns, perhaps becomes plausible. It is also alleged that the ATF records of the assault on the Branch Davidian complex in Waco, Texas, were stored in the Murrah Federal Building. These possibly embarrassing records would have been subpoenaed by Congress in scheduled hearings on ATF participation at Waco and Ruby Ridge. [4]

Whether by happenstance or "enemy action," the timing on the Oklahoma bombing could not have been better for Establishment talking heads Bill and Hillary Clinton. Chicago-based investigator Sherman Skolnick provides a comprehensive run-down on what was going on at the time of the bombing, an event that perhaps provided at least a slight respite from prosecution for the President and First Lady. Skolnick reports:

"On Monday, April 17, 1995, a Federal Grand Jury in Little Rock, Arkansas handed up some 16 sealed Grand Jury Indictments according to those close to the matters. Among those reportedly named, Jim Guy Tucker, current Arkansas Governor, reportedly charged with bank fraud; Thomas 'Mac' McClarty, Clinton White House Counsel, formerly White House Chief of Staff and previously CEO of ARCLA — one of the largest natural gas public utility firms; and, Hillary Rodham Clinton. The First Lady is reportedly charged with two counts of federal criminal offenses: (1) Bank fraud, causing the loss or misapplication of between 47 and 60 million dollars of federally insured funds (Madison Guaranty S&L's); and (2) Obstruction of justice. Hillary reportedly ordered Webster Hubbell while he was third in command at the Justice Department to remove documents from the office of White House Aide Vincent Foster,

Jr., following his death at a time when such records were ordered by a Federal Magistrate in Little Rock to be turned over to Federal authorities in the then pending criminal case of U.S. vs. David Hale, a former Arkansas judge accused of defrauding the Small Business Administration. "Hubbell was ordered to deliver or cause to be delivered such records to the private White House quarters of Hillary. She later ordered Hubbell to arrange for the destruction of these records. After resigning from the Justice Department, Hubbell entered into a guilty plea with the independent prosecutor, Kenneth Starr, to Federal charges against Hubbell. Part of the Plea Bargain required that Hubbell fully cooperate in the on-going Whitewater probe. Persuant to that, Hubbell turned over the Foster office records to the Grand Jury. Hubbell had earlier led the First Lady to believe that they had been destroyed. They weren't.

"On April 22, 1995, Kenneth Starr questioned under oath both the President and the First Lady. A superseding Federal Grand Jury Indictment will reportedly be brought accusing Hillary of perjury, an additional count to the indictment. Starr's White House questions also seem designed to assist a pending secret Congressional Impeachment Investigation directed against the President. Starr's Grand Jury probe overlaps the impeachment matter.

"On Sunday, April 23, 1995, the President's announcement on CBS' 60 Minutes program was just short of declaring martial law, no doubt to save himself from impeachment, and Hillary from jail.

"The bombing of the federal building in Oklahoma City, to some sources, seems to somehow serve the purpose of delaying the unsealing by the Chief Federal District Judge in Little Rock of these indictments. The bombing, two days after the sealed indictments were handed down, reportedly involves one or more DEA undercover agents acting as provocateurs within the citizens' militias. Records highly critical to the role of Janet Reno and Clinton in the 1993 Waco assault, killing women and children, were reportedly stolen from the Oklahoma federal building just prior to the bombing.

"The First Lady is reportedly giving consideration to a nolo contendre plea, 'no contest,' which might include no jail time and the surrender of her license to practice law, or agreement for temporary disbarment. Most of the other 13 indictments are against other White House aides for perjury and obstruction of justice in the Foster matter." [5]

Making the possibility of government involvement more credible are the historical circumstances. Over the years we have seen American police and intelligence agencies involved in numerous circumstances in which individuals and groups have been encouraged to perform illegal operations by paid agent provocateurs. A few of these instances include the infiltration of the Black Power movement and radical student movement during the 1960s, the setting up of the Symbionese Liberation Army by the CIA-manufactured Cinque, and the infiltration of various rightist organizations such as the CSA, the Silent Brotherhood, the Aryan Nations, and the Ku Klux Klan. Other recent examples include the government penetration of agent provocateurs into Islamic organizations, Earth First, animal rights organizations, and Latin American solidarity movements. Compelling evidence also links the CIA, the FBI, and other American intelligence agencies to numerous political assassinations and attempted assassinations, including those of Martin Luther King, John F. Kennedy, Robert F. Kennedy, and Malcolm X, as well as to other crimes such as international drug-running and the laundering of drug monies, as alleged to have taken place in Mena, Arkansas, on the watch of then-Governor Clinton. The CIA and other agencies of American intelligence have long been compromised by international criminal and intelligence elements including the Mafia, the Nazi International, and the Mossad, and to imagine that these agencies always work in the interest of America is rash indeed. J. Edgar Hoover, for his part, always maintained that the Mafia did not exist. It was only after his death that his close association with Mafia figures became public.

Although it is almost never reported in the United States, the CIA has been linked to numerous incidents of terrorism worldwide, including incidents in Spain, Libya, Guatemala, Germany, Iran, and France. One car bombing in Lebanon attributed to a joint CIA-Mossad team resulted in the killing of 91 innocent bystanders.

According to French author on foreign affairs Alaine de Segonzac, over the last 25 years "the CIA became known, not as a security agency, but as an outlaw instigator of state-sponsored terrorist outrages." Is the bombing at Oklahoma City so difficult to understand, or at least conceive, in this context? Those who reject out of hand that the American government or American intelligence could possibly have been involved in the Oklahoma City bombing are either ignorant of the misdeeds of the controllers, or they work for them.

The timing on the bombing is all too convenient for those who would like to further consolidate government, police, and intelligence agency control over the American people. The Oklahoma City bombing appears to have been, although it has not been proven to have been, a Reichstag-like attack whose purpose was to provide the justification for further consolidating a police state in America. With the Oklahoma City bombing we now have the justification for a further demonizing of the populist right and the militias, thus putting a checkmate to the only forces with any intention of opposing the plans of Bill Clinton and his intelligence agency and internationalist cronies, and to the New World Order one-world government scheme of the controllers.

One compelling "coincidence" in the Oklahoma City bombing, linking it to the government, is the mostly non-discussed background of Frank Keating, the governor of Oklahoma. Keating is a political insider and alleged to be a "fixer" in the CIA-connected "Bush league." Keating's father, Anthony, was a wealthy Texas oilman, and his wife Cathy was the daughter of another rich oilman; might this have been the connection that spawned his association with oil man George Bush? [6]

Frank Keating started out his career as a special FBI agent in Seattle, San Francisco, and Berkeley between 1969-71, astoundingly "investigating terrorist activities, bombings, and bank robberies." [7] According to People magazine, "One of Keating's assignments was to infiltrate underground groups like the Black Panthers and the Weathermen. Though these groups never staged an attack on the scale of the Oklahoma City bombing, Keating says he sees only superficial differences between them and the right-wing militias. 'The leftists I dealt with would never consider themselves patriots, and they had contempt for the government,' he says. 'The right-wing crowd has contempt for the government, and yet see themselves as patriots. It's a curious anomaly, but both of them are very similar.'" [8]

In 1988 George Bush selected Keating as assistant Attorney General under Edwin Meese, then as assistant Secretary of the Treasury under James Baker, where he supervised the department's 94 attorneys, as well as the Federal Bureau of Prisons, and the Marshall's Service. Keating was allegedly used for damage control in scandals in which Bush was intimately connected, such as the Savings and Loan failures (which benefited two of Bush's sons to the tune of millions of dollars, along with many of Bush's CIA cronies), the BCCI investigation, the Inslaw conspiracy, and the treasonous Iran-contra "parallel government" plot.

Keating was allegedly sent to Oklahoma as part of a long-term plan, beginning with his taking of the Oklahoma governorship. According to this theory Keating is being groomed to take the office of President or Vice-President of the United States in the year 1996 or 2000. This theory is unintentionally verified by the statements of men like Frosty Troy, the editor of the *Oklahoma Observer* magazine. Troy's view, trumpeted widely in national newspapers, is that "I've covered Oklahoma politics, man and boy, for 40 years, and Frank Keating is the first Republican of national stature who ought to be on a national ticket." Troy's view of Keating is not shared by all Oklahomans, however. Oklahoma City-based journalist J.D. Cash calls Keating "a carpetbagger... a sleazeball," and he is not alone in this view, from my conversations with other Oklahomans. [9]

According to a private investigator who investigated the Keating-Bush connection in 1988, "The word in Tulsa [Oklahoma] is that [George] Bush is his 'political godfather'; that Keating got his job in the Treasury Department through Bush's good offices and that Bush 'loves Keating.'" [10]

Keating had been in office in Oklahoma for only three months when the bomb at the federal building went off. [11] It is also alleged that Keating was the man ultimately responsible for ordering the demolition of the Murrah Building, preventing further investigation of the bombing site. [12]

Is it not more than convenient, if there is a government or intelligence agency conspiracy in the Oklahoma City bombing, that Keating should be the governor of Oklahoma, in a position to shepherd the investigation and prosecution of the case in virtually whatever direction is desired? Is it not highly interesting that Keating should have been in the FBI, involved in the infiltration and investigation of "terrorist" groups and bombers, and undoubtedly familiar with FBI agent provocateurs, their controlling agents and tactics?

There is a final, strange connection of the Oklahoma City bombing to Frank Keating. The governor's brother, Martin Keating, seven years before the bombing, penned an unpublished fictional thriller titled *The Final Jihad*. In the book, "Tom McVey" or "Tom McVeigh" (depending on the source quoted) is a terrorist who bombs a federal building in Oklahoma, and is arrested on a routine traffic stop. In the first draft of the book there was also a bombing at the World Trade Center and an airplane that crashes at the White House, both penned prior to the fact, but the incidents were later removed from the book because "it was too close to reality."

The following is a transcript of a CNN interview with Martin Keating and Governor Frank Keating:

Tony Clark, Correspondent: "When a bomb destroyed the federal building in Oklahoma City, Martin Keating was personally shocked and grieved. But as an author, he was not completely surprised. Four years ago, Keating finished writing a novel called *The Final Jihad*. It deals with terrorist bombings across the U.S. The terrorists in Keating's book are based in Oklahoma."

Martin Keating: "The reason I based my terrorists in Oklahoma was precisely that, because it was a place you would overlook. And this would be an ideal place."

Tony Clark: "The similarities between fact and fiction are striking. For example, the prime bombing suspect in the Oklahoma City bombing is named Tim McVeigh. One of Keating's characters is Tom McVeigh. In real life, McVeigh was arrested by highway patrol trooper Charlie Hanger for a traffic violation. In the novel..."

Martin Keating: "We also have a highway patrolman who, doing his job, pulls over a suspicious vehicle and makes a discovery, which at the time he doesn't understand fully the significance of, and it breaks the case open. Of course, that happened in real life with Charlie Hanger."

Tony Clark: "Keating started his as of yet unpublished novel in 1988. Over the years he's had to make several revisions, as fictional events he wrote about became reality — the fall of the Berlin Wall; Gorbachev's resignation and the breakup of the Soviet Union; the attack on the World Trade Center, and an airplane crashing into the White House."

Martin Keating: "When those things happened, I had to go back and change the book, make past tense out of what I had as future tense."

Tony Clark: "However, Keating's bombers were international terrorists financed by hard line communists, a group not suspected in the real bombing. But the similarities between Keating's fiction and reality have been grist for the Internet, fueling the suspicion of some conspiracy theorists. Some even see a conspiracy connection because Keating's brother is Oklahoma's governor."

Governor Frank Keating: "You know there are silly people who say silly things. There are dumb people who say dumb things, and to suggest that there is any connection or similarity is very, very remote."

Tony Clark: "The author, Martin Keating, is already planning a sequel to *The Final Jihad*. Because at the end of *The Final Jihad*, one of the bad guys gets away. That's one piece of Keating's fiction people here hope doesn't come true." [13]

Since Martin Keating discussed the book on Cable News Network there has been very little media exposure of this "amazing coincidence." Naturally, it is impossible that a crime such as the Oklahoma City bombing would be discussed in a novel prior to the event... isn't it? Apparently it has happened before. In the early 1970s a book by the title of

Black Abductor was published in a miniscule print run in Berkeley, California. Some researchers allege that the book was written by the CIA's own E. Howard Hunt, although I have no proof of this. *Black Abductor* contained what has been described as a near-letter perfect account of the Patty Hearst abduction by the Symbionese Liberation Army; like *The Final Jihad*, written prior to the fact. Little noted is the fact that the SLA was run by Donald De Freeze (aka General Cinque Mtume), who was a member of the Los Angeles Police Department's Public Disorder Unit between 1967-1969. DeFreeze's controlling agent was apparently Colston Westbrook, a veteran of the CIA's PHOENIX murder program, while De Freeze was an organizer of the CIA-run Black Cultural Association behavior modification program at Vacaville prison in California. Cinque's crime spree, including the kidnapping of Hearst, was apparently a CIA-based program to test mind control operations and to discredit the left wing in the 60s. [14]

Sometimes the truth is concealed in the open.

NOTES:

1. Janofsky, Michael. "Militia plotted assault on military base," *San Francisco Examiner*, June 25, 1995
2. "The Bomb... in Oklahoma," video by *Star Investigative Reports*, 1995
3. Kovaleski, Serge F. "Oklahoma Bombing Conspiracy Theories Ripple Across the Nation," *Washington Post*, July 9, 1995
4. McAlvany, Donald S. "The Oklahoma City Tragedy: Implications for Free Speech, Political Dissent, and Liberty in America (A Clear and Present Danger)," *The McAlvany Intelligence Advisor*, May/June 1995
5. "More Proof Oklahoma City Bombing was an Inside Job!", Citizens for a Constitutional Washington, April 27, 1995
6. *People* magazine, June 12, 1995
7. Hamilton, Arnold, and Jennings, Diane, *Dallas Morning News*, May 7, 1995
8. *People* magazine, June 12, 1995
9. Hamilton; Cash, J.D. Interview conducted by Jim Keith, September 26, 1995
10. Wheaton, Gene. "Another Bush Boy," *Portland Free Press*, July/August 1995
11. *People* magazine, June 12, 1995

12. Sherrow, Rick. Spoken presentation at the University of Nevada in Reno, October 5, 1995
13. Keating, Martin. Interview conducted by Tony Clark on Cable News Network, "Book Shares Similar Facts of Oklahoma City Bombing," July 7, 1995
14. Hayes, Ace R. "The CIA Cons the Cult-Fighters," *Portland Free Press*, January/February 1995; Krawczyk, Glenn. "The New Inquisition, Cult Awareness or the Cult of Intelligence?", *Nexus*, December 1994/January 1995; Briley, Pat. Interview in *The Spotlight*, October 2, 1995

26

McVeigh As Agent

Examining facts and connections in the Oklahoma City bombing case, a familiar outline appears that seems to discredit the media version of the event, and also to put in doubt the familiar and simplistic conception of Timothy McVeigh and Terry Nichols as right-wing monsters, motivated only by hatred for the excesses of the government. There is the possibility that McVeigh, as well as his alleged cohorts, are military intelligence agency provocateurs, or are manipulated by same.

The first objection to this interpretation would be that, if McVeigh was indeed a member of military intelligence, then he would not have been captured after the bombing, would not be currently incarcerated, and would not be waiting to stand trial. But the same argument could be used in the case of Lee Harvey Oswald, whom abundant evidence suggests was an agent of the CIA and possibly other intelligence agencies. We know what happened to Oswald, who proclaimed himself to be "a patsy" and was subsequently silenced by a bullet from the gun of Jack Ruby. Is McVeigh a patsy? Is the McVeigh who is in prison the same man who was responsible for the Oklahoma City bombing? And will he share the evil fate of Oswald, silenced before he has an opportunity to defend himself in court?

The FBI, CIA, and military intelligence have a long history of creating enemies and groups who are on the surface anti-Establishment, and this is sometimes accomplished through the use of agent provocateurs within those groups.

Lieutenant Colonel James "Bo" Gritz, currently a high profile representative of the populist right, has discussed his own experience with agent provocateurs:

"During the 60s and early 70s I knew of many young officers assigned to infiltrate fringe and militant organizations. The Army Counter-Intelligence Corps (CIC) saturated campus clubs, penetrated political organizations, intruded into private lives, filtered through church and civic orders, and in general invaded the American public! Nothing was exempt!... CIA programs' seeds were carefully planted into front organizations to spur and slant the growth of various viewpoints."

Gritz describes the alleged infiltration by the CIA of two right-wing groups:

"The United States Information Agency is an official State Department overt voice for disseminating propaganda overseas. The CIA employs a wide variety of non-violent [and sometimes violent] covert means to help undermine various target groups. As Americans, we tend to overlook the fact that as much, or even more, brainwashing is focused on the U.S.!

"I summarily rejected the suggestion by a CIC colleague back in 1971 — that the John Birch Society was established as a gray-level diversionary front organization to devitalize Americans with strong nationalistic ideals... To me the JBS provided its membership with dedicated patriotic awareness, education, and direction. People like Ezra Taft Benson, Eisenhower's Secretary of Agriculture, had spoken out strongly for the Constitution and against Communism at Boston JBS rallies.

"Still, those over me who knew the magnitude of classified compartmented campaigns, advised us to remain insulated from the JBS. Even then, I secretly supported what the rank and file Birchers openly advocated — and still do. But my intelligence colleague back in 1971 was correct — the Birch Society is a diversionary front — to devitalize Americans with strong nationalistic instincts.

"One day, following a heated discussion over the merits of the John Birch Society, I was told that the JBS was an "antithetical" model to the Ku Klux Klan. The Cold War KKK had been infiltrated by Communist organizers who sought to use its secrecy as a cover to foment un-American activities. The JBS I was told — on the other hand — had been re-tooled toward a more subtle purpose.

"Like a tar baby, it attracted and regulated the actions and attitudes of conservatives. I wasn't convinced then, but after reading the JBS story on the [Randy] Weaver atrocity, I join... others in questioning the true intent of those now at the helm..." [1]

What evidence is there to suggest that Timothy McVeigh might have been an intelligence agency spook engaged in infiltrating the right wing? According to David Hackworth, who interviewed McVeigh in prison for *Newsweek* magazine:

"I had reviewed his Army records before we got together in the prison's small visiting room. His test scores are collectively the highest I've ever seen. An Army personnel expert says his entrance test scores were 'brilliant.' He rated in the 'top five percent' and had the potential to be 'a great combat officer.' His electronic aptitude qualified him for the most complex communication training." [2]

Sheffield Anderson, who was in the Army at the same time as McVeigh, has stated, "The Army really liked Tim McVeigh. And Tim McVeigh really liked the Army. He was real career-oriented at the time. He was a real good soldier." [3]

Tim McVeigh was, in all ways, an exemplary member of the Army. He studied, read, and trained for combat continuously. His zeal resulted in promotions to corporal, to sergeant, and then to platoon leader. Is it possible that the image of McVeigh as a disgruntled military man conceals another reality? Initial media reports stated that McVeigh was disappointed when he was unable to complete the strenuous 21-day "assessment period" for Army Special Forces at Fort Bragg, North Carolina. "Preliminary psychological testing had shown him to be unfit," and "a road march with a 45-pound rucksack was too arduous." Still, Lieutenant Colonel Ken McGraw, a spokesman for the Army's Special Operations, said that McVeigh voluntarily withdrew from the course. As researcher John Judge has pointed out in an unpublished interview, one is given psychological testing before being sent to Special Forces Assessment, not after. Asked to produce documentation of McVeigh's psychological failure, the Army was unable to do so. Later they offered a letter supposedly penned by McVeigh, stating that he "just couldn't cut it." [4]

It has been said that the reason McVeigh failed the test was that he was out of shape because of his service in the Gulf War, but also because he was wearing new boots. This, in itself, hints of a set-up. Who takes an Army Special Forces physical wearing new boots?

It also seems debatable as to whether McVeigh was depressed after his voluntary withdrawal from the Special Forces. "He didn't seem terribly depressed," fellow soldier William Dilly said. "He was more worried at the time about the cutbacks they were making, and he would have been stuck at Fort Riley, which is no place to be stuck."

After Timothy McVeigh left the Army he joined the National Guard at Tonawanda, New York. Is that the action of a man disillusioned with the military? [5]

Interestingly, Terry Nichols left the Army under unexplained circumstances. "In the spring of 1989, Nichols was discharged because of a family emergency that has not been publicly explained by military authorities." Nichols ex-wife Lana Padilla voiced her own suspicions about the discharge in her book: "I've always wondered just why he was released, less than a year after enlisting, and always been told it was because he had to take care of Josh. But this theory never washed with me because he'd had Josh with him all along." [6]

McVeigh's failure of the Special Forces test and Nichols' unexplained leaving of the Army have their parallels. One of these is with Lee Harvey Oswald, whose "hardship discharge" from the Army has never been explained. Another example is that of Thomas Martinez, the FBI infiltrator within the radical right Silent Brotherhood, who was given an honorable discharge during Army basic training. The Army chooses not to explain why.

The case of David Lewis Rice also bears certain similarities. Rice was a dedicated survivalist and right winger who allegedly murdered lawyer Charles Goldmark and his family in Seattle in 1985. The day after the murder, Rice dropped into the home of the president of the local populist Duck Club, Homer Brand. "Hey, Homer," Rice is reported to have said, "it's me. The cops are after me. They could be arriving any minute. I've just dumped the top Communist. There were four involved." The court psychologist who later examined Rice stated that Rice told him that he had killed the Goldmarks because friends from outer space told him to do so. Rice, like Martinez, had been released from Navy boot camp with an honorable discharge, for "unstated reasons." [7]

McVeigh may not have failed the Special Forces training at all. He had apparently passed every other test that he had taken in the Army with flying colors, and had been promoted to the rank of sergeant ahead of the rest of his platoon. It is possible that McVeigh's outstanding performance and early promotion to sergeant drew the attention of military intelligence, and that he was approached at the time of his Special Forces training and offered a berth in a secret operational unit more elite than the Green Berets, perhaps a unit with responsibilities including domestic operations. McVeigh may have been activated as an agent provocateur to infiltrate the populist right.

We do know that at least in Vietnam Special Forces added a psychological operations group, termed a "five function." According to retired Lieutenant Colonel Daniel Marvin, "Almost all of the independent operations within the Green Berets were run by the CIA." [8]

Researcher John Judge has reached similar conclusions. Judge has stated that, "He seems to have played the same role that [Lee Harvey] Oswald did with the right wing Cubans, of being someone who came into their midst and promised a little more violence than they were ready for, and had been tossed out. This is also the way that the classic provocateur established a legend and a connection to groups that they eventually want to hang with [i.e., be associated with] at the particular crime." [9]

The memories of an acquaintance of McVeigh's seem to bear out the possibility of Timothy McVeigh as an intelligence asset. The man told me during an interview that McVeigh was "always asking questions, trying to find things out" at the gun shows he attended. He also stated that McVeigh seemed to have a high-photographic memory, because when you spoke to him months after an encounter, he would quote back information that you had told him, "almost verbatim." [10]

Walter "Mac" McCarty remembers McVeigh and Michael Fortier from their days in Kingman, Arizona, and from a handgun self-defense course that they took under his instruction during the Summer of 1994. McCarty found it strange that the two men, both proficient in the use of guns, would have taken the course in the first place. He came to suspect that they had other reasons.

"They wanted to hear certain things from me to see if they could get me involved," McCarty states. "They definitely liked what they heard. We were on the same page about the problems of America." McCarty wonders whether McVeigh and Fortier were able to recruit others in their plans, plans that apparently involved the bombing of the Oklahoma City federal building. [11]

McVeigh is reported to have been a bodyguard for Mark Koernke, a member of the patriot movement who states that he was trained in Army intelligence. Koernke is an example of the more excitable end of the spectrum in the patriot movement, along with lawyer Linda Thompson, the self-styled "Acting Adjutant General of the Unorganized Militia," who in 1994 called for an armed patriot march en masse upon Washington, D.C. to arrest members of Congress. Thompson also required people contacting her American Justice Federation bulletin board to fill out a computerized questionnaire that asked how the person would benefit the movement: could they provide safe houses, guns, training, ammunition? Anyone for self-incrimination?

Both Thompson's radical style and her prior military background as "assistant to the U.S. Army Commanding General, NATO, Allied Forces

Central Europe" with "Cosmic Top Secret/Atomal security clearance" render her suspect as a member of the populist right. Another individual of this sort is Thompson's associate, William Cooper, self-proclaimed to have been a member of military intelligence, who began his career by calling an alert against an invasion by extraterrestrial aliens, and is now more focused on excesses of the government, rather than on the imminent threat of flying saucer abduction.

These are the individuals who garner most of the attention from the above-ground media. This strategy, of providing media access to the more radical, wacko, and emotional (and in certain cases, controlled) voices, is easily seen as an effort by the government to broadly paint the right end of the political spectrum in the public's mind, to characterize members of these groups as armed crazies, as well as to kindle armed confrontations with the government. Persons on the right with more reasoned approaches are simply ignored by the media. This is the same strategy, along with the use of paid agent provocateurs, that was employed by the government to create armed confrontations, and to discredit and bring down the Black Power and leftist student movements during the 1960s.

There is no overestimating the amount of infiltration that the U.S. government has done into populist right wing groups, as shown by the employment of agent provocateurs in the CSA, the KKK, Aryan Nations, White Aryan Resistance, and other groups. It has been assumed that McVeigh, Nichols, and their associates were simply garden variety right wingers with a grudge against the government, but there is the strong possibility that they were influenced by or were members of government anti-right infiltration programs.

It is not necessary that McVeigh have been deceived, if he was indeed on an intelligence mission. While researching his book *Operation Mind Control*, Walter Bowart interviewed a high-ranking military man, who had put in thirty years in the service. During the latter years of his service, the officer had performed assassinations and had gained knowledge of sophisticated spy operations. The anonymous informant stated:

"Let me tell you something: the cheapest commodity in the world is human beings. Most assassins don't need to be programmed to kill. They're loyal to command. They're conditioned first by the circumstances of their own early life, then by a little 'loyalty training.' The command is their only justification for living. It is also their only protection once they're into it..." [12]

McVeigh and Terry Nichols were both stationed at Fort Riley, Kansas, where 15,000 men are stationed, and remained in contact with the area long after their discharges. There is the possibility that they engaged in recruiting in that area, as well. According to a report in *USA Today*, federal investigators investigating the Oklahoma City bombing "are going door-to-door in Junction City, Kansas, displaying snapshots of five men dressed in military uniform..." *USA Today* also stated, "The latest investigative effort in Kansas appears rooted in the military backgrounds of McVeigh and Nichols..." [13]

Whether McVeigh and his comrades engaged in recruiting among the military or not, there may be a connection between Fort Riley and the ingredients that were used in the OKBomb. According to federal investigators, the ammonium nitrate bomb was set off with Primacord detonator (or Primadet). This detonating cord is not available to the public because of the extreme danger of accidental detonation; even static electricity will set it off. If Primacord was used in the bomb, Fort Riley is the most likely location where it was obtained. An ex-CIA agent, who wishes to remain anonymous, confirmed in an interview with the author that there has been a thriving illegal diversion of weaponry taking place at Fort Riley for a very long time. [14]

It is interesting that no one seems to have mentioned that there had been strange, unexplained things going on at Fort Riley around the time of the Oklahoma City bombing. Four soldiers are dead and one wounded, after two shootings which took place in the vicinity of the Custer Hill barracks at Fort Riley. On April 6, Specialist Brian Stoutenburg was found dead, an apparent suicide by gunshot. On March 2, Private First Class Maurice Wilford killed two other soldiers and wounded another with a 12-gauge shotgun, before he killed himself. Is there any connection to McVeigh, Nichols, and the Oklahoma City bombing in these killings? Is a cover-up going on? So far there is no proof of such, although recent events have been of great concern to the men stationed at the base. Scott Sanders, who was stationed at Fort Riley stated, "It's making us all look bad, like this is some center to train terrorists." [15]

There is no question that the CIA and other intelligence agencies have historically been engaged in manipulating the radical elements of the American conservative populist movement, the militant Islamic, and other movements with puppetmaster facility. They have created, encouraged, and funded individuals and groups with radical political agendas, and have sometimes used those individuals to precipitate violence — opening the door to politically profitable retribution.

The entirety of the previous chapter had been written when I received an article which noted Jennifer McVeigh's testimony to the grand jury:

"Despite being a government witness, Ms. McVeigh read a letter from her brother claiming that he was a member of a military Special Forces Group involved in criminal activity." [16]

NOTES:

1. Gritz, James "Bo." "The Birch Society's Twisted Version of the Weaver Family Atrocities!," *Criminal Politics*, January 1993
2. Hackworth, David H. "Talking 'Soldier to Soldier' Behind Bars," *Newsweek*, July 3, 1995
3. "McVeigh a dedicated soldier and a loner," *Associated Press*, August 11, 1995
4. McFadden, Robert D., "The troubled life of Tim McVeigh," *The Arizona Republic*, May 7, 1995; Komarow, Steve and Spitzer, Kirk. "Past offers a few clues into psyche," *USA Today*, May 2, 1995
5. McFadden, Robert D. "How Lonely Soldier McVeigh Became Suspect in Bombing," *New York Times*, May 5, 1995; Loe, Victoria, and Parks, Scott. "McVeigh Fits pattern of notorious killers, expert says," *Dallas Morning News*, July 9, 1995
6. McFadden. Padilla, Lana and Delpit, Ron. *By Blood Betrayed,* Harper Paperback, New York, 1995
7. Coates, James. *Armed and Dangerous, the Rise of the Survivalist Right*, Hill and Wang, New York, New York 1987
8. Anderson, Scott. "*Globe* publishers' Viet tour took in mind warfare," *Now Magazine*, Toronto, Canada, May 26, 1994
9. Judge, John. Unpublished interview conducted by Kenn Thomas, June 8, 1995. Copy in the author's possession
10. Anonymous acquaintance of Tim McVeigh, interviewed by Jim Keith on July 14, 1995
11. Shaffer, Mark. "Gun class sheds new light on McVeigh," *The Arizona Republic*, May 28, 1995
12. Bowart, Walter. *Operation Mind Control*, Dell Publishing Co., Inc., New York, New York, 1978
13. Johnson, Kevin. "Blast investigators' pace slows to a walk," *USA Today*, May 18, 1995
14. Anonymous ex-CIA agent, interviewed by Jim Keith on August 12, 1995

15. "Fort Riley regiment stunned by McVeigh ties to bombing," *Los Angeles Times*, April 30, 1995; Terry, Don. "Proud Base Faced With Notoriety by Association," *New York Times,* April 28, 1995
16. Myers, Lawrence W. "OKC Bombing Grand Jurors Claim 'Cover-Up'," *Media Bypass*, November 1995

27

A McVeigh Double?

F or those familiar with the investigation of the John F. Kennedy
assassination, there are aspects of the Oklahoma City bomb case
that are curiously reminiscent. Some researchers have charged
that there was more than one "Lee Harvey Oswald" in action prior to
the Kennedy assassination, and that several look-alike individuals were
used to confuse the trail, and to implicate a patsy, the real Oswald, in the
crime. It may be that the same is true of Timothy McVeigh. Another
wild conspiracy theory? If so, then it is being offered by federal investigators in the case.

According to the *Los Angeles Times*, "The investigators said authorities theorize that John Doe 2 could be two people, and that McVeigh and
his alleged conspirators could have used different men to accompany him
in order to serve as 'decoys' and confuse investigators trying to trace his
movements." [1]

Cited earlier is the information from the *New York Times* about
Timothy McVeigh ("or a look-alike," according to the *Times)* and a
friend trying to get haircuts on the day before the bombing. According to
the hairdresser, neither of the men needed haircuts.

This account sounds almost as if McVeigh and his companion, or
whoever he was, wanted to be noticed, to establish his whereabouts on
the day before the bombing. Certainly it would have made more sense
for McVeigh to be getting some sleep prior to the long trip to Oklahoma
City, and his reported flight after the bombing, rather than worrying
about his buzz cut. The "haircut" incident provides a macabre echo of a
Lee Harvey Oswald double, alleged to have been William Seymour, who
made pro-Castro remarks in an Irving, Texas barber shop and at shops

around Dallas, and did target shooting at ranges in Dallas in the month prior to the Kennedy assassination. [2]

McVeigh and Fortier casing the Murrah Federal Building prior to the bombing, flashing dog tags, and wearing camouflage clothing also challenges credulity, leading one to think that a double may have been implicating McVeigh, at least.

As cited earlier, Jerry Bohnen of K-TOK radio in Oklahoma City was contacted by a homeless man who stated that while at the McDonalds restaurant at Sheridan and Western streets in Oklahoma City the night before the bombing, Timothy McVeigh drove by and asked him if he wanted to have some beers with him, which the man did. Here is another incident of McVeigh apparently wanting to be noticed and remembered. The employee in the nearby Total Store verifies the man bought beer, and that a Ryder truck was parked at the McDonalds at the time. According to David Hall, Terry Nichols told him that McVeigh was at the McDonalds on the 18th in order to receive $2,000 from Middle Eastern contacts. Another source verifies the meeting, based upon the account of a "Middle Eastern source" and other witnesses in Oklahoma City. [3]

Shortly after the capture of Timothy McVeigh, the recollections of Bob Regin, a Kingman, Arizona trailer park owner, were given wide coverage in the press. According to the *New York Times*,

"*The Arizona Republic* in Phoenix reported in its Sunday issue that Mr. McVeigh lived in the Kingman area for a year until he was evicted from a trailer park last June. The owner of the trailer park said Mr. McVeigh had lived there from February to June 1994. Residents of the Canyon West Mobile Park drew a picture of an arrogant loner who worked as a security guard for a now-defunct trucking company, lived with his pregnant girlfriend, expressed deep anger against the federal government and often caused trouble for his neighbors." [4]

Not so widely noted was the fact that the trailer park owner shortly recanted his story, and stated that although a Timothy McVeigh had indeed lived in his trailer park, it had not been the man who he had originally described. "They were the same height, the same age, they looked alike," Mr. Regin stated, and also added that both men had recently been released from the Army. [5]

Speaking with people who knew McVeigh, it sometimes seems as if they are talking about two different people. Some, like Chuck Halley, mention an extremely intelligent, fast-talking individual — Halley specifically mentioned to me in an interview that he talked fast. [6] Others, like

Matt, who met McVeigh at a gunshow in Utah, journalist J.D. Cash, who was present when McVeigh was indicted, and Terry Nichols' ex-wife Lana Padilla say that they don't think McVeigh was smart enough to carry out a bombing on his own. [7]
Some call McVeigh extremely talkative. The owner of one motel where McVeigh rented a room calls him "a talker," and he was listed as "most talkative" in his high school yearbook. Others call him taciturn, withdrawn, silent.

Another case of a possible McVeigh double was revealed when *Soldier of Fortune* magazine printed a photo of an unidentified ATF agent escorting Robert Rodriguez to court during the trial of the Branch Davidians in Waco. The ATF agent looks remarkably like McVeigh, as evidenced by the large number of readers who contacted *Soldier of Fortune* bringing the matter to their attention. When asked, Jack Killorin, an ATF public affairs official, denied that the agent was McVeigh (which is irrelevant in the case of a double), but would only say that the man was assigned to a California ATF office. [8]

If proof could be found that there was a double of McVeigh, then an amazing number of questions might be answered. Now we would understand why McVeigh left a trail implicating himself and others in the bombing, flashing his dogtags and identifying himself as being from Fort Riley at the Oklahoma City federal building when casing it. We would understand why McVeigh would sign his real name at a motel immediately prior to the bombing when he could have used false I.D. We would know why he gave the address of James Nichols when he was arrested, and dropped a card mentioning a TNT order in the police car. We would understand why McVeigh would be carrying damning evidence of his intentions in the form of letters in his glove compartment, and would accommodate the prosecution by penning "a large body of writings about his ideological leanings." We might understand why McVeigh would need to ask directions of a number of people while travelling to the Murrah Building, when he had been there in the past, and why he would call Elohim City after reserving the Ryder truck, thus incriminating members of that group. We might understand why McVeigh drove the Mercury Marquis, observed at the crime site, instead of changing to another car that wouldn't have been recognized, and why McVeigh "forgot" to put license plates on the car prior to his flight from Oklahoma City. We would understand why McVeigh did not shoot the policeman who stopped him in Perry, Oklahoma, but instead volunteered the information that he was carrying a concealed gun before the officer had drawn his own pistol. We would understand why three witnesses state that McVeigh was not in the Perry, Oklahoma jail the day of the bombing, or the following day. These are only some of the questions that proof of a McVeigh double would answer. After those questions were answered we might even come to the conclusion that the Timothy McVeigh who is currently in custody might be innocent of the Oklahoma City bombing.

NOTES:

1. "Feds charge Terry Nichols in bombing," *Los Angeles Times*, May 10, 1995
2. Torbitt, William. *Nomenclature of an Assassination Cabal*, Prevailing Winds, Santa Barbara, California
3. Rappoport, John. *Oklahoma City Bombing, The Suppressed Truth*, Blue Press, Los Angeles, 1995
4. "Timothy James McVeigh: Tracing One Man's Complex Path to Extremism," *New York Times*, April 23, 1995
5. Kifner, John. "Arizona Trailer Park Owner Remembered the Wrong Man," *New York Times*, April 25, 1995
6. Halley, Chuck. Interview conducted by Jim Keith, July 29, 1995
7. Interview with "Matt," conducted by Jim Keith, June 15, 1995; Cash, J.D. Interview conducted by Jim Keith, September 26, 1995; Padilla, Lana and Delpit, Ron. *By Blood Betrayed*, Harper Paperback, New York, 1995
8. "Timothy McVeigh A BATF Agent?", *Soldier of Fortune*, September 1995

28

McVeigh and the Controllers

Given the curious behavior of Timothy McVeigh and many other contradictions and inexplicable aspects in the OKBomb case, an incredible possibility presents itself: that Timothy McVeigh was a mind-controlled intelligence agency asset. The Oklahoma City bombing has intelligence agency and Psy-ops fingerprints all over it, and even the name of one of the motels McVeigh stayed at in Kansas — Dreamland — is a macabre echo of the top secret military installation in Nevada otherwise known as Area 51.

I would like to emphasize that the possibility of mind control in the case of Timothy McVeigh is at this time only speculation on my part — repeat, a speculation. This will not prevent those wishing to paint this book as wild-eyed conspiracy mongering from doing so, maintaining that I believe against all evidence in the science fictional impossibility that McVeigh was a mind control subject. This is just another means of discrediting anyone who projects anything but the standard government and controlled media line, but when this does take place at least we will know the identity of some of those who wish to see the truth suppressed and the official line and official lies furthered.

Mind control as a subject has been, perhaps purposefully, shunted by the media into the realm of science fiction and horror movies, thus preventing the public from gaining a true understanding of the hidden history of the world, and the ways in which people have been controlled. An even cursory study of the subject of mind control, however, will show that the subject is not science fiction, is not fantasy, and that it may have been employed to program Timothy McVeigh into the murder of 169 persons in Oklahoma. Before you discount the possibility entirely, examine the facts.

The following is a brief sketch of the feasibility and history of mind control as practiced by American intelligence agencies during the latter part of the twentieth century. The research begins with Stanley Lovell, who ran research and development in the OSS, the predecessor agency to the CIA, during World War II. His idea was to hypnotize German prisoners of war of high rank, implanting the mission of assassinating Hitler, then returning them to Germany. Shortly thereafter, George "Esty" Estabrooks, director of the Colgate University Psychology Department, was suggesting to the OSS that an experiment be conducted to see if a normal person could be turned into a murderer through hypnosis. Estabrooks stated that "Any accidents that might occur during the experiments will simply be charged to wastage in human life which is part and parcel of war." [1]

After the war, intelligence agency research continued into the modification of behavior. Such research included OSS research into chemical means of mind control, using marijuana, mescaline, barbiturates, scopolomine, and peyote. The OSS and CIA were happy to employ a number of Nazi chemical warfare specialists in their endeavors to develop full-blown mind control. These men included Karl Tauboeck, Friedrich Hoffman, Theodore Wagner-Jauregg, Karl Rarh, and Hans Turit. [2]

April 1950 saw the birth of the CIA's PROJECT BLUEBIRD, which transmuted into PROJECT ARTICHOKE, meant to "exploit operational lines, scientific methods and knowledge that can be utilized in altering the attitudes, beliefs, thought processes and behaviour patterns of agent personnel. This will include the application of tested psychiatric and psychological techniques including the use of hypnosis in conjunction with drugs." According to researcher Martin Cannon, the investigation of electronic means for behavior modification was a high priority for both ARTICHOKE and BLUEBIRD.

The Bureau of Social Science Research, a subcontracting agency for the Rand Corporation obtaining funding from the government, provided a report to the Air Force in 1958 titled "The Use of Hypnosis in Intelligence and Related Military Situations." The report said that:

"In defense applications, subjects can be specifically selected by a criterion of hypnotizability, and subsequently trained in accord with their anticipated military function... Personnel entrusted with particularly sensitive material could be prepared against possible capture in many different ways: (a) by simple hypnotic suggestion, they could be 'immunized' against hypnotic interrogation and suggestion by the enemy; (b) with posthypnotic and autosuggestive training, appropriately timed amnesias could be induced; (c) posthypnotic depersonalization and related dissociative states could be built into the subjects so that if they fall into enemy hands, they would no longer function as rational, integrated individuals..." [3]

ARTICHOKE turned into MKULTRA in 1953, which, over the next 20 years and perhaps to the present day, engaged in at least 187 projects dealing with mind control, including further experimentation and utilization of psycho-electronics. [4]

A small step forward for mankind, and a great step forward for techno-fascism was taken with the research of Dr. Jose Delgado, who developed the 'stimoceiver' in the late 1950s and was funded by the CIA and the U.S. Office of Naval Research. The stimoceiver is a tiny electronic receiver and transmitter which can be implanted into the head of the control subject. The stimoceiver can be used to stimulate emotions and control behavior, and according to Delgado, "Radio Stimulation of different points in the amygdala and hippocampus [areas of the brain] in the four patients produced a variety of effects, including pleasant sensations, elation, deep, thoughtful concentration, odd feelings, super relaxation, colored visions, and other responses." [5] Delgado stated that "brain transmitters can remain in a person's head for life. The energy to activate the brain transmitter is transmitted by way of radio frequencies."

Also according to Delgado, "One of the possibilities with brain transmitters is to influence people so that they conform with the political system. Autonomic and somatic functions, individual and social behaviour, emotional and mental reactions may be invoked, maintained, modified, or inhibited, both in animals and in man, by stimulation of specific cerebral structures. Physical control of many brain functions is a demonstrated fact. It is even possible to follow intentions, the development of thought and visual experiences." [6]

Dr. Stuart Mackay's 1968 textbook *Bio-Medical Telemetry* reported, "Among the many telemetry instruments being used today, are miniature radio transmitters that can be swallowed, carried externally, or surgically implanted in man or animal. They permit the simultaneous study of behavior and physiological functioning. The scope of observations is too broad to more than hint at a few examples. The possibilities are limited only by the imagination of the investigator." [7]

By 1973 Dr. Joseph Sharp, of the Walter Reed Army Institute of Research, was demonstrating that spoken words could be projected directly to a subject's brain via microwave broadcasting. Becker offered the comment that, "Such a device has obvious applications in covert operations designed to drive a target crazy with 'voices' or deliver undetectable instructions to a programmed assassin." [8]

Former FBI agent Lincoln Lawrence, in his 1969 book *Were We Controlled?*, described a technology termed RHIC-EDOM, or Radio Hypnotic Intracerebral Control and Electronic Dissolution of Memory. According to Lawrence:

"It is the ultra-sophisticated application of post-hypnotic suggestion triggered at will by radio transmission. It is a recurring state, re-induced automatically at intervals by the same radio control. An individual is brought under hypnosis. This can be done either with his knowledge — or without it — by use of narco-hypnosis, which can be brought into play under many guises. He is then programmed to perform certain actions and maintain certain attitudes upon radio signal." The RHIC-EDOM technology also involves the electronic dissolution of memory, so that the subject does not remember what he has done in response to the controllers' whims.

Lawrence stated that Lee Harvey Oswald had been implanted with an electronic mind control device when he had been in a hospital in Minsk: "After he was placed under anaesthesia, advanced technique was employed to implant a miniaturized radio receiver which would produce a muscular reaction in his cerebral region." According to Lawrence, Oswald would "remain for the rest of his life — without his knowledge — a completely efficient human tool... subject to 'control'!" [9]

Impossible? The CIA didn't think so at the time. In 1964 CIA Director McCone sent a memo to Secret Service Chief James Rowley, in which McCone stated that Oswald might have been "chemically or electronically 'controlled'... a sleeper agent. Subject spent 11 days hospitalized for a 'minor ailment' which should have required no more than three days hospitalization at best." [10]

Lincoln Lawrence believed that Jack Ruby, the alleged assassin of Oswald, was also "placed under hypnosis... perhaps at a party or perhaps by some 'performer' who was pretending to offer a casual audition for the Carousel Club [which Ruby owned]." It is interesting that the featured performer at Ruby's club the week of the JFK assassination was a hypnotist.

Colonel William Bishop provided information about his own involvement in the MKULTRA program to journalist Dick Russell. Bishop stated:

"That was how, after the Korean War, I got involved with CIA. I have been subjected to every known type of drug. The medical doctors connected with the agency found that certain drugs work quite well in conjunction with hypnosis — hypnotic power of suggestion — with some subjects. It did with me. I speak with absolute certainty and knowledge and experience that this is not only possible, but did and is taking place today.

"I never understood why they selected me personally. There were any number of psychological or emotional factors involved in people's selection. Antisocial behavior patterns, paranoid or the rudiments of paranoia, and so on. But when they are successful with this programming — or, for lack of a better term, indoctrination — they could take John Doe and get this man to kill George and Jane Smith. He will be given all the pertinent information as to their location, daily habits, etc. Then there is a mental block put on this mission in his mind. He remembers nothing about it.

"Perhaps a month or a year later — rarely over a year, at least back in those days — the phone rings. A code word will be read to him in a voice that John Doe recognizes. That will trigger the action. John Doe will commit the assassination, return home, and remember absolutely nothing of it. It is totally blank space.

"Now there is a problem with this, and they never found a way that I know of to overcome it. From time to time — it happens to me now — I will see faces, names, places, gunfire, for which there is no rational explanation. I went back for deprogramming. In these sessions, they explain that this does happen from time to time, not to worry about it, just clear your mind and forget it." [11]

Although MKULTRA was said to have been terminated in 1973, we know that research into mind control and, specifically, the creation of mind controlled assassins did continue. In July 1975 Thomas Narut, a U.S. naval psychologist, addressed a conference in Oslo, Norway, on the subject of "The Use of a Symbolic Model and Verbal Intervention in Inducing and Reducing Stress." During private questioning Narut talked about programming "combat readiness units" (which he also termed "hit men and assassins") to kill, and described his participation in US Naval Intelligence operations in which convicted murderers from military prisons were hypnotically programmed as assassins and deployed to American embassies worldwide. After Narut's statements were published, both he and the US Navy issued official denials. [12]

As an example of the mindset which may have gone into the creation of a mind-controlled Timothy McVeigh is that of the Human Resources

Research Office, described by Dr. John Coleman:
"This is an Army research establishment dealing in 'psychotechnology.' Most of its personnel are Tavistock-Institute, specializing in psychological warfare, trained [in England]. 'Psychotechnology' covers GI motivation, morale and music used by the enemy. In fact a lot of what George Orwell wrote about in his book *1984* appears to be remarkably similar to what is taught at HUMRRO... It is the largest behavioral research group in the U.S.

"One of its specialties is the study of small groups under stress, and HUMRRO teaches the Army that a soldier is merely an extension of his equipment and has brought great influence to bear on the 'man/weapon/system' and its 'human quality control,' so widely accepted by the United States Army. HUMRRO has had a very pronounced effect on how the Army conducts itself. Its mind-bending techniques are straight out of Tavistock. HUMRRO's applied psychology courses are supposed to teach Army brass how to make the human weapon work. A good example of this is the manner in which soldiers in the war against Iraq were willing to disobey their field manual standing orders and bury 12,000 Iraqi soldiers alive.

"This type of brainwashing is terribly dangerous because, today, it is applied to the Army, the Army applies it to brutally destroy thousands of 'enemy' soldiers, and tomorrow the Army could be told that civilian population groups opposed to government policies are 'the enemy.' We are already a mindless brainwashed flock of sheep, yet it seems that HUMRRO can take mind bending and mind control a step further. HUMRRO is a valuable adjunct to Tavistock, and many of the lessons taught at HUMRRO were applied in the Gulf War, which makes it a little easier to understand how it came to be that American soldiers behaved as ruthless and heartless killers, a far cry from the concept of the traditional American fighting man." [13]

The above offers a demonstration that the CIA or another intelligence agency in all probability has the techological expertise and possibly the will to activate Timothy McVeigh as a mind controlled assassin. But is there any suggestion that this might have actually taken place?

The clearest evidence of the possibility of mind tampering or electronic monitoring (or telemetry) of McVeigh comes from the statements of friends and acquaintances. According to reporter Sally Barclay, "Something strange... happened to McVeigh after he was with a psychologist during a mysterious counselling testing-session, prior to his aborted attempt to enter Special Forces (after the Persian Gulf War).

McVeigh's Army associates noted: 'He seemed quite a bit different than he'd been before... He wasn't the same McVeigh, didn't have the same drive...'"

Phil Morawski, a friend of McVeigh's, states that he complained that he had a microchip implanted in his buttocks by the Army. McVeigh apparently thought that it had been implanted in order to monitor his movements, although at least one source has stated that McVeigh believed he was being mind controlled through the use of the microchip. [14] Another acquaintance, Dan Stomber, says that McVeigh mentioned the microchip to him, as well. [15]

Sally Barclay notes, "Timothy McVeigh told people in Decker, Michigan, that his government-implanted microchip was causing real sharp pain in his buttocks. McVeigh said that the biochip was implanted 'so the all-seeing eye of the government could watch him and know his location.'

"After he was arrested, one of the few things McVeigh spoke about was to complain about the continuing pain from his implant."

If McVeigh did believe that he had been implanted with a microchip, would he have engaged in a plot to bomb the Oklahoma City federal building? Wouldn't he have thought that the government might become aware of what he was doing, and could easily capture him if he engaged in the crime?

Had McVeigh gone off the deep end in his belief about being implanted? Perhaps not. A significant detail about McVeigh's past that is never mentioned by the media is that, after his stint in the Army, McVeigh was employed as a guard with Burns International Security Services at the Calspan facility in Buffalo, New York. Calspan is a division of the Fortune 500 company Arvin, which manufactures automobile parts, but the lower profile Calspan, according to the InvestText database, "provides technological services to the United States government and various industries." More precisely, according to industry sources, Calspan does research into aeronautics, electronic warfare, microwave technology, and electronic telemetric devices. Microchip implants are by definition electronic telemetric devices, and this technology is anything but science fiction.

While Calspan publicly claims to primarily be engaged in aeronautics research, the topics addressed during their yearly seminar series are a remarkably mixed bag. Here are a few of the topics and speakers that have been featured at Calspan seminars:

August 14, 1972, Science and Control of Social Behavior, Dr. Israel

Goldiamond, Prof. of Psychology at the University of Chicago; July 8, 1974, The Great World Transformation Today, Dr. John Platt; December 8, 1975, Genetic Engineering — How Great is the Danger? Dr. Bernard D. Davis, Harvard Medical School; October 26, 1976, The Mood of the Nation, Dr. George H. Gallup; October 14, 1977, Terrorism and Law Enforcement, Sir Robert Mark, New Scotland Yard; September 27, 1979, Some Problems of Freedom, Dr. William F. Buckley; January 16, 1984, Macromachined Smart Silicon Sensors, Prof. James B. Angell; April 11, 1988, Perfectly Engineered Viruses, Dr. Iain Hay; and March 15, 1994, Crime and the Information Society, Marc Rotenberg, Georgetown University. [16]

There is a possibility that McVeigh was purposely washed out of his Special Forces training and was recruited into a secret specialized unit, then sent to Calspan for indoctrination, training, or, as he believed was performed on him, the implanting of a microchip. The letter from Tim McVeigh read by Jennifer McVeigh at the grand jury hearings, in which McVeigh indicates that he was a member of a "military Special Forces Group involved in criminal activity," substantiates this possibility.

It may be relevant that at least two government scientists researching microwave and laser weapons were in touch with members of the rightist Silent Brotherhood, and expressed an interest in sharing weapons technology with them. An initiative was brought before the Brotherhood leadership to provide the scientists with living and research expenses, false I.D., and relocation, and the initiative was agreed to. A Silent Brotherhood member was given $100,000 to finance the scientists, according to court testimony, although no further information on the extent of collaboration between these government scientists and the Silent Brotherhood has been uncovered. [17]

Providing further information on implanted microchips is Dr. Carl Sanders, a 32-year engineering veteran and the designer of the Intelligence Manned Interface (IMI) biochip:

"There are new satellites going up [such as the] sixty-six satellites that Motorola is putting up in conjunction with the Russians. These are low orbiting satellites," which according to Sanders, can monitor ground-based microchips. "We used this with military personnel in the Iraq War where they were actually tracked using this particular type of device."

Speaking of his research with Motorola, General Electric, and the Boston Medical Center, Sanders explains, "We noticed that the frequency of the chip had a great effect upon behavior and so we began to branch off and look possibly at behavior modification... the project almost turned into electronic acupuncture because what they ended up with was embedding a microchip to put out a signal which affected certain areas. They were able to determine that you could cause a behavioral change."

Sanders has also spoken about a "Rambo chip," which stimulates adrenaline and turns humans into fighting machines, the technology reportedly developed under the auspices of "the Phoenix Program." The Rambo chip has reportedly been tested on soldiers.

EYE magazine provides more information about the biochips: "Sematech in Austin, Texas, developed a computer chip this year that is only 0.35 microns wide; roughly 1/200th the size of a human hair. Sematech is the maker of components for the advanced weapons systems used in the Gulf War, and will supply American companies with the tools necessary to manufacture these chips."

EYE also reports, "Tracking objects with implantable transponders is... a growing field, usually involving what is known as radio-frequency identification (RFID). The idea is that tiny transponders — now small enough to be inserted into a variety of objects including animals [and humans] — are programmed with unique codes as well as data about the object if desired. The transponders remain passive until scanned, allowing the data to appear on a computer screen. Hughes Identification Devices, a division of GM Hughes Electronics, is using RFID transponders or 'tags' that can be embedded into objects for industrial applications. One of the company's glass-encapsulated transponders, model TX1400, is so small (11 mm x 2.1 mm) that it can be used in applications where automatic identification would normally be impossible. Literature from the California-based company explains: 'It can be molded into plastic objects or inserted into predrilled holes. It can also be injected with a syringe in materials soft enough for needle penetration.'" *EYE* wryly notes, "And one wonders just what that soft material might be."

McVeigh is not the only person to claim that he has been implanted with a monitoring or mind control device. There are, in fact, several support groups internationally that have been formed to help the thousands of people who believe they have been electronically implanted.

An example of one person who believes that he is electronically mind controlled is detailed in the March 17, 1984 *San Francisco Chronicle*, in which a would-be assassin arrested at the White House claimed that he had been injected with a telemetry device in the form of a crystalline implant. He believed that he was receiving commands to kill through the device. Although voices in the head are the hallmark of those society thinks of as crazy, this provides deniability for clandestine operations of this sort. It is well within the capability of intelligence agencies to electronically install those voices in subjects.

On May 5, 1991, Carl Campbell approached Navy Commander Edward J. Higgins in the Pentagon parking lot. Campbell shot Higgins in the chest five times, killing him, and was arrested by federal police. In a psychological report penned about Campbell it was revealed that he believed that he had been injected with a microchip by the CIA which controlled his mind. [18]

Lynda Haner-Mele supervised McVeigh while he worked for the Burns organization in New York. Substantiating that something very strange was going on with McVeigh at the time, she says that, "That guy did not have an expression 99 percent of the time. He was cold. He didn't want to have to deal with people or pressure. Timmy was a good guard, always there prompt, clean and neat. His only quirk was that he couldn't deal with people. If someone didn't cooperate with him, he would start yelling at them, become verbally aggressive. He could be set off easily. He was quiet, but it didn't take much." His supervisor states that she doesn't believe that McVeigh was capable of carrying out the Oklahoma bombing by himself. "Timmy just wasn't the type of person who could initiate action. He was very good if you said, 'Tim, watch this door — don't let anyone through.' The Tim I knew couldn't have masterminded something like this and carried it out himself. It would have had to have been someone who said, 'Tim, this is what you do. You drive the truck...'"

Journalist J.D. Cash, who was present at the indictment of McVeigh, states that the accused killer is "just a kid, very boyish, very juvenile..." and "not the mastermind." Cash sees McVeigh's probable role in the bombing as that of a patsy. [19]

A similar estimation of McVeigh was offered to the author by another acquaintance who chooses to remain anonymous. "He didn't seem like he was capable of doing the bombing on his own," the man says.

"He was real different," said Todd A. Regier, a man who served with McVeigh in the military. "Kind of cold. He wasn't enemies with anyone. He was kind of almost like a robot. He never had a date when I knew him in the Army. I never saw him at a club. I never saw him drinking. He never had good friends. He was a robot. Everything was for a purpose." [20]

McVeigh's behavior while staying at the Imperial Motel in Kingman, Arizona, from March 31 until April 12 is also exceedingly odd. According to the owner of the motel, McVeigh "didn't go out, he didn't make phone calls, he didn't do anything. He just sat up there and brooded." [21]

Walter "Mac" McCarty, the gun course instructor who felt that McVeigh and Fortier were trying to recruit him into a plot in Kingman, Arizona, has another intriguing observation about the alleged conspirators. McCarty says of McVeigh, "He was upset about things happening in this country to the point of being disoriented." He was "wandering around in a flux with no goals or bounds to his hatred." And where does McCarty speculate that this disorientation and hatred came from? "I know brainwashing when I see it," McCarty says. "Those two boys had really gotten a good case of it." [22]

I have already recounted the suspicious circumstances of Timothy McVeigh failing his Special Forces testing, as well as McVeigh's statement that he had been recruited into a Special Forces Group involved in criminal activity. I have also mentioned other instances where honorable discharges were given to individuals who later turned into murderers, or were involved in surveillance of populist right groups.

An interview conducted by the author with an ex-CIA agent in August 1995 confirmed certain suspicions I had about Fort Riley as a center for somewhat unusual military activities. Fort Riley, the ex-agent stated, had been a facility where biological warfare testing had taken place "since World War II." According to the former agent, there are also "special medical and Psy-ops [psychological operations] facilities at Fort Riley," and he stated that experimentation is often done "in collaboration with the whole range of intelligence agencies, FBI, CIA, NSA, the works." My informant also stated that he had seen the results of some kind of special psychological operation performed on the crew members of the Pueblo naval vessal at Fort Riley, and also at Fort Benning, Georgia (where McVeigh did his basic training), prior to the ship's capture by the North Koreans. Fort Benning is also known as the location where military death squad leaders like El Salvador's Roberto D'Aubisson, Haiti's Emmanuel Constant, and Guatemala's General Hector Gramajo were trained.

The ex-CIA agent I spoke to recounted having seen several men at Fort Riley who had been recruited for special training operations, and then had come back "with a completely different, unemotional mindset." [23]

After his arrest, McVeigh was taken to Tinker Air Force Base. It is possible that a debriefing or brainwashing was done at Tinker. After his transfer to the Federal Correctional Institute at El Reno, Oklahoma, McVeigh was placed in a 12-by-12 foot cell which was continually illuminated — suggesting that he was purposely being deprived of sleep — and he was observed 24 hours a day. This, in itself, might be construed as psychological warfare against McVeigh, and might be enough to cause a prisoner to break down and confess to anything. [24]

Researcher Texe Marrs points out an additional matter of interest regarding Timothy McVeigh. He states, "Two attorneys from Houston, Texas mysteriously showed up in Oklahoma City shortly after his arrest claiming to represent Mr. McVeigh. They said the defendant's family had asked them to take the case. But McVeigh denied it and sent a letter to the federal judge in the case insisting that the two were not his attorneys." Marrs adds, quite correctly, "This fits the CIA pattern in which hapless patsies are assigned CIA-related attorneys — who promptly sell them down the river!" [25]

Sometimes intelligence agency operations are complex enough to defy the assigning of responsibility. The dividing lines between both public and private intelligence agencies are somewhat hazier than is generally acknowledged, and private concerns may have been the real motivating force behind the Oklahoma City bombing. Walter Bowart's anonymous military informant provides insight into what deceased journalist Danny Casolaro called the Octopus, a control structure that exceeds formal intelligence agency boundaries and mixes with private concerns:

"This country is controlled by the Pentagon. All the major decisions in this country are made by the military, from my observations on the clandestine side of things.

"The CIA's just the whipping boy. NSA [National Security Agency] are the ones who have the hit teams. Look into their records — you won't find a thing. Look into their budget — you can't. For the life of you, you can't find any way they could spend the kind of money they've got on the number of people who're supposed to be on their payroll. Even if they had immense research and development programs, they couldn't spend that kind of money.

"The CIA's just a figurehead. They are more worldwide — like the FBI is. They're accountants, lawyers, file clerks, schoolboys. They are information-gatherers. They've pulled a lot of goddamned shenanigans — I'm not going to deny that — but as far as intelligence goes, the NSA's far, far superior to them — far in advance in the 'black arts.'

"The CIA gets blamed for what NSA does. NSA is far more vicious and far more accomplished in their operations. The American people are kept in ignorance about this — they should be, too."

According to Bowart's informant, "There is a group of about eighteen or twenty people running this country. They have not been elected. The elected people are only figureheads for these guys who have a lot more power than even the President of the United States." He continues by saying, "What people don't know is that the global corporations have their own version of the CIA. Where they don't interface with the CIA, they have their own organizations — all CIA trained. They also have double-agents inside CIA and other intelligence organizations who are loyal to those corporations — I mean where's the bread buttered? Would you rather take the government pensions or would you rather work a little for the corporation on the side and get both government pensions and corporate benefits after you retire? Most men retire after twenty years, and they're only in their mid-forties, then they go to work for the corporation they've been working for while they were in government service. They get both the pension and the corporate paycheck that way!

"Together with what the corporations do on their own, they have a worldwide espionage system far better than the CIA's. There is a network of what amounts to double-agents — they do work for the government, and may appear to be government agents, but they are first loyal to the corporations. They report to those corporations on the government and on what foreign governments might be planning which would interfere with those corporations' foreign investments. These guys are strictly free enterprise agents."

Bowart sums up the situation: "The assassin confirmed many of my own conclusions which had been based only on research: that an invisible coup d'etat had taken place in the United States; that the CIA is only the tip of the cryptocracy [or secret government] iceberg; and that ultrasonic and electrical memory erasure was used to protect 'search and destroy' operators from their own memories. I had some indication that the cryptocracy had investigated such techniques (a 1951 CIA document had briefly cited the need for such research), but the assassin's disclosure that the cryptocracy had developed invisible forms of sonics and electronic stimulation of the brain for mind control sent me back to the libraries." [26]

The information in this chapter is highly speculative, but is based upon aspects of Timothy McVeigh's behavior and other evidence which have been otherwise unexplained and unexplored.

NOTES:

1. Bresler, Fenton. *Who Killed John Lennon?*, St. Martin's Press, New York, NY, 1989

2. Cannon, Martin. "Mind Control and the American Government," *Lobster* magazine, issue 23
3. Russell, Dick. *The Man Who Knew Too Much*, Carroll & Graf, 1994
4. Bresler
5. Cannon; Delgado, J.M.R., "Intracerebral Radio Stimulation and Recording in Completely Free Patients," in Schwitzgebel and Schwitzgebel (eds.)
6. Krawczk, Glenn. "Mind Control & the New World Order," *Nexus*, February-March 1993
7. Ibid.
8. Cannon
9. Cannon; Russell
10. Russell
11. Ibid.
12. Bresler
13. Coleman, Dr. John C., *Conspirators' Hierarchy: The Story of the Committee of 300*, America West Publishers, Carson City, Nevada, 1992
14. "Bombing manhunt goes on," *Associated Press*, April 23, 1995
15. Thomas, Evan, et al. "The Plot," *Newsweek*, May 8, 1995
16. Information obtained off Calspan Internet site.
17. Coates, James. *Armed and Dangerous, the Rise of the Survivalist Right*, Hill and Wang, New York, New York 1987
18. Constantine, Alex. *Psychic Dictatorship in the U.S.A.*, Feral House, 1995
19. McFadden, Robert D., "The Troubled Life of Tim McVeigh," *The Arizona Republic*, May 7, 1995
20. McFadden, Robert D., *New York Times,* May 14, 1995
21. Kifner, John. "Agents Fan Out in a Town in Arizona, Retracing the Trail of the Jailed Suspect," *Associated Press*, April 29, 1995
22. Shaffer, Mark. "Gun class sheds new light on McVeigh," *The Arizona Republic*, May 28, 1995
23. Anonymous, interview with an ex-CIA agent, August 12, 1995
24. Thomas, Evan, et al. "The Plot," *Newsweek*, May 8, 1995
25. Marrs, Texe. *Flashpoint* newsletter, July 1995
26. Bowart, Walter. *Operation Mind Control*, Dell Publishing Co., Inc., New York, New York, 1978

29

Terms of the Agreement

T
he following press release, dated August 10, 1995, was issued by Stephen Jones, McVeigh's attorney. The document speaks for itself, and is reprinted in its entirety:

In the second week of September 1994, the Office of the United States Attorney for a District within the Tenth Circuit entered into a formal written agreement between a specific individual, an informant, and the United States of America. The terms of the agreement provided that the individual had contacted the U.S. Marshall's Service indicating that he had information concerning a conspiracy to destroy United States court facilities in that city and possibly other cities. The United States agreed that any statement or information that this individual provided relevant to the conspiracy would not be used against him in any criminal proceedings and that no evidence derived from the information or statements provided by him would be used against him in any way.

In return for this grant of immunity, the informant agreed to fully and completely cooperate with all federal law enforcement authorities regarding his knowledge of and participation in any crimes or related activities. The agreement further provided that if the individual made any false statement or testimony, at any time, the agreement became null and void, and that the decision as to whether a violation of the agreement had occurred remained solely in the discretionary judgement of the Office of the United States Attorney for the District. The individual executed his signature, as did the Assistant United States Attorney.

Copies of this formal letter of immunity are available to you this afternoon.

In reliance upon this grant of immunity, the informant met with agents of the Federal Bureau of Investigation and provided relevant information. Thereafter, he continued to provide relevant information about the conspiracy to bomb and destroy federal buildings, including the following:

1. That he made at least one trip to Kingman, Arizona, where he met individuals concerning a conspiracy to bomb federal buildings.

2. That he was asked to carry, and did carry, certain packages back to the city of his residence which contained explosive material.

3. That these individuals were a combination of American citizens, and he thought, either Latin Americans or Arabs. The individuals were identified by Arabic names.

4. This individual has a prior non-violent felony.

5. After the appearance of the *Newsweek* article with our client's face on the cover, this individual voluntarily contacted our office. Representatives from our office flew to the city of his residence and interviewed the individual at length. They confirmed the existence of the letter of immunity and the original is in our possession. They confirmed this individual's representations that he had contacted a United States Attorney's Office through an attorney. We spoke with that attorney who confirmed the terms and grant of the letter of immunity.

6. We asked the individual to furnish us certain information in order to verify the accuracy of his story. He supplied evidence in the form of receipts that he had been in Kingman, Arizona, provided a map of Kingman, provided an accurate description of certain street addresses in Kingman that are relevant to this investigation, and identified certain photographs of individuals.

7. This individual was subsequently interviewed by myself and another attorney, and then interviewed by a private investigator. He also provided information indicating an ability to make false identification papers.

8. The individual further related that in the spring, that is to say in the months of March and April of 1995, he provided additional information to the Federal Bureau of Investigation and to the Office of the U.S. Marshall concerning more specific information; to wit, that a federal building in the Midwest would be blown up or destroyed by a bomb during the middle of April 1995.

9. During the course of our investigation of the credibility of this informant, our attention was drawn to an article which appeared to corroborate the accuracy of his information in the *Star Ledger* of Newark,

New Jersey. A copy of this article was furnished to us on August 5, 1995. The lead paragraph reads:

"U.S. law enforcement authorities have obtained information that Islamic terrorists may be planning suicide attacks against federal courthouses and government installations in the United States.

"The attacks, it is feared, would be designed to attract world-wide press attention through the murder of innocent victims.

"*The Star Ledger* has learned that U.S. law enforcement officials have received a warning... against federal authorities as a result of an incident during the trial last year of four persons in the bombing of the World Trade Center in New York."

The article relates that the memo to all U.S. Marshalls was issued by the Director of the U.S. Marshall's Service, Eduardo Gonzalez, and the memo warned that attacks may be designed to "target as many victims as possible and draw as much media coverage as possible."

We do not have sufficient information to determine whether there is a direct link between the information furnished by an informant, who received a grant of immunity, and the information relayed in the Newark *Star Ledger*. However, the closeness in time of the two pieces of information, and in turn, their proximity in time to the bombing of a Federal Building in Oklahoma in the middle of April, raises serious and troubling questions.

Among those questions are the following:

1. Was the day care center in the Alfred P. Murrah Building and similar day care centers in other federal buildings specifically notified of the threat?

2. Were appropriate federal security personnel in Oklahoma City made aware of the threat as we believe they were? If not, why not? If so, what additional security measures were taken, if any?

There has been a consistent "spin" on an "off-the-record" basis by the Department of Justice that the bombing in Oklahoma City was the result of two "drifters" who had no training, education, or employment history in the planning and construction of explosive devices.

We have repeatedly expressed our concern that there is a rush of judgment in this matter and that for political reasons, the indictments and prosecutions of a limited number of "drifters" will be passed off to the public as a completely successful investigation resulting in the arrest of all concerned. These assurances are, to be certain, not credible.

We make the public, including the families of the victims, aware of information that we are reasonably confident they have not been made aware of, but certainly are entitled to be informed about.

It is important to understand what the grand jury has done today. Having heard from witnesses selected by the prosecution and without cross examination, without the motives, credibility, or bias of the witnesses explored, this federal grand jury meeting in secrecy at an undisclosed location and hearing only one side of the story, and probably only a limited version of the entire investigation, has indicted our client.

No matter how thin we may make our pancakes, they always have two sides. We urge the public not to accept the grand jury's actions as the final or definitive answer as to who is behind the Oklahoma City bombing.

The guilt of our client is to be determined by a jury trial in open court, with the public and press in attendance, hearing the evidence and the witnesses who can be examined and cross examined by both sides. Almost always, the first instruction given a trial jury by a judge is that there is no inference of guilt by the return of an indictment or the arrest of a defendant. This basic fair principle of law should be observed in reality as well as in the abstract.

We ask the members of the press and the public to remember this wise counsel. Every year, hundreds of people indicted by grand juries are found not guilty.

We have been repeatedly asked about the theme or theory of the defense. Let me just say that the parameters of the defense will be to insist that our client, consistent with his constitutional rights, receives a fair trial and due process of law. This concept, while deeply honored as a fine principle, is often observed more in the breach than in the observation. We hope this will not be true in our case.

After the release of the above document, the identity of the confidential informant was identified by a Denver, Colorado television station. He is 51-year old Cary Gagan of Denver. According to attorney Henry D. Solano, who has been in touch with Gagan, the man first contacted federal authorities in September 1994, but that they did not believe the "totality of [Gagan's] claims to be credible." Gagan states that on April 1, 1995 he warned federal authorities in even more specific terms in the following letter. Although the U.S. Marshall's Service denies ever receiving the letter, Gagan says he can prove that they signed for the letter. The following is the text of Gagan's handwritten warning:

Tina Rowe, U.S. Marshall, April 1, 1995, Dear Ms Rowe: After leaving Denver for what I thought would be for a long time, I returned here last night because I have specific information that within two weeks a federal building(s) is to be bombed in this area or nearby. The previous requests I made for you to contact me, 25th & 28th of April 1995 were ignored by you, Mr. Allison and my friends at the FBI. I would not ignore the specific request for you personally to contact me immediately regarding a plot to blow-up a federal bldg. If the information is false request Mr. Allison to charge me accordingly. If you and/or your office does not contact me as I so request herein, I will never again contact any law enforcement agency federal or state, regarding those matters set out in the letter of immunity. Cary Gagan

Call 832-4091 (Now) [1]

NOTES:

1. Myers, Lawrence. "OKC Update," *Media Bypass*, October 1995

30

Control Structure

❝ For those conducting a covert action, there are three layers of protection against disclosure. First, there is the culture of secrecy surrounding such operations. People are sworn to silence, and they take their oaths with the utmost seriousness. Second, there is compartmentalization. Ideally, in a covert action almost no one should have the whole picture. Especially those at a lower level should have as little information as possible about any activities except those required to fulfill their mission. The third layer of protection is culpability. If the covert operation involves criminal actions, the source will be reluctant to subject himself to possible prosecution. That inhibition is greatly strengthened if those he is accusing happen to be in positions of great political power."

— Gary Sick, *October Surprise*

Amid conflicting theories and allegations about who was responsible for the Oklahoma City bombing, facts and real connecting links can be discerned, with some of the most important leads apparently being purposely ignored and even covered up by the major media and by government investigators. From available evidence it appears that Oklahoma City was a surgical strike against freedom in America, with the real perpetrators almost undoubtedly hidden behind layerings of command structure, doubles, and deception.

Although we may never be able to point to a credible confession or piece of evidence that provides undeniable responsibility in the bombing (what collaborator in the murder of 169 people is likely to come forward and volunteer such information?), we can offer both facts and speculation on the case, and provide markers for future research.

Examining the most likely perpetrators of the Oklahoma City bombing, significant examples of foreknowledge, collaboration between foreign and domestic militant groups and government intelligence agencies, and a possible top-down control emerges from the morass of competing theories in the case. There are numerous indications that patsies and provocateurs, probably including Timothy McVeigh, Terry Nichols, Michael Fortier, John Doe 2, and others, were tuned to a fever pitch by some controlling entity, and then turned loose to destroy the lives of 169 persons and their families in Oklahoma City.

The Oklahoma City bombing seems to have been a politically motivated terrorist operation involving pliant elements among the radical right (with a possible focus in individuals connected to the group that met at Hayden Lake, Idaho in 1983), as well as a possible collaboration with Islamic terrorist networks. These factions may have worked in collaboration with or have been controlled by American or international intelligence or criminal agencies, as evidenced by the infiltration of informants and agent provocateurs into Islamic and rightist groups with which McVeigh and others may have been associated. Sources also inform us that one Iraqi seen with McVeigh in Oklahoma City, and identified as a "possible John Doe 2" by Oklahoma City investigators, may have been an informant for the Bureau of Alcohol, Tobacco, and Firearms. The activities of the ATF in recent years have increasingly seemed bloodthirsty and "rogue," and this is an agency whom witnesses suggest may have been warned at Oklahoma City prior to the bombing.

The connection of seemingly unrelated groups and individuals is, in itself, a form of "compartmentalization" which makes a crime more difficult to understand and to solve. How could groups and individuals so disassociated, so at odds in terms of personnel and purposes, rationally be linked? As evidenced by the scalpel-dissection performed on the John Kennedy assassination by "William Torbitt," in the classic book *Nomenclature of an Assassination Cabal*, these sorts of disparate groups can be utilized as foot soldiers as well as for concealment of those actually responsible for a crime.

McVeigh and Nichols seem most likely to have been offered up as unwitting "expendables" to conceal the actual collaborators in the crime, a control mechanism camouflaged by a confederacy of dupes. In published accounts even agents of the FBI admit that this is the most probable scenario. Given the enormous amount of conflicting data and apparent cover-up in the Oklahoma City bombing case, I am forced to believe that there was an unseen control structure existing octopus-like above the visible machinations which we see. Despite suspicions, at this time I do not have sufficient evidence or certainty to name that entity.

With this book I have attempted to follow up leads that are being ignored by the mainstream media, and to alert the public to what has been discovered by myself and other investigators. What I have offered should be only the beginning of the search for the guilty parties in the bombing. Through time, clues will continue to be located and analyzed, and the court trial of McVeigh and Nichols, if it ever takes place, may provide a wealth of information, whether or not it illuminates what really happened. There is the possibility, judging from statements of federal investigators and their media mouthpieces, that the trial will be a limited showcase intended to promote the lone, crazed assassin theory, which would certainly be a boon for forces wishing to conceal the truth. Even those who wish to aid in the discovery of the truth may ultimately assist in concealing it. McVeigh's attorney, Stephen Jones, has already privately informed independent investigator Karl Granse that he is "not going to put the government on trial." [1]

Additional research is necessary and will be continued by myself and other investigators. These efforts should be augmented by independent studies commissioned by government and other persons. I would particularly like to applaud the efforts of Oklahoma Representative Charles Key in attempting to obtain independent investigations in both Washington, D.C. and in Oklahoma. I would suggest that those conducting investigations should be scrupulously screened to disqualify those with vested interests, in particular, and those who have prior connections to political factions, to the military, and to intelligence agencies. Better that there should be no investigation than there be a clone of the Warren Commission.

Above all, the Oklahoma City bombing case should not be forgotten until it is solved, and until those who are responsible — and who are not just patsies — are brought to justice.

NOTES:

1. Granse, Karl. Interview conducted by Jim Keith on September 25, 1995

Aftermath

With the aftermath of the Oklahoma City bombing, we see another crime of perhaps even greater long-term significance taking place. Bill Clinton and his internationalist crowd in Washington are using Black PR to destroy their enemies — not the entrenched Republicans on Capitol Hill, but the conservative pro-Constitutionalists, Christian religious fundamentalists, Second Amendment militia movement, and other adversaries to the New World Order — who they characterize as violent, armed hatemongers, dangerous crackpots, and rabid followers of "Hate Radio" (i.e., advocates of free speech). Even the Republicans on Capitol Hill are in a stampede to crucify these same "radicals" in this society for the purpose of obtaining funding for their draconian social policies.

It is imperative to see through all of the lies and the pre-prepared script served up in newspapers and on the nightly news. We must question these controllers who are so eager to take advantage of the deaths which occurred at Oklahoma City, and we must question their media and political representatives, regardless of which side of the mostly illusory right/left political spectrum they reside on. At stake is not just the solution to the murder of 169 men, women, and children at Oklahoma City, but the tradition of freedom in the United States.

And through it all, the bombing and the shrill, self-interested screaming which erupted afterward in the media, the controllers linger, generally unnoticed, in the shadows. The controllers, the ones who actually steer the ship of state, believe that they did their job well at Oklahoma City. They believe that a bribe here, a cover-up there, and an assassination whenever needed will quickly right the lumbering moron of public opinion when it falters, when too many facts come to light.

Perhaps they are right. But perhaps they are dead wrong, elitist dinosaurs who are already faltering and destined to fall prey to the exposure of their lies and to their own inner moral decay. It is my belief that the public is beginning to awaken to the ways in which they are lied to and manipulated; that they are beginning to see, understand, and undermine the techniques of parasitic control, and to pinpoint the identities of those who would manipulate them. With that recognition, let us all insist that the truth about Oklahoma City is brought to light, and assist in bringing to an end a tyranny of lies in America.

Appendix 1

Three Letters by Timothy McVeigh

L etter sent to the Lockport, New York, *Union-Sun and Journal*, February 11, 1992:
America Faces Problems

Crime is out of control. Criminals have no fear of punishment. Prisons are overcrowded so they know they will not be imprisoned long. This breeds more crime, in an escalating cyclic pattern.

Taxes are a joke. Regardless of what a political candidate "promises," they will increase. More taxes are always the answer to government mismanagement. They mess up, we suffer. Taxes are reaching cataclysmic levels, with no slowdown in sight.

The "American Dream" of the middle class has all but disappeared, substituted with people struggling just to buy next week's groceries. Heaven forbid the car breaks down!

Politicians are further eroding the "American Dream" by passing laws which are supposed to be a "quick fix," when all they are really designed for is to get the official reelected. These laws tend to "dilute" a problem for a while, until the problem comes roaring back in a worsened form (much like a strain of bacteria will alter itself to defeat a known medication).

Politicians are out of control. Their yearly salaries are more than an average person will see in a lifetime. They have been entrusted with the power to regulate their own salaries and have grossly violated that trust to live in their own luxury.

Racism on the rise? You had better believe it! Is this America's frustrations venting themselves? Is it a valid frustration? Who is to blame for the mess? At a point when the world has seen communism falter as an imperfect system to manage people; democracy seems to be headed down the same road. No one is seeing the "big" picture.

Maybe we have to combine ideologies to achieve the perfect utopian government. Remember, government-sponsored health care was a communist idea. Should only the rich be allowed to live long? Does that say that because a person is poor, he is a lesser human being; and doesn't deserve to live as long, because he doesn't wear a tie to work?

What is it going to take to open up the eyes of our elected officials? America is in serious decline!

We have no proverbial tea to dump; should we instead sink a ship full of Japanese imports? Is a Civil War imminent? Do we have to shed blood to reform the current system? I hope it doesn't come to that! But it might. Tim McVeigh

Letter sent to Representative John LaFalce, New York, February 16, 1992:

Dear Mr. LaFalce:

Recently, I saw an article in the *Buffalo News* that detailed a man's arrest; one of the charges being "possession of a noxious substance" (CS gas). This struck my curiousity, so I went to the New York State Penal Law. Sure enough, section 270 prohibits possession of any noxious substance, and included in section 265 is a ban on the use of "stun guns." Now I am a male, and fully capable of physically defending myself, but how about a female?

I strongly believe in a God-given right to self-defense. Should any other person or governing body be able to tell another person that he/she cannot save their own life, because it would be a violation of a law? In this case, which is more important: faced with a rapist/murderer, would you pick to a.) die, a law-abiding citizen, or b.) live, and go to jail?

It is a lie if we tell ourselves that the police can protect us everywhere, at all times. I am in shock that a law exists which denies a woman's right to self-defense. Firearms restrictions are bad enough, but now a woman can't even carry Mace in her purse?!?! Tim McVeigh

Letter sent to the Lockport, New York, *Union-Sun and Journal,* March 10, 1992:

Meat Insured Survival

Since the beginning of his existence, man has been a hunter, a predator. He has hunted and eaten meat to insure his survival. To deny this is to deny your past, your religion, even your existence.

Since we have now established that about every human being on this planet consumes meat, we in America are left with two choices, buy your meat from a supermarket, or harvest it yourself.

We will, for now, discuss that fact that in many areas of the world, there is no "supermarket."

We know the choice these people make; their lives, or the lives of meat, a good hunter enters the woods and kills a deer with a clean, merciful shot. The deer dies in his own environment, quick and unexpected.

To buy your meat in a store seems so innocent, but have you ever seen or thought how it comes to be wrapped up so neatly in cellophane?

First, cattle live their entire lives penned up in cramped quarters, never allowed to roam freely, bred for one purpose when their time has come.

The technique that I have personally seen is to take cattle, line them up side by side with their heads and necks protruding over a low fence, and walk from one end to the other, slitting their throats with either machete or power saw. Unable to run or move, they are left there until they bleed to death, standing up.

Would you rather die while living happily or die while leading a miserable life? You tell me which is more "humane."

Does a "growing percentage of the public" have any pity or respect for any of the animals which are butchered and then sold in the store?

Or is it just so conveniently "clean" that a double standard is allowed? Tim McVeigh

Appendix 2

FBI Arrest Warrant Affidavit

I , Henry C. Gibbons, being duly sworn, do hereby state that I am an agent with the Federal Bureau of Investigation, having been so employed for 26 years and as such am vested with the authority to investigate violations of federal laws, including Title 18, U.S. Code, Section 844 (f).

Further, the Affiant states as follows:

1. The following information has been received by the Federal Bureau of Investigation over the period from April 19 through April 21, 1995:

2. On April 19, 1995, a massive explosive detonated outside the Alfred P. Murrah Building in Oklahoma City, Oklahoma, at approximately 9:00 a.m.

3. Investigation by Federal agents at the scene of the explosion have determined that the explosive was contained in a 1993 Ford owned by Ryder Rental company.

    a. A vehicle identification number (VIN) was found at the scene of the explosion and determined to be from a part of the truck that contained the explosive.

    b. The VIN was traced to a truck owned by Ryder Rentals of Miami, Florida.

4. The rental agent at Elliot's Body Shop in Junction City, Kansas, was interviewed by the FBI on April 19, 1995, and advised that two persons had rented the truck on April 17, 1995. The individuals who signed the rental agreement provided the following information:

    a. The person who signed the rental agreement identified himself as BOB KLING, SSN: 962-42-9694, South Dakota's driver's license YF942A6, and provided a home address of 428 Malt Drive, Redfield, South Dakota. The person listed the destination 428 Maple Drive, Omaha, Nebraska.

    b. Subsequent investigation conducted by the FBI determined all this information to be bogus.

5. On April 20, 1995, the rental agent was recontacted and assisted in the creation of composite drawings. The rental agent has told the FBI

that the composite drawings are fair and accurate depictions of the individuals who rented the truck.

6. On April 20, 1995, the FBI interviewed three witnesses who were near the scene of the explosion at the Alfred P. Murrah Federal Building prior to the detonation of the explosives. The three witnesses were shown a copy of the composite drawing of Unsub #1 and identified him as closely resembling a person the witnesses had seen in front of the Alfred P. Murrah Federal Building where the explosion occurred on April 19, 1995, when they entered the building. They again observed Unsub #1 at approximately 8:55 a.m., still in front of the 5th Road entrance of the building when they departed just minutes before the explosion.

7. The Alfred P. Murrah Building is used by various agencies of the United States, including Agriculture Department, Department of the Army, the Defense Department, Federal Highway Administration, General Accounting Office, General Service Administration, Social Security Administration, Housing and Urban Development, Drug Enforcement Administration, Labor Department, Marine Corps, Small Business Administration, Transportation Department, United States Secret Service, Bureau of Alcohol, Tobacco and Firearms, and Veteran's Administration.

8. The composite drawings were shown to employees at various motels and commercial establishments in the Junction City, Kansas, vicinity. Employees of the Dreamland Motel in Junction City, Kansas, advised FBI agents that an individual resembling Unsub #1 depicted in the composite drawings had been a guest at the Motel from April 14 through April 18, 1995. This individual had registered at the Motel under the name of Tim McVeigh, listed his automobile as bearing an Arizona license plate with an illegible plate number, and provided a Michigan address, on North Van Dyke road in Decker, Michigan. The individual was seen driving a car described as a Mercury from the 1970s.

9. A check of Michigan Department of Motor Vehicle records shows a license in the name of Timothy J. McVeigh, date of birth April 23, 1968, with an address of 3616 North Van Dyke Road, Decker, Michigan. This Michigan license was renewed by McVeigh on April 8, 1995. McVeigh had a prior license issued in the state of Kansas on March 21, 1990, and surrendered to Michigan in November 1993, with the following address: P.O. Box 2153, Fort Riley, Kansas.

10. Further investigation shows that the property at 3616 North Van Dyke Road, Decker, Michigan, is associated with James Douglas Nichols and his brother Terry Lynn Nichols. The property is a working farm.

Terry Nichols formerly resided in Marion, Kansas, which is approximately one hour from Junction City.

11. A relative of James Nichols reports to the FBI that Tim McVeigh is a friend and associate of James Nichols, who has worked and resided at the farm on North Van Dyke Road in Decker, Michigan. This relative further reports that she had heard that James Nichols had been involved in constructing bombs in approximately November 1994, and that he possessed large quantities of fuel oil and fertilizer.

12. On April 21, 1995, a former co-worker of Tim McVeigh's reported to the FBI that he had seen the composite drawing of Unsub #1 on the television and recognized the drawing to be a former co-worker, Timothy McVeigh. He further advised that McVeigh was known to hold extreme right-wing views, was a military veteran, and was particularly agitated about the conduct of the federal government at Waco, Texas, in 1993. In fact, the co-worker further reports that McVeigh had been so agitated about the deaths of the Branch Davidians in Waco, Texas, on April 19, 1993, that he had personally visited the site. After visiting the site, McVeigh expressed extreme anger at the federal government and advised that the government should never have done what it did. He further advised that the last known address for McVeigh is 1711 Stockton Hill Road, No. 206, Kingman, Arizona.

13. On April 21, 1995, investigators learned that a Timothy McVeigh was arrested at 10:30 a.m. on April 19, 1995, in Perry, Oklahoma, for not having a license tag and for possession of a weapon approximately one hour after the detonation of the explosive device at the Alfred P. Murrah Federal Building in Oklahoma City, Oklahoma. Perry, Oklahoma, is approximately a 1 1/2 hour drive from Oklahoma City, Oklahoma. McVeigh, who has been in custody since his arrest on April 19, 1995, listed his home address as 3616 North Van Dyke Road, Decker, Michigan. He listed James Nichols of Decker, MI, as a reference. McVeigh was stopped driving a yellow 1977 Mercury Marquis.

14. The detonation of the explosives in front of the Alfred P. Murrah Federal Building constitutes a violation of 18 U.S.C. S. 844 (f), which makes it a crime to maliciously damage or destroy by means of an explosive any building or real property, in whole or in part owned, possessed, or used by the United States, or any department or agency thereof.

Further, your affiant sayeth not. HENRY C. GIBBONS, Special Agent Federal Bureau of Investigation subscribed and sworn before me this 21st day of April 1995, RONALD L. HOWLAND, UNITED STATES MAGISTRATE JUDGE, Western District of Oklahoma

Appendix 3

Affidavit of Charles J. Hanger. The State of Oklahoma, plaintiff
McVeigh, Timothy James, 04-23-68, defendant

AFFIDAVIT

1. That your affiant, Charles J. Hanger, is employed as an Oklahoma State Trooper, and has been so employed since September 1976.

2. That on 04-19-95 I was northbound on I-35 at a point approximately 1 mile south of S.H. 15 when I observed a yellow 1977 Mercury 4DR (four door) also traveling north and was not displaying a tag. This was at approximately 1020 hrs.

3. That I stopped the vehicle and the defendant was the driver and only occupant of the vehicle.

4. That I told the defendant why I had stopped him and asked him for his DL (drivers license).

5. That as the defendant was getting his billfold from under his right rear pocket I noticed a bulge under the left side of his jacket and I thought it could be a weapon.

6. That I then told the defendant to pull his jacket back and before he did he said, I have a gun under my jacket.

7. That I then grabbed a hold of the left side of his jacket and I drew my weapon and pointed it at the back of his head and instructed him to keep his hands up and I walked him over to the trunk of his car and had him put his hands on the trunk. I removed the weapon which was a chambered and magazine loaded 45-caliber Glock model 21, SER-VW769, along with another loaded clip and shoulder holster rig, also on his belt was a brown leather scabbard containing a single blade knife 5 1/8 inches in length.

8. That I took him into custody and then did a search of his person and did not find any other weapon.

9. That I also made a search of the car and did not find any weapon.

10. That the defendant did not have any proof of insurance.

11. That based on this information I feel like the defendant committed the following offenses. A.) Unlawfully carrying a weapon. B.) Transporting a loaded firearm in a motor vehicle. C.) Failure to display a current number plate. D.) No license plate. E.) No insurance on the car.

Appendix 4

I ndictment Against McVeigh & Nichols in the United States District Court for the Western District of Oklahoma.

United States of America, Plaintiff, vs. Timothy James McVeigh and Terry Lynn Nichols, Defendants. Filed August 10, 1995.

Indictment Count One

(Conspiracy to Use a Weapon of Mass Destruction)

The Grand Jury charges:

1. Beginning on or about September 13, 1994 and continuing thereafter until on or about April 19, 1995, at Oklahoma City, Oklahoma, in the Western District of Oklahoma and elsewhere, Timothy James McVeigh and Terry Lynn Nichols, the defendants herein, did knowingly, intentionally, willfully and maliciously conspire, combine and agree together and with others unknown to the Grand Jury to use a weapon of mass destruction, namely an explosive bomb placed in a truck (a "truck bomb"), against persons within the United States and against property that was owned and used by the United States and by a department and agency of the United States, namely, the Alfred P. Murrah Federal Building at 200 N.W. 5th Street, Oklahoma City, Oklahoma, resulting in death, grievous bodily injury and destruction of the building.

2. It was the object of the conspiracy to kill and injure innocent persons and to damage property of the United States. Among the manner and means used by the defendants to further the objects of the conspiracy were the following:

3. MCVEIGH and NICHOLS planned an act of violence against persons and property of the United States.

4. MCVEIGH and NICHOLS selected the Alfred P. Murrah Federal Building and its occupants as the targets of their act of violence and MCVEIGH attempted to recruit others to assist in the act of violence.

5. MCVEIGH and NICHOLS obtained and attempted to obtain the components of a truck bomb, including a truck, ammonium nitrate, racing and diesel fuel, detonation cord and other explosive materials.

6. MCVEIGH and NICHOLS used storage units to conceal the truck bomb components and stolen property.

7. MCVEIGH and NICHOLS used stolen property and its proceeds to help finance their act of violence.

8. MCVEIGH and NICHOLS made calls with a telephone calling card that they had acquired in a false name as a means of concealing their true identities and as a means of preventing calls from being traced to them.

9. MCVEIGH and NICHOLS used different false names in business transactions as a means of concealing their true identities, their whereabouts and the true intent of their activities.

10. MCVEIGH and NICHOLS constructed an explosive truck bomb, and MCVEIGH placed it outside the Alfred P. Murrah Federal Building in downtown Oklahoma City, where he detonated the bomb. To further the conspiracy and to achieve its objectives, MCVEIGH and NICHOLS committed and caused to be committed the following acts, among others, in the Western District of Oklahoma and elsewhere:

11. On or about September 22, 1994, MCVEIGH rented a storage unit in the name of "Shawn Rivers" in Herington, Kansas.

12. On or about September 30, 1994, MCVEIGH and NICHOLS purchased forty fifty-pound bags of ammonium nitrate in McPherson, Kansas under the name of "Mike Havens."

13. In or about late September 1994, MCVEIGH made telephone calls in an attempt to obtain detonation cord and racing fuel.

14. On or about October 1, 1994, MCVEIGH and NICHOLS stole explosives from a storage locker (commonly referred to as a magazine) in Marion, Kansas.

15. On or about October 3, 1994, MCVEIGH and NICHOLS transported the stolen explosives to Kingman, Arizona.

16. On or about October 4, 1994, MCVEIGH rented a storage unit in Kingman, Arizona for the stolen explosives.

17. On or about October 16, 1994, NICHOLS registered at a motel in Salina, Kansas under the name of "Terry Havens."

18. On or about October 17, 1994, NICHOLS rented storage unit #40 in Council Grove, Kansas, in the name of "Joe Kyle."

19. On or about October 18, 1994, MCVEIGH and NICHOLS purchased forty fifty-pound bags of ammonium nitrate in McPherson, Kansas under the name of "Mike Havens."

20. In or about October 1994, MCVEIGH and NICHOLS planned a robbery of a firearms dealer in Arkansas as a means to obtain moneys to help finance their planned act of violence.

21. On or about November 5, 1994, MCVEIGH and NICHOLS caused firearms, ammunition, coins, United States currency, precious metals and other property to be stolen from a firearms dealer in Arkan-

sas.

22. On or about November 7, 1994, NICHOLS rented storage unit #37 in Council Grove, Kansas in the name of "Ted Parker" and used the unit to conceal property stolen in the Arkansas robbery.

23. On or about November 16, 1994, NICHOLS rented a storage unit in Las Vegas, Nevada and stored, among other items, a ski mask.

24. On or about November 21, and prior to departing for the Philippines, NICHOLS prepared a letter to MCVEIGH, to be delivered only in the event of NICHOLS' death, in which he advised MCVEIGH, among other matters, that storage unit #37 in Council Grove, Kansas had been rented in the name "Parker" and instructed MCVEIGH to clear out the contents or extend the lease on #37 by February 1, 1995. NICHOLS further instructed MCVEIGH to "liquidate" storage unit #40.

25. On or about December 16, 1994, while en route to Kansas to take possession of firearms stolen in the Arkansas robbery, MCVEIGH drove with Michael Fortier to the Alfred P. Murrah Federal Building and identified the building as the target.

26. In early 1995, following NICHOLS' return from the Philippines, firearms stolen in the Arkansas robbery were sold and MCVEIGH, NICHOLS and Michael Fortier obtained currency from those sales.

27. On or about February 9, 1995, NICHOLS, using currency, paid for the continued use of storage unit #40 at Council Grove, Kansas in the name of "Joe Kyle."

28. In or about March 1995, MCVEIGH obtained a driver's license in the name of "Robert Kling" bearing a date of birth of April 19, 1972.

29. On or about April 14, 1995, MCVEIGH, using currency, purchased a 1977 Mercury Marquis in Junction City, Kansas.

30. On or about April 14, 1995, MCVEIGH called the NICHOLS residence in Herington, Kansas from Junction City, Kansas.

31. On or about April 14, 1995, MCVEIGH called a business in Junction City and, using the name "Bob Kling," inquired about renting a truck capable of carrying 5,000 pounds of cargo.

32. On or about April 14, 1995, MCVEIGH, using currency, rented a room at a motel in Junction City, Kansas.

33. On or about April 15, 1995, MCVEIGH, using currency, placed a deposit for a rental truck, in the name "Robert Kling."

34. On or about April 17, 1995, MCVEIGH took possession of a 20-foot rental truck in Junction City, Kansas.

35. On or about April 18, 1995, at Geary Lake State Park in Kansas, MCVEIGH and NICHOLS constructed an explosive truck bomb

with barrels filled with a mixture of ammonium nitrate, fuel and other explosives placed in the cargo compartment of the rental truck.

36. On April 19, 1995, MCVEIGH parked the truck bomb directly outside the Alfred P. Murrah Federal Building, located within the Western District of Oklahoma, during regular business and day-care hours.

37. On April 19, 1995, MCVEIGH caused the truck bomb to explode.

38. As intended by MCVEIGH and NICHOLS, the truck bomb explosion resulted in death and personal injury and the destruction of the Alfred P. Murrah Federal Building, located within the Western District of Oklahoma. The following persons were present at the Alfred P. Murrah Federal Building on April 19, 1995, and were killed as a result of the explosion: Charles E. Hurlburt, 73; John Karl Vaness III, 67; Anna Jean Hurlburt, 67; Donald Lee Fritzler, 64; Eula Leigh Mitchell, 64; Donald Earl Burns, Sr., 63; Norma Jean Johnson, 62; Calvin C. Battle, 62; Laura Jane Garrison, 61; Olen Burl Bloomer, 61; Luther Hartman Treanor, 61; Rheta Ione Bender Long, 60; Juretta Colleen Guiles, 59; Robert Glen Westberry, 57; Carolyn Ann Kreymborg, 57; Leora Lee Sells, 57; Mary Anne Fritzler, 57; Virginia Mae Thompson, 56; Peola Y. Battle, 56; Peter Robert Avillanoza, 56; Richard Leroy Cummings, 55; Ronald Vernon Harding, 55; LaRue Ann Treanor, 55; Ethel Louise Griffin, 55; Antonio C. Reyes, 55; Thompson Eugene Holdges, Jr., 54; Alvin Junior Justes, 54; Margaret Goodson, 54; Oleta Christine Biddy, 54; David Jack Walker, 54; James Anthony McCarthy, 53; Carol L. Bowers, 53; Linda Coleen Housley, 53; John Albert Youngblood, 52; Robert Nolan Walker, Jr., 52; Thomas Lynn Hawthorne, Sr., 52; Dolores Marie Stratton, 51; Jules Alfonso Valdez, 51; John Thomas Stewart, 51; Mickey Bryant Maroney, 50; John Clayton Moss III, 50; Carole Sue Khalil, 50; Emilio Tapia-Rangel, 50; James Everette Boles, 50; Donald R. Leonard, 50; Castine Deveroux, 50; Clarence Eugene Wilson, 49; Wanda Lee Watkins, 49; Michael Lee Loudenslager, 48; Carrol June Fields, 48; Frances Ann Williams, 48; Claudine Ritter, 48; Ted Leon Allen, 48; Linda Gail Griffin McKinney, 47; Patricia "Trish" Ann Nix, 47; Betsy Janice McGonnell, 47; David Neil Burkett, 47; Michael George Thompson, 47; Catherine May Leinen, 47; Ricky Lee Tomlin, 46; Larry James Jones, 46; Richard Arthur Allen, 46; Harley Richard Cottingham, 46; Lanny Lee David Scroggins, 46; George Michael Howard, 45; Lerry Lee Parker, 45; Judy Joann Fisher, 45; Diane Elaine Hollingsworth Althouse, 45; Michael D. Weaver, 45; Robert Lee Luste, Jr., 45; Peter Leslie DeMaster, 44; Katherine Ann Finley, 44; Doris

Adele Higginbottom, 44; Steven Douglas Curry, 44; Michael Joe Carrillo, 44; Cheryl E. Bradley Hammon, 44; Aurelia Donna Luste, 43; Linda L. Florence, 43; Claudette Meet, 43; William Stephen Williams, 42; Johnny Allen Wade, 42; Larry Laverne Turner, 42; Brenda Faye Daniels, 42; Margaret Louise Clark Spencer, 42; Paul Gregory Boxterman, 42; Paul Douglas Ice, 42; Woodrow Clifford "Woody" Brady, 41; Claude Arthur Medearis, 41; Theresa Lea Lauderdale, 41; Terry Smith Ress, 41; Alan Gerald Whicher, 40; Lola Renee Bolden, 40; Kathy Lynn Seidl, 39; Kimberly Kay Clark, 39; Mary Leasure Rentie, 39; Diana Lynn Day, 38; Robin Ann Huff, 37; Peggy Louise Jenkins Holland, 37; Victoria Jeanette Texter, 37; Susan Jane Ferrell, 37; Kenneth Glenn McCullough, 36; Victoria Lee Sohn, 36; Pamela Denise Argo, 36; Rona Linn Chafey, 35; Jo Ann Whittenberg, 35; Gilbert Xavier Martinez, 35; Wanda Lee Howell, 34; Saundra Gail "Sandy" Avery, 34; James Kenneth Martin, 34; Lucio Aleman, Jr., 33; Valerie Jo Koelsche, 33; Theresa Antoinette Alexander, 33; Kim Robin Cousins, 33; Michelle Ann Reeder, 33; Andrea Y. Blanton, 33; Karen Gist Carr, 32; Christi Yolanda Jenkins, 32; Jamie Lee Genzer, 32; Ronota Ann Woodbridge, 31; Benjamin Laranzo Davis, 29; Kimberly Ruth Burgess, 29; Tresia Jo Mathes-Worton, 28; Mark Allen Bolte, 28; Randolph Guzman, 28; Sheila R. Gigger Driver, 28; Karan Denise Shepherd, 27; Sonja Lynn Sanders, 27; Derwin Wade Miller, 27; Jill Diane Randolph, 27; Carrie Ann Lenz, 26; Cynthia Lynn Campbell Brown, 26; Cassandra K. Booker, 25; Shelly Deann (Turner) Bland, 25; Scott Dwain Williams, 24; Dana LeAnne Cooper, 24; Julie Marie Welch, 23; Frankie Ann Merrell, 23; Christine Nichole Rosas, 22; Lakesha Levy, 21; Cartney J. McRaven, 19; Aaron M. Coverdale, 5; Ashley Megan Eckles, 4; Zackary Taylor Chavez, 3; Kayla Marie Haddock, 3; Peachlyn Bradley, 3; Chase Dalton Smith, 3; Anthony Christopher Cooper II, 2; Colton Smith, 2; Elijah Coverdale, 2; Dominique R. London, 2; Baylee Almon, 1; Jaci Rae Coyne, 1; Blake Ryan Kennedy, 1; Tevin D'Aundrae Garrett, 1; Danielle Nicole Bell, 1; Tylor S. Eaves, 8 months; Antonio Ansara Cooper, Jr., 6 months; Kevin Lee Gottshall II, 6 months; and Gabreon Bruce, 4 months.

All in violation of Title 18, United States Code, Section 2332a.

Count Two (Use of a Weapon of Mass Destruction)

The Grand Jury further charges: On or about April 19, 1995, at Oklahoma City, Oklahoma, in the Western District of Oklahoma, TIMOTHY JAMES MCVEIGH and TERRY LYNN NICHOLS, the defendants herein, did knowingly, intentionally, willfully, and maliciously use, aid and abet the use of, and cause to be used, a weapon of mass destruction, namely an explosive bomb placed in a truck, against persons within the United States, resulting in death to the persons named in Count One, Paragraph 38 (which is expressly incorporated by reference herein) and personal injury to other persons.

All in violation of Title 18, United States Code, Sections 2332a and 2 (a) & (b).

Count Three (Destruction by Explosive)

The Grand Jury further charges: On or about April 19, 1995, at Oklahoma City, Oklahoma, in the Western District of Oklahoma, TIMOTHY JAMES MCVEIGH and TERRY LYNN NICHOLS, the defendants herein, did knowingly, intentionally, wilfully and maliciously damage and destroy, aid and abet the damage and destruction of, and cause to be damaged and destroyed, by means of an explosive, namely, an explosive bomb placed in a truck, a building and other personal and real property in whole and in part owned, possessed and used by the United States and departments and agencies of the United States, that is, the Alfred P. Murrah Federal Building, 200 N.W. 5th Street, Oklahoma City, Oklahoma, causing, as a direct and proximate result, the death of the persons named in Count One, Paragraph 38 (which is expressly incorporated by reference herein) and personal injury to other persons. All in violation of Title 18, United States Code, Sections 844 (f) and 2 (a) & (b).

Counts Four Through Eleven (First Degree Murder)

The Grand Jury further charges: On or about April 19, 1995, at Oklahoma City, Oklahoma, in the Western District of Oklahoma, TIMOTHY JAMES MCVEIGH and TERRY LYNN NICHOLS, the defendants, herein, did unlawfully, wilfully, deliberately, maliciously, and with premeditation and malice aforethought, kill, and aid, abet and cause the killing of, the following persons while they were engaged in and on account of the performance of their official duties as law enforcement officers: Count Four Mickey Bryant Maroney, Special Agent, United States Secret Service; Count Five Donald R. Leonard, Special Agent, United States Secret Service; Count Six Alan Gerald Whicher, Assistant Special Agent in Charge, United States Secret Service; Count Seven Cynthia Lynn Campbell-Brown, Special Agent, United States Secret Service; Count Eight Kenneth Glenn McCullough, Special Agent, United States Drug Enforcement Administration; Count Nine Paul Douglas Ice, Special

Agent, United States Customs Service; Count Ten Claude Arthur Medearis, Special Agent, United States Customs Service; Count Eleven Paul G. Broxterman, Special Agent, Department of Housing and Urban Development, Office of Inspector General. All in violation of Title 18, United States Code, Sections 1114, 1111 and 2 (a) & (b); and Title 28, Code of Federal Regulations, Section 64.2 (h). A TRUE BILL: Don Frantz, Foreperson of the Grand Jury. Patrick M. Ryan, United States Attorney

Appendix 5

I ndictment Against Michael J. Fortier in the United States District Court for the Western District of Oklahoma.

United States of America, Plaintiff, vs. Michael J. Fortier, Defendant. Filed August 10, 1995.

Indictment Count One (Conspiracy to Transport Stolen Firearms)

The Grand Jury charges:

1. Beginning in or about October 1994 and continuing thereafter until in or about March 1995, in the Western District of Oklahoma and elsewhere, MICHAEL J. FORTIER, the defendant herein, did knowingly, intentionally and willingly conspire, combine and agree with Timothy James McVeigh and Terry Lynn Nichols, unindicted co-conspirators herein, and others known to the Grand Jury to commit offenses against the United States, to-wit: a. To transport stolen firearms in interstate commerce, knowing and having reasonable cause to believe that the firearms were stolen; in violation of Title 18, United States Code, Section 922 (i); and b. To receive, possess, conceal, store, sell and dispose of stolen firearms which had been transported in interstate commerce, knowing and having reasonable cause to believe that the firearms were stolen; in violation of Title 18, United States Code, Section 922 (j); Among the manner and means used by the defendant to further the objects of the conspiracy were the following:

2. FORTIER obtained firearms which he knew and had reason to believe McVeigh and Nichols had caused to be stolen in a robbery.

3. FORTIER transported and caused to be transported in interstate commerce the stolen firearms.

4. FORTIER sold and caused to be sold the stolen firearms.

5. FORTIER delivered a portion of the proceeds from the sale of the stolen firearms to McVeigh and Nichols. To further the conspiracy and to achieve its objectives, the following acts, among others, were committed and caused to be committed in the Western District of Oklahoma and elsewhere.

6. On November 5, 1994, McVeigh and Nichols caused firearms, ammunition, coins, United States currency and other property to be stolen in a robbery in Arkansas.

7. On or about November 7, 1994, Nichols rented a storage unit in

Council Grove, Kansas to conceal the stolen property.

8. On or about December 16, 1994, FORTIER and McVeigh traveled through Oklahoma City en route to Kansas for the purpose of taking possession of some of the stolen firearms.

9. On or about December 17, 1994, FORTIER transported the stolen firearms through the Western District of Oklahoma to Arizona.

10. In early 1995 FORTIER sold the stolen firearms and provided a portion of the currency proceeds to McVeigh for Nichols. All in violation of Title 18, United States Code, Section 371.

Count Two (Transporation of Stolen Firearms)

The Grand Jury further charges: On or about December 17, 1994, in the Western District of Oklahoma and elsewhere, MICHAEL J. FORTIER, the defendant herein, did knowingly, intentionally, and willfully transport firearms in interstate commerce from Kansas through the Western District of Oklahoma to Arizona, knowing and having reasonable cause to believe that the firearms were stolen. All in violation of Title 18, United States Code, Sections 922 (i) and 924 (a) (2).

Count Three (False Statement)

The Grand Jury further charges: 1. At all times material to this investigation: a. The Federal Bureau of Investigation (hereafter "FBI") was a bureau within the Department of Justice, which was a department of the United States; b. The investigation of the bombing of the Alfred P. Murrah Federal Building in Oklahoma City, in the Western District of Oklahoma on April 19, 1995, was a matter within the jurisdiction of the Department of Justice. 2. Between April 21 and April 24, 1995, at Kingman, Arizona, and affecting the federal investigation within the Western District of Oklahoma, MICHAEL J. FORTIER, the defendant herein, did knowingly and wilfully make a materially false statement in the matter within the jurisdiction of the Department of Justice in that he falsely stated to agents of the FBI that he had no prior knowledge of the plans of Timothy James McVeigh and Terry Lynn Nichols to bomb the Alfred P. Murrah Federal Building in Oklahoma City. All in violation of Title 18, United States Code, Section 1001.

Count Four (Commission of Felony)

The Grand Jury further charges:

1. A felony cognizable by the United States District Court for the Western District of Oklahoma was actually committed, in that persons

conspired to use and did use a weapon of mass destruction on April 19, 1995, against persons within the United States and against property owned and used by the United States, in violation of Title 18, United States Code, Section 2332a.

2. Prior to April 19, 1995, MICHAEL J. FORTIER had actual knowledge of the plans of Timothy James McVeigh and Terry Lynn Nichols to explode a truck bomb at the Alfred P. Murrah Federal Building but did not disclose that knowledge to law enforcement officials.

3. Between April 21 and May 17, 1995, at Kingman, Arizona and affecting the federal investigation of said felony within the Western District of Oklahoma, MICHAEL J. FORTIER, the defendant herein, having knowledge of the actual commission of the felony as described hereinabove in paragraph 1, did knowingly and willfully make a false material statement to agents of the Federal Bureau of Investigation and further did knowingly and intentionally conceal physical evidence and thereby did affirmatively conceal said knowledge and evidence and did not as soon as possible make known the same to a judge or a person in civil authority under the United States; All in violation of Title 18, United States Code, Section 2332a.

4. A TRUE BILL: Don Frantz, Foreperson of the Grand Jury. Patrick M. Ryan, United States Attorney

Index

For a copy of our current catalog
write to:

IllumiNet Press
P.O. Box 2808
Lilburn, Georgia   30226